THE SEVENTH
INNING STRETCH

THE SEVENTH INNING STRETCH

Baseball's Most Essential and Inane Debates

JOSH PAHIGIAN

LYONS PRESS
Guilford, Connecticut
An imprint of Globe Pequot Press

Lyons Press is an imprint of Globe Pequot Press.

Project editor: David Legere
Text design: Sheryl Kober
Layout artist: Kevin Mak

All photos by Josh Pahigian except where noted.

Library of Congress Cataloging-in-Publication Data is available on file.

ISBN 978-1-59921-805-2

Printed in United States of America

10 9 8 7 6 5 4 3 2 1

TABLE OF CONTENTS

ACKNOWLEDGMENTS

I extend my most sincere debt of gratitude to all my family members and friends, especially my wife, Heather. Your encouragement has made all the difference.

I also thank my literary agent, Colleen Mohyde at the Doe Coover Agency, and the fine editors I've had the opportunity to work with at Globe Pequot Press through the years, most recently Tom McCarthy and Keith Wallman. Thank you for believing in this book.

INTRODUCTION

We baseball fans are philosophical creatures, prone to engaging our fellow devotees of the Grand Old Game in a wide range of inherently subjective, often ridiculous, and always thoroughly enjoyable debates. Whether sitting by the hot stove waiting impatiently for the new season to begin, munching peanuts at the local Little League field on an April afternoon, or rubbing elbows with friends at the neighborhood sports bar, we find immeasurable delight and satisfaction in immersing ourselves in the minutia of the game. Our ruminations involve topics concerning baseball's teams, players, memorable games, ballparks, and intersections with popular culture. Our discussions begin easily enough and then tend to jump from topic to topic with the unpredictability of a fluttering knuckleball.

Imagine two fans sitting in the bleachers at the local big league park on a steamy summer night watching the final innings of a blowout. A batter lifts what at first appears to be a harmless fly ball to leftfield, but then the ball catches a breeze and drifts, and drifts, and drifts some more, until it unexpectedly disappears over the fence. One fan turns to the other and says, "Too bad it's not a closer game."

"Yeah," the other fan agrees, "That's a homer that really doesn't matter."

"Here's one for you," the first fan says. "What would be your pick for the homer that mattered the most, the most dramatic, most important, most memorable long ball ever?" Then, if his friend doesn't answer correctly within a reasonable time frame of, say, about three seconds, Fan One will inform Fan Two that in *his* opinion Carlton Fisk's twelfth-inning walk-off shot against the Reds in Game Six of the 1975 World Series ranks number one in the all-time dinger diary.

After mulling this over for a minute or two, his friend will reply, perhaps, by pointing out that the Red Sox went on to lose Game Seven that fateful October. He'll say Fisk's dramatic homer really didn't make a difference in the final outcome of the World Series, at least not in the same way Kirk Gibson's opening-game winner against Dennis Eckersley and the A's did in 1988, since that homer set the stage for a stunning five-game Dodgers win against their heavily favored foes.

As the friends deconstruct the relative merits of these two memorable October jacks, a voice from a few rows behind them will suddenly boom, "You two are both wrong. Hank Aaron's 715th home run was more important in the grand scheme of things than either of those two taters." Thus, Fan Three joins the fray, becoming a fast friend, as he makes the case for the most famous milestone homer of all time.

Another fan seated nearby will pipe up with a vote for Roger Maris's 61st homer in 1961. And other fans in surrounding seats will join in with votes for the clinching homers hit by Bobby Thomson, Bill Mazeroski, and Bucky Dent. These new friends will happily show off their historical knowledge of the game's four-baggers, until a manager trots out to the mound to change pitchers, prompting one of them to wonder aloud, "Who was the best manager ever?" Then, during the game's closing salvo, the fans will weigh in with their picks for the savviest skippers of all time.

Eventually, when the last out is recorded and the ballpark PA announcer declares that Roy "Doc" Halladay has earned the win, another fan will comment that Doc is a pretty clever nickname for a pitcher named Halladay, but not as clever as the one once carried by the often traded Harry "Suitcase" Simpson, or the one bequeathed upon Ted "Double Duty" Radcliffe after he caught the first game and pitched the second game of a Negro League doubleheader. As the fans file out of the park, they'll each offer their thoughts regarding the best player nicknames. Then, as they settle onto stools at the local watering hole, their talk might turn to the best minor league team names: the Altoona Curve? Modesto Nuts? Montgomery Biscuits? Auburn Doubledays?

Even after they've dispersed and headed home for the night, chances are the discussion they've begun will remain alive. The next day, when new insights strike them as they try to concentrate on supposedly more important matters at work, they'll continue their debates via email or text messages. You see, we baseball fans never run out of topics to discuss when it comes to the game we love. And our discussions rarely reach conclusive end points.

The essays in this book address some of the classic baseball debates, as well as many that fans have probably never stopped to consider before. Often, the book takes a contrary approach to a familiar line of discourse. For example, instead of pondering which player deserves to be called the *best* hitter ever, one query within these pages asks: Who was the *worst* hitter to play major league baseball for an extended period of time? Another essay seeks to identify not the best, but the worst no-hit game ever pitched. Another searches for the worst team to win a World Series. Another acknowledges the best player who has been left out of the Hall of Fame.

In total, the fifty chapters explore a wide array of topics related to the game's most magical and most disappointing moments, its ballparks, fans, traditions, and even its representation in pop culture. One chapter is dedicated to the worst baseball-card error of all time, one to the best baseball prank, one to the manager who had the most trouble keeping a lid on his volatile temper, one to the most hideous uniform a big league owner ever forced his players to wear, and so on.

After introducing readers to a new topic at the start of each chapter, the essays that follow review the cases to be made for several leading candidates for the best or worst distinction in the category. Then, toward the conclusion of each chapter, your humble author weighs in with his choice. Although I've tried to put aside my personal preferences and rooting interests and to be as objective as possible, most of the inquiries pursued in this book delve into inherently subjective territory, so please do feel free to disagree with as many of my picks as you'd like. The fact is, if each essay merely explored a question with an obvious answer or one that could be looked up and solved in a book of baseball statistics, then the reading experience wouldn't be very much fun. The enjoyment derived from a spirited baseball debate is found, instead, in the gray area that exists between the obvious points upon which we fans can all agree.

I hope the pages that follow will provide you with new food for thought regarding some of the more interesting baseball debates—some that you've considered previously, and surely too, some that you and your friends have never taken the time to ponder. Enjoy!

THE BEST TRAILBLAZERS

THE BEST HANDICAPPED PLAYER

He Challenged Both Hitters and Stereotypes

The debate concerning the best physically handicapped player in baseball history is easier to settle than some of the other questions posed within this book, owing largely to the fact that very few individuals with serious physical disadvantages have ever suited up for big league teams. As we all know, baseball is an exceedingly difficult sport to play at the highest level even for those individuals with two fully functional arms, two working legs, and all senses intact. That's why 99.9 percent of twelve-year-olds who dream of playing big league ball as they're swatting prodigious home runs over their moms' azalea bushes wind up teaching school, or building houses, or washing windows, or writing books for a living instead. That's why we fans realize when we see J. D. Drew pull up lame on his way to first base that he'll likely be spending some time in the near future on the disabled list—that metaphoric convalescent home for players who aren't in peak physical condition. And that's why it's all the more remarkable to fans and fellow players alike when along comes that once-in-a-generation player who demonstrates that he can succeed in the bigs despite a significant physical disadvantage.

The first notable record of such a player in baseball's storied past appears back in the 1880s, when William "Dummy" Hoy became the third deaf player to play big league ball and the first to flourish at the sport's highest level. Hoy, who'd lost his hearing after a childhood bout with meningitis, broke in with the Washington Nationals in 1888 and, despite never hearing the crack of the bat, the encroaching footsteps of another outfielder, or the roar of the crowd, batted .287 and amassed 2,044 lifetime hits and 594 stolen bases over fourteen major league seasons. Hoy is sometimes credited with inventing the hand signals that umpires use to call balls and strikes, as well as the signs third base coaches use to relay instructions to batters, but there are also competing "theories of evolution" for both of these baseball conventions. What we do know for certain is that Hoy helped pave the way for Luther "Dummy" Taylor, a deaf pitcher who won 116 games in a career spent mostly with the Giants between 1900 and 1908, and more recently for Curtis Pride, a deaf outfielder, who appeared in 421 big league games between 1993 and 2006, batting .250.

A journeyman who played for six different teams, Pride was born deaf. He starred in soccer, basketball, and baseball in high school, and then, after being drafted by the Mets in the tenth round of the 1986 amateur draft, played his first minor league season as a seventeen-year-old. Simultaneous to his minor league career, he enrolled at the College of William and Mary and played four years at point guard on the hardwood. Although Pride's accomplishments are to be commended, Hoy's more impressive statistical body of work, and role as a trailblazer who debunked social stereotypes that were more prevalent in his era than in Pride's, make him a stronger nominee in our quest to crown the best handicapped player.

Another player deserving of our consideration is Mordecai "Three Finger" Brown, the Hall of Fame pitcher who suffered a serious injury at age seven when he accidentally put his right hand in a corn shredder. Brown's index finger was severed just above the first joint and his little finger was paralyzed. Kiss those baseball dreams goodbye? Not so fast. It may have taken him longer than most big league hopefuls, but Brown eventually reached the majors as a twenty-six-year-old with the Cardinals in 1903. He went on to win 239 games in a fourteen-year career spent mostly with the Cubs, while compiling a minuscule 2.06 ERA. Now, as any person who's ever tried to throw a curveball, changeup, or splitter will attest, the index finger has an important role to play in gripping every pitch. So how did Brown succeed when his index finger and pinkie were considerably less than fully functional? Well, his best pitch was a natural knuckleball, which he'd throw by putting the stub of his index finger to good use in taking the rotation off the ball. This raises the question of whether Brown's mangled right

Historians have debated whether Mordecai "Three Finger" Brown's missing digits were actually a handicap when he took the mound.
COURTESY OF THE LIBRARY OF CONGRESS

hand actually represented a handicap. Sure, the lost fingers may have made him ineligible to serve in World War I, but did they detract from his baseball aptitude, or did they enhance it by giving him a trick pitch unlike anything opposing hitters had ever seen?

A generation later, the most severely physically challenged player yet, Pete Gray, became one of baseball's primary drawing cards at a time when many of the regulars were overseas participating in World War II. Gray was born right-handed but lost his right arm when he fell off the running board of a truck as a youngster. Undeterred, he learned to throw left-handed and to bat from the left-handed batter's box. He won the Southern League MVP Award in 1944, when he hit .333 with 63 stolen bases, prompting the St. Louis Browns to buy his contract. The scouting report on Gray was that he covered a lot of ground in the outfield and transferred the ball from his glove to bare hand with amazing acuity. At the plate, though, the thirty-year-old rookie struggled, particularly against off-speed pitches, since he had trouble slowing down his bat once he began a swing. With the War ending upon Japan's surrender in August, 1945 would be Gray's lone season in the big leagues. In seventy-seven games he tallied 51 hits and a .218 average. Those numbers may sound paltry, and it's true that with the stars abroad the level of competition Gray faced was not as high as usual, but considering that Gray had only one arm, a .218 batting average is pretty amazing. Not convinced? Try swinging a baseball bat with just one arm—not a Wiffle Ball bat, a 33-ounce Louisville slugger—in your backyard and imagine trying to hit an 85-mile-per-hour fastball or diving curve that way.

To this point in our review, it seems clear that Gray was the player who overcame the greatest physical limitation to play in the major leagues, while Brown enjoyed greater success than any other physically impaired player—although it's debatable just how impaired he was. But what if there were a player who overcame a seemingly insurmountable physical impairment in the way Gray did, while also posting good statistics, which Gray didn't do? What if there were a handicapped player who competed for a Rookie of the Year Award, and nearly won a Cy Young, and pitched a no-hitter, and was just as dominant as the best pitchers of his era? Well, in fact, there was one such player, and not too long ago. You may remember Jim Abbott, the one-handed pitcher who made the leap directly from college ball to the big leagues in 1989 without tossing a single inning in the minors. Abbott's right arm extended only to where a person's wrist normally appears, leaving him without a right hand. But that didn't stop him from excelling on the gridiron as a quarterback and on the diamond as a pitcher in high school. And it didn't slow him down at the University of Michigan, where he used a powerful fastball and devastating array of breaking pitches to lead the Wolverines to two Big Ten championships in three years. But Abbott was just getting started. Next, he pitched Team USA to the Gold in the 1988 Olympics, beating Japan 5–3 in the finale. The Angels selected him with the eighth overall pick of the 1988 draft, and Abbott won a job in the big league rotation as a twenty-one-year-old the next spring.

He was one of the better pitchers in the American League during his first four seasons, then his production tailed off over the latter years of his career. For anyone who'd ever been told their ambitions exceeded their potential, Abbott's delivery was an inspiration. To throw a pitch, he would tuck his glove under his right arm. Then, immediately after releasing the ball he would slide his hand up into the glove, leaving him positioned to field balls back through the box. At first, teams tried to bunt on him, but they quickly realized that he fielded his position quite well.

The talk of baseball throughout his first season, Abbott finished 12-12 with a 3.92 ERA in 1989. Pretty impressive for a guy who skipped the minors. Really impressive for a guy with one hand who skipped the minors. For his efforts, he placed fifth in the Rookie of the Year balloting. Two years later, he finished third in the Cy Young Award voting, after an 18-11 season in which he logged 243 innings and posted a 2.89 ERA. In 1993 as a member of the Yankees, he tossed a no-hitter against the Indians, spinning a 4–0 masterpiece at Yankee Stadium. Like a lot of pitching phenoms though, Abbott threw too many pitches at too young an age, and his stuff deteriorated prematurely. After returning to the Angels for a dreadful 2-18 season in 1996, sitting out the 1997 season, doing a stint in the minors in 1998, and suffering through a 2-8 season with the Brewers in 1999, he retired at age thirty-one. His career record of 87-108 with a 4.25 ERA belies just how effective he was in the early 1990s when he staked his claim as not just the best handicapped baseball player who ever lived, but as one of the best pitchers of the day. For refusing to accept the supposed limitations of his "disability," and for excelling to the extent that he did, Jim Abbott is our pick.

[2]

THE BEST FEMALE PLAYER

The Diamond Was This Girl's Best Friend

In recent years we've witnessed the continued dismantling of many gender barriers in American sports. Female hoopsters now have a nationally prominent sister league to the NBA. The USA women's soccer team has held a place in our hearts ever since 1999, when Brandi Chastain famously ripped off her shirt after kicking the game winner against China to win the World Cup. College hockey squads are sprouting up for women across America, as are semipro football circuits. Women's tennis is thriving. And even though golfer Michelle Wie has struggled, her presence on the world scene has prompted fans and pundits to wonder if there might come a time when the best ladies and gents tee it up together in the PGA. Then there's Danica Patrick, who burst onto the Indy racing scene in 2005 when she won Rookie of the Year honors, and then became the first female to win an Indy race in 2008. Unfortunately, baseball doesn't currently have any gender benders in the public eye, but that's not to say women have never challenged the Grand Old Game's status quo. In fact, some females have made genuine progress in infiltrating the game and in proving that they can play too. And they are the subjects of this essay, which seeks to determine who among them deserves credit as the best woman hardballer that America has yet known.

When the topic of women in baseball comes up, most of today's fans immediately think of the All-American Girls Professional Baseball League (AAGPBL), which formed during World War II, faded when the men came home, and was chronicled decades later by Tom Hanks, Madonna, and Rosie O'Donnell in the 1992 film *A League of Their Own*. But even before the league's creation in the 1940s, there were females who strived to compete—against prevailing social mores—in the semipro leagues and barnstorming competition of earlier times. During those days, one young lady stood above the rest and in so doing, made hers a household name. The story of Jackie Mitchell's claim to baseball fame dates back to April 1931 when the New York Yankees arrived in Chattanooga, Tennessee, for a spring exhibition game against the local minor league team. Unbeknownst to the wayfaring Yankees, shortly before their arrival Chattanooga Lookouts owner Joe Engel offered a contract to the seventeen-year-old Mitchell, a left-handed pitcher who had been making the local boys look bad ever since she'd learned to throw.

Mitchell entered the game against the Yankees in the first inning, after the Lookouts starter surrendered base hits to the first two batters. The southpaw—who relied on a sidearm sinker and impeccable control—would have to face three straight future Hall of Famers: Babe Ruth, Lou Gehrig, and Tony Lazzeri.

Ruth took Mitchell's first offering for a ball, then swung and missed at Mitchell's second pitch, evoking a gasp from the crowd. The Bambino swung and missed again on the next pitch, then took the next one only to hear the home plate umpire bark, "Strike three." Ruth kicked the dirt and flung his bat to the ground in disgust, then headed back to the Yankees dugout. Next, Gehrig stepped into the batter's box and struck out on three consecutive pitches, swinging too early each time. Afraid of being similarly embarrassed himself, Lazzeri ran up to bunt on Mitchell's first offering to him, but the ball somehow eluded his bat. Then the star second baseman worked a walk, prompting the Lookouts manager to remove Mitchell from the game.

It didn't take long for footage of Babe Ruth whiffing against the teenage girl to turn up at movie houses across the country. Nor did much time pass before baseball commissioner Kenesaw Mountain Landis voided Mitchell's contract with the Lookouts and declared that there was no place for women in organized baseball. Nonetheless, Mitchell would forever be known as the Girl Who Struck Out Babe Ruth. She played for a female team in Chattanooga for a while, and then toured with the famous House of David barnstorming team.

So how good was Mitchell? Baseball historians have debated whether the successive strikeouts of Ruth and Gehrig were authentic or staged, but the prevailing sentiment seems to be that they were real. The events of that inning lead us to wonder whether Mitchell might have served as a viable situational lefty for the Lookouts, at least for one trip around the Southern Association until hitters figured out her repertoire. Skeptical? The Chattanooga History Center still has video footage of the Ruth at-bat, so perhaps a visit to Chattanooga will convince you.

A decade after Mitchell's mythical accomplishment, the AAGPBL was born. Many men had been drafted into military service, causing most minor leagues to disband. But no sooner than this void in the world of American entertainment had been created did a group of forward-thinking Midwestern businessmen that included Chicago Cubs owner Phillip K. Wrigley found the country's first professional women's baseball league. The game these ladies played during the inaugural 1943 season was essentially softball, owing to a shorter-than-normal distance between the bases, an oversize ball, and an underhand pitching requirement. Each subsequent season brought gradual rule changes though. By the final season, 1954, the baselines had been extended from an original distance of 65 feet to a nearly official 85, the distance between the pitching rubber and home plate had grown from 40 feet to a more familiar 60, and the ball had evolved from a circumference of 12 inches to a baseball-size 9. The pitching style also changed by degrees—from underhand to sidearm to three-quarters to overhand.

In short, before long the women of this groundbreaking league were playing baseball or something pretty close to it. It makes sense, therefore, to weigh more heavily the exploits of players who stood out during the league's latter years than those who excelled when it was still essentially a softball circuit. By this measure then, Joanne Weaver was probably the league's best hitter. "Joltin' Jo," whose two sisters also played for her Fort Wayne Daisies, led the league in batting average in all three of its final three seasons. In 1954 she pounded pitchers to the tune of a .429 mark, becoming the only player in league history to top .400. She also set records that year with 29 home runs and 254 total bases. On the mound, meanwhile, South Bend Blue Sox right-hander Jean Faut was the class of the league. After debuting in 1946 when sidearm pitching was first legalized, she compiled a 1.23 ERA over eight seasons. Faut twice won the Player of the Year Award, threw two perfect games, and even won the league batting title in 1949 when she hit .291.

It is impossible to project, of course, how these ladies and the several other stars of the AAGPBL would have fared against male competition, a possibility baseball commissioner Ford Frick preemptively dismissed in 1952 when the success of the AAGPBL prompted him to reiterate Landis's ban on teams signing female players. And so, once the men came home from war, the women played for a few more seasons before retreating to the traditional roles assigned to them in 1950s America.

A more recent stride on the diamond for female players occurred in 1989 when Julie Croteau became the first woman to play NCAA baseball, lacing up her spikes for Division III St. Mary's College of Maryland. Croteau, who served as a backup first baseman for the Seahawks, batted .222 as a first-year student and played a total of three seasons before graduating in 1992. The next year, she and Lee Anne Ketcham became the first women to play in the Hawaii Winter League.

lie Croteau played for the St. Mary's College ahawks and Coors Silver Bullets. COURTESY OF ST. RY'S COLLEGE

As members of the Maui Stingrays, Croteau went 1-for-12 in the Major League Baseball–sanctioned developmental league, while Ketcham posted a 6.75 ERA in nine games, allowing six earned runs in eight innings.

Both Croteau and Ketcham later played for the Colorado Silver Bullets, an all-female team sponsored by the Coors Brewing Company and managed by Hall of Famer Phil Niekro. From 1994 through 1997, the Bullets traveled the country competing against male city-league teams, college teams and summer league teams. After struggling during their first few years, the Bullets finished with a winning record for the first time in 1997, but soon after lost their funding from Coors and disbanded.

Finally, in 1997, America witnessed the arrival of the first female minor leaguer. Ila Borders didn't make it to the big leagues, but she took an important leap for young women everywhere, or rather several important leaps, during her four-year minor league career. Like the trailblazing Mitchell, who had shocked the baseball world decades before, Borders was a left-handed pitcher who relied on guile. It is worth noting, however, that the 5-foot 10-inch Californian possessed a fastball that consistently sat in the high seventies and topped out in the low eighties, making her a considerably harder thrower than the typical American male.

After pitching for the ordinarily all-male teams at Southern California College (1994–1996) and Whittier College (1997), Borders became the first female to play for a men's pro team when she signed with the St. Paul Saints of the Northern League. The bush league circuit was, and still is, unaffiliated with Major League Baseball's farm system. But it is generally viewed as comparable to organized baseball's low Class A.

Borders appeared in her first game on May 31, 1997, and suffered an abysmal debut. Facing the Sioux Falls Canaries, she hit the first batter and then committed a balk, en route to allowing three runs without recording an out. Two weeks later she was traded to the Duluth-Superior Dukes, for whom she struggled during the season's final two and a half months to finish her rookie year with no decisions and a 7.53 ERA in fifteen games. Although the Northern League was using her, at least in part, as a publicity stunt, Borders had talent. When she kept the ball down in the strike zone she could induce batters to hit ground balls. Pitching for the Dukes the next season, she recorded her first win when she held Sioux Falls scoreless on three hits over six innings in a 3–1 win. She finished 1998 with a 1-4 record and an 8.66 ERA in forty-four innings. In 1999 she enjoyed her most successful stretch after an early-season trade to the Madison Black Wolf. In Madison, she was used mainly as a three-inning starter and flourished in the role, posting a 1-0 record and 1.67 ERA in fifteen outings. Counting the first three games she had pitched that season with Duluth-Superior, her 1999 totals included

Ila Borders, shown warming up for the Duluth Superior Dukes, pitched for three minor league teams. COURTESY OF THE SAINT PAUL SAINTS

a 3.63 ERA in thirty-five innings. After playing the next season in the ill-fated Western Baseball League, Borders retired at age twenty-six with a career mark of 2-4 and a 6.73 ERA.

Clearly, this baseball debate seems to boil down to which lefty pitcher was the better player, Mitchell or Borders. While it's tempting to give the nod to Mitchell—she did strike out the greatest player ever, after all—Borders is our choice, for submitting a more extensive body of work and for challenging assumptions that other female players will hopefully continue to debunk in the years ahead. It would seem to be only a matter of time before the gains female athletes have made in other sports are also reflected in our baseball world, and Borders has done more than any other female player to date to pave the way.

[3]

THE BEST GAIJIN

His Star Rose in the Land of the Rising Sun

As American baseball fans, our current interest in Japanese players most commonly concerns how the latest imports will affect the big league teams we follow. If we wanted to step back and appraise the last decade's emigration of Nippon Professional Baseball League (NPBL) stars to the major leagues, we could surely debate the relative merits of such past and present ballers as Hideo Nomo, Kazuhiro Sasaki, Ichiro Suzuki, Takashi Saito, Hideki Matsui, Daisuke Matsuzaka, and Kosuke Fukudome, but of course we'd eventually recognize Ichiro Suzuki's greatness above all others.

Although the infusion of Japanese players into our national pastime is a relatively recent phenomenon, the effect of American players on Japanese baseball dates back more than five decades to when Wally Yonamine, who had never played in the major leagues but had played in the minors, became Japan's first foreign-born—or *gaijin*—star in 1951. This chapter celebrates the careers of all those trailblazers like Yonamine, who have made the trek from America to Japan to play, in the hope of identifying the American player who has enjoyed the most success in Japan.

Some cultural and historical perspective will inform our discussion, so let's begin by noting that although we Americans are far less interested in the daily intricacies of the Japanese leagues than the Japanese are in how their former stars are doing over here, American players have profoundly influenced the evolution of the NPBL through the years. They have set several Japanese records, won their share of MVP Awards, and played starring roles in many Japan Championship Series since Yonamine's debut. And they've done so despite their limited representation in the league, as NPBL teams have traditionally been permitted to carry only two or three gaijin at any one time on their twenty-five-man rosters. Although this foreign-players rule was recently relaxed to allow up to four gaijin per club, a fair number of these spots are taken by relatively low-salaried players from Taiwan or South Korea, leaving just a few openings for the American and Latin-American visitors who draw the largest contracts.

Although Yonamine, whose career we'll discuss in greater detail shortly, was an important figure in establishing the baseball bond between the United States and Japan, he was not the first baseball ambassador to the island nation. In fact, the hardball connection between the two countries began in 1873 when Horace Wilson, an English professor from Maine, accepted a job at Tokyo University and carried with him to Japan not only a love of Shakespeare but of the American game as well. Wilson introduced the sport to his students, and before long it had spread across the island.

By the 1920s dozens of Japanese teams were playing under an array of loosely organized leagues, similar to how American teams organized prior to the formation of the National League. And during those Roaring Twenties and Thrifty Thirties, the two nations' sporting interests were more closely fused by marauding American All-Stars who visited Japan during the off-season to promote the game and reap appearance fees. Headliners like Casey Stengel, Ty Cobb, Lou Gehrig, Jimmie Foxx, and Babe Ruth all made voyages to Japan.

The country's first major league made its debut in 1936 when the Japan Pro Baseball League formed, but the onset of World War II caused interest in the sport to wane and the bombings of 1945 resulted in the league's dissolution. When it came time to restore play as part of Japan's postwar rebuilding in 1950, large corporations bankrolled the effort and the NPBL came into existence. The circuit was, and still is, composed of twelve teams: six in the Central League and six in the Pacific League.

Now then, let's begin our review of the better American players who have influenced Japanese hardball in the years since. The first, Yonamine, was a Hawaiian-born ethnic Japanese. He served the United States in the war and then played semipro football with a barnstorming Hawaiian team before spending the 1947 season as a halfback for the San Francisco 49ers of the early NFL. After suffering an injury on the gridiron, he decided to devote himself to baseball. He played one season for a Class C team, and then had the good fortune of meeting legendary Pacific Coast League manager Lefty O'Doul, who had toured Japan with Ruth and others, and was committed to doing his part to help repair the fissure between the United States and Japan. In concert with Matsutaro Shoriki, the NPBL's first commissioner, O'Doul convinced Yonamine to sign a contract with the Tokyo Giants. This was no small cultural phenomenon, given the anti-American sentiment in Japan at the time, and the conflicted feelings many Japanese citizens had for Japanese-Americans. Nonetheless, Yonamine made his debut in 1951 and excelled

A plaque honoring Wally Yonamine hangs in the Japanese Baseball Hall of Fame. COURTESY OF THE BASEBALL HALL OF FAME AND MUSEUM OF JAPAN

immediately, finishing runner-up for the batting crown with a .354 average. Then the speedy outfielder led the Central League in hitting in 1954, 1956, and 1957. He became the first gaijin to win an MVP Award in 1957. He won four Japan Championship Series with the Giants, made eight All-Star teams, and stole home a league record eleven times. He played through 1962, finishing with a .311 average, good for the sixth-best mark in league history, then spent several seasons as a coach and manager. For his efforts he was elected to the Japanese Baseball Hall of Fame in 1994, becoming the first and only American player to be thus honored (O'Doul is also a member, but he never played in Japan).

Following in Yonamine's footsteps, a pair of former major leaguers headed off to play Nippon pro baseball in 1962, as Don Newcombe and Larry Doby, both products of the Negro Leagues and pioneers in the integration of Major League Baseball, signed with the Chunichi Dragons. Doby batted .225, while Newcombe, who'd always been known as a good-hitting pitcher, played the outfield and batted .262 with 12 homers in eighty-one games.

By the 1970s American players were heading east regularly, usually for brief stopovers during transitional phases of their careers, but sometimes for longer stays. In general, the Americans heading to Japan could, and still can, be classified into three groups. First are the so-called "Four-A" players who perform well at the higher minor league levels but aren't able to establish themselves in the American big leagues. They head to Japan hoping to get steady playing time, showcase their skills, and then return with a big league contract. The classic example would be Cecil Fielder, who bounced back and forth between the Toronto Blue Jays and the minors from 1985 to 1988, hit 38 homers for the Hanshin Tigers in 1989, earning a contract with the Detroit Tigers, for whom he hit 51 home runs with 132 RBIs in 1990. Some of these players don't come back to the States so soon, concluding that they'd prefer to be stars in Japan than benchwarmers in America. Charlie Manuel, for example, was content to stay in Japan where he twice led the Pacific League in home runs and won the MVP Award in 1979 after he had batted just .198 over parts of six seasons in the big leagues. He eventually returned to the States as a manager, after batting .303 with 189 home runs and 491 RBIs over six seasons with the Yakult Swallows and Kintetsu Buffaloes. Similarly Alonzo Powell, who never could stick with a big league club, found the prospect of perennially vying for batting titles in Japan—he won three straight Central League crowns between 1994 and 1996—more appealing than signing another minor league deal back home.

The second commonly observed gaijin group is composed of established big leaguers suddenly foundering midway through their careers. They head to Japan looking to reassert their previous form against slightly lesser competition, and to do so for substantially more money and fewer eight-hour bus rides than the American minor leagues offer. Warren Cromartie, Julio Franco, Goose Gossage, Bill Gullickson, Shane Mack, and Steve Ontiveros all fall into this class, as well as Bob Horner, who was so peeved when the colluding Major League owners refused to offer him a big free agent contract in 1987 that he headed to Japan after a season in which he had hit 27 homers and driven in 87 runs for the Atlanta Braves. In Japan, Horner hit 31 long balls for the Swallows, before promptly signing with the St. Louis Cardinals in 1988.

The third group of players who consider Japan a viable professional option consists of prominent big leaguers nearing the ends of their careers, looking for one last payday and perhaps some cultural enlightenment. In addition to Newcombe and Doby, others who have headed to Japan in the later stages of their playing days include Matty Alou, Glenn Davis, Rob Deer, Mike Greenwell, Pete Incaviglia, Davey Johnson, Bill Madlock, Kevin Mitchell, Larry Parrish, Joe Pepitone, and Roy White.

As for the Americans from these three groups who have enjoyed the most success overseas, brothers Leron and Leon Lee—the uncle and father, respectively, of current big leaguer Derrek Lee—Randy Bass, and Karl "Tuffy" Rhodes stand above the rest. All four were power hitters who made prodigious marks in the NPBL record books.

Leron Lee sits atop Japan's all-time batting list with a .320 average, while brother Leon ranks eighth all-time among NPBL hitters (among players with at least 4,000 at-bats) with a .308 average. The brothers' odyssey began when, after playing eight seasons with the Cardinals, Padres, Indians, and Dodgers and collecting just 404 hits and amassing only a .250 average, Leron Lee signed with the Lotte Orions in 1977. He led the Pacific League with 34 home runs and 109 RBIs as a rookie, then won the batting title with a .358 mark in 1980. Over ten seasons he never batted below .300, while racking up 283 homers and 912 RBIs. His lifetime average is fractionally better than Tsutomu Wakamatsu's.

After his brother's successful debut, Leon Lee, who had previously played five minor league seasons in the Cardinals system, joined the Orions. Leon Lee enjoyed his best season in 1980 when he batted .340 with 41 home runs and 116 RBIs. In a ten-year career he had 268 home runs and 884 RBIs. Of the two Lee brothers, Leron, whose life story inspired the 1992 movie *Mr. Baseball,* was the better gaijin player.

Another player of the era, who enjoyed even more success but over a shorter period of time, was Randy Bass. The slugging first baseman had made the Twins roster in 1977, but he never claimed a starting job in six seasons. At age twenty-nine he joined the Hanshin Tigers and blossomed, displaying a combination of power and discipline from the left side of the plate that Japanese fans had scarcely seen. He won back-to-back Triple Crowns in 1985 and 1986. During his first such season, he hit 54 homers and appeared on his way to breaking the legendary Sadaharu Oh's single-season record of 55 until a conspiracy orchestrated by Oh's Yomiuri Giants resulted in Bass being repeatedly intentionally walked during the final week of the season. Bass was, however, honored with an MVP trophy for his efforts and his Tigers won the Championship Series. In 1986 he broke the single-season batting record, hitting .389 to unseat Isao Harimoto. Then he continued to rake for Hanshin for another season and a half before being granted his release midway through 1988 amid a contract dispute. Over three and a half seasons, Bass batted .337 with 202 homers and 486 RBIs. With just 2,208 at-bats he comes up considerably short of the 4,000 required to rank among Japan's all-time batting leaders, but it is worth noting that only Ichiro Suzuki (.353) had a higher average among NPBL players with at least 2,000 at-bats. After Bass's fleeting career, he returned to Oklahoma and became a state senator.

While Bass challenged Oh's single-season long-ball record, Tuffy Rhodes did him one better. The outfielder, who had batted .224 with just 14 home runs in 225 major league games spent mostly with the Astros and Cubs, tied Oh in 2001 when he hit 55 big flies for Kintetsu. Then, the very next year, Alex Cabrera, who had played briefly with the Arizona Diamondbacks in 2000 after spending ten seasons in the minors, tied the record as well, playing for the Seibu Lions. Cabrera was later named in baseball's Mitchell Report, which alleged that he had purchased and possessed large quantities of performance-enhancing drugs. Rhodes has not been linked to steroid use and continues to play in Japan where he batted .284 with 442 homers and 1,207 RBIs through 2008.

Rhodes's power totals are impressive, but he hasn't been able to match Bass's average. Bass too is a flawed candidate for best-gaijin bragging rights, since his career was so short. Thus, we must conclude that while Rhodes, Bass, and both Lee brothers made profound contributions to the NPBL, none has duplicated the success of Yonamine, who made those eight All-Star squads and won those four championship rings. Thus, the first gaijin—and the only one in the Japanese Baseball Hall of Fame—is our pick.

[4]

THE BEST TWO-SPORT PLAYER

He Was a Man for Two Seasons

Since the days of Jim Thorpe—the Olympic hero and star of the early NFL who also played six seasons as a member of the Giants, Reds, and Braves during the 1910s—athletes skilled enough to play professionally in more than one sport have continued to fascinate us Americans. Through the years more than two dozen Major League Baseball players have done just that. But before we get to this essay's main task, which involves determining which of these versatile athletes was the best baseball player of the lot, let's first tip our caps to some familiar players who had the talent to play professionally in two sports but instead chose to star in just one.

The ranks of highly regarded amateurs who were drafted by major league teams but didn't sign include: Archie Manning, who was selected in four different baseball drafts, including in 1971 by the Royals who picked him in the second round; Ken Stabler, who was selected three times, including in 1968 by the Astros who picked him in the second round; Dan Marino, who was selected in the fourth round in 1979 by the Royals; and Tom Brady, who was picked in the eighteenth round in 1995 by the Expos. And there have been plenty of others. Those are just the more recognizable footballers who had the opportunity to try their hands at pro baseball if they'd so chosen.

Stars of other sports who did play minor league baseball before, during, or after their more noteworthy accomplishments include: Michael Jordan, whose midlife-crisis tour of the Southern League saw him bat .202 and commit 11 errors as an outfielder for the Birmingham Barons in 1994; John Elway, who batted .318 with a .432 on-base percentage and 13 steals in forty-four New York–Penn League games in 1982; John Lynch, who posted a 1-3 record and 2.36 ERA over eleven minor league starts in the Marlins system; Ricky Williams, who batted .211 over four minor league baseball seasons while simultaneously playing college football; Chris Weinke, who batted .248 with 69 home runs over six minor league seasons before playing quarterback at Florida State University; and Javon Walker, who batted .153 over parts of three minor league seasons while playing college football.

On the other hand, here's a list of prominent baseball players whom the scouts believed were talented enough to play other sports: Dave Winfield, who was drafted by the NFL's Vikings, NBA's Hawks, and ABA's Utah Stars; Tom Glavine, who was a fourth-round selection of the L.A. Kings in the 1984 NHL

Basketball legend Michael Jordan played for the Birmingham Barons in 1994. COURTESY OF THE BIRMINGHAM BARONS

draft; Kenny Lofton, who played in the Final Four as a member of the Arizona Wildcats in 1988; Kirk McCaskill, who was a fourth-round pick of the Winnipeg Jets in 1981 and played one minor league hockey season; and the great Jackie Robinson, who lettered in baseball, football, basketball, and track at UCLA.

While speculation regarding amateur players' two-sport potential is an intriguing topic each year as the baseball draft approaches, the occurrence of an athlete actually playing at the highest level in two sports is, of course, rare. But some recent players have reached the pinnacle of two professional sports. Eventual NBA All-Star Danny Ainge, for instance, played two seasons with the Toronto Blue Jays, batting .220 over the 1980 and 1981 seasons, while simultaneously playing basketball at Brigham Young University. NFL running back D. J. Dozier had a similarly forgettable baseball career, batting .191 in twenty-five games with the Mets in 1992, before joining the Vikings. Future NFL quarterback Chad Hutchinson posted a 24.75 ERA in three games with the Cardinals in 2001 before joining the Cowboys. Josh Booty, another future NFL signal caller, hit .269 in twenty-six at-bats with the Marlins in the late 1990s, prior to playing for the Browns. And still another future NFL QB, Drew Henson, batted .111 in eight big league games with the Yankees before joining the Cowboys. And current big league southpaw Mark Hendrickson played four years in the NBA in the 1990s, averaging 3.3 points per game for four different teams, before embarking upon a baseball career that has yielded 56 big league wins through 2009.

As for the two-sport players who have *starred* on the baseball field, two names usually come immediately to mind when the topic comes up: Bo Jackson and Deion Sanders. Both became media darlings during their forays into both the baseball and football worlds during the 1980s and 1990s. Jackson was a full-time baseball player and part-time football player. Sanders was a full-time football player and part-time baseball player. Both were very good at both sports, and Jackson, in fact, may have become better than just "very good" in both, if he hadn't suffered a career-ending injury as far as football was concerned, and career-altering injury as far as baseball was concerned, during a Raiders playoff game in 1991.

After the Royals selected Jackson in the fourth round of the 1986 draft, he played fifty-three minor league games before appearing in twenty-five big league contests later that same summer. The next season, he began a stretch of four years in which he hit at least 22 homers and struck out at least 128 times. He quickly became a fan favorite, owing to his prodigious long balls and spectacular plays in the outfield. Once, he literally ran up an outfield fence while making a difficult catch. Another time, he threw out a runner who was attempting to score on an apparent sacrifice fly that had carried all the way to the leftfield warning track. Even in failure, Jackson put on a good show, snapping bats over his knees or even his muscle-bound neck in frustration. His best year was 1989, when he batted .256 with 32 homers, 105 RBIs, and 26 stolen bases. He was also named MVP of the All-Star Game that season, after hitting a tremendous home run to centerfield at Anaheim Stadium in the first inning and later beating out an infield hit and stealing a base. The next year, he raised his average to .272 with 28 home runs and 78 RBIs in just 111 games. Simultaneously, he played about ten games per season at tailback for the Raiders from 1987 to 1991, averaging 5.4 yards per carry and racking up 2,782 yards and 16 touchdowns. After injuring his femur so badly that he needed to have artificial hip replacement surgery, he remarkably returned to the baseball diamond in 1993 as a designated hitter for the White Sox and hit a home run in his first at-bat in two years. He was named Comeback Player of the Year after batting .232 with 16 homers and 45 RBIs. He played one more mediocre season with the Angels, and then retired. His lifetime stat line includes a .250 average, 141 home runs, and 415 RBIs over eight seasons.

Sanders made eight Pro Bowls in his fourteen-year NFL career, won Defensive Player of the Year honors in 1994, and won a Super Bowl ring with the 49ers. He may be the best football player ever to play big league baseball, although a case could also be made for Thorpe—a .252 hitter over six big league seasons—who played fifty-two games in the early NFL and eventually became league president. On the diamond, Sanders was a speedy outfielder, electric base runner, and mediocre hitter. A few months before beginning his career at cornerback for the Atlanta Falcons in 1989, he got his first taste of the Show with the Yankees, batting .234 in fourteen games. As his NFL career progressed, he continued to return to the diamond for the first several months each season, before hustling back to the gridiron. When his Braves made the playoffs in 1992 and 1993, he stuck around longer than usual and shuttled back and forth between the two sports, once famously arriving for a Sunday night World Series game via helicopter after playing football that same day. He led the National League with 14 triples in 1992, despite playing just ninety-seven games. He finished second in the league in stolen bases twice, swiping 38 bags in 1994 and 56 in 1997. He batted .348 in thirteen postseason games. Over nine seasons with four different teams, he batted .263 with 43 triples, 39 home runs, 168 RBIs, and 186 stolen bases.

A less-heralded teammate of Sanders in the Falcons' defensive backfield was also playing both baseball and football in 1989, 1990, and 1991. Brian Jordan received much less fanfare than Sanders and Jackson but eventually became a better baseball player than either of them. A first-round draft pick of the Cardinals in 1988, Jordan started at cornerback for the Falcons for two full seasons while toiling in the St. Louis farm system. After getting his first cup of coffee in the big leagues in 1992, he decided to give up football, which proved to be a good decision. He batted .309 with 10 home runs and 44 RBIs in sixty-seven games for St. Louis in 1993 and became a steady offensive producer throughout the rest of the 1990s, later playing for the Braves and Dodgers. He finished eighth in the NL MVP balloting in 1996, when he batted .310 with 17 homers and 104 RBIs. He made the All-Star team in 1999, when he batted .283 with 23 home runs and 115 RBIs. In thirty-eight postseason games, he batted .250 with 6 homers and 27 RBIs. Over a fifteen-year career he had 1,454 hits—nearly three times as many as Jackson or Sanders, while batting .282, with 184 home runs, 821 RBIs, and 119 stolen bases.

In baseball history, no other two-sport player has excelled to the extent that Jordan did when it comes to hitting big league pitching and driving in runs. But two pitchers, who succeeded both on the mound and on the hardwood, also deserve our consideration. The only man to win a championship in two major sports, Gene Conley, tasted autumn champagne with the Milwaukee Braves in 1957 and then spring champagne with the Boston Celtics in 1959, 1960, and 1961. After displaying his skills as a power forward during a collegiate career at Washington State University, the 6-foot 9-inch Conley was selected in the tenth round of the 1952 NBA draft. By then, he had already signed a contract with the Boston Braves and had played two seasons in the minors. At age twenty-two he appeared in four games for the Braves at the tail end of the 1952 season, then that same year he averaged 2.3 points per game in thirty-nine outings for a Celtics squad that starred Bob Cousy, Ed MacCauley, and Bill Sharman. After the Braves convinced Conley to focus exclusively on baseball, he finished third in the National League Rookie of the Year balloting in 1954 (one spot behind Ernie Banks and one ahead of Hank Aaron), going 14-9 with a 2.96 ERA. He also made the NL All-Star team as a rookie, and then made it again the next year. In the 1955 Midsummer Classic, he earned the victory by striking out Al Kaline, Mickey Vernon, and Al Rosen in succession. In 1957, he went 9-9 with a 3.49 ERA for the Aaron- and Warren Spahn–led Braves who won the World Series. Then, despite the Braves' discouragement of his two-sport aspirations, Conley rejoined the Celtics, to join Bill Russell and Tom Heinsohn in the Boston frontcourt for the 1958-59 season. In fifty regular-season appearances for Red Auerbach's budding dynasty, Conley averaged 4.2 points per game, then he played in all eleven playoff games, averaging 4.9 points as the Celtics won their first of eight consecutive NBA titles. The peeved Braves responded by trading him to Philadelphia, where he played five more seasons (and four more basketball seasons) before retiring from both sports. It can be truly said that he was Bo Jackson before Bo Jackson. In six NBA seasons, Conley averaged 5.9 points and 6.3 rebounds. In eleven baseball seasons, he enjoyed five campaigns in which he won in double figures, he made three All-Star teams, and he went 91-96 with a 3.82 ERA.

Conley, Jackson, and Sanders can quibble over which of them best excelled in two major sports simultaneously—indeed all three have impressive resumes, though none was as good a baseball player as Brian Jordan. But our search for the best baseball player who also played at the highest level of another sport would not be complete if we didn't first consider another pitcher: Ron Reed, a tall right-hander whose short tenure on the hardwood and long career in the big leagues began after he starred in both sports at Notre Dame. The Detroit Pistons selected Reed twentieth overall in the 1965 NBA draft. Meanwhile, he signed a contract with the Milwaukee Braves, who had apparently forgotten by then their frustration with Conley's forays into a second sport. The 6-foot 5-inch Reed appeared in fifty-seven games for the Pistons during the 1965-66 season and in sixty-two more the next season, averaging 8.0 points and 6.4 rebounds. At the same time, he was quickly working his way up the Braves' minor league ladder, posting an ERA in the 1.00s at three of his first four stops. After making a brief appearance in the bigs late in 1966, Reed decided to focus solely on baseball. And by 1968, when he went 11-10 with a 3.35 ERA as a rookie, he was an All-Star. Although he never made another All-Star team, Reed stuck around in the big leagues for nineteen seasons and had a number of excellent campaigns. He was a starter for the Braves during his first eight years, and won at least ten games on six different occasions, including a high-water mark of 18-10 in 1969 when the Braves won the NL West. After being traded to the Cardinals, who then shipped him to the Phillies in 1975, Reed became a dominant reliever, registering at least fourteen saves in each of his first three seasons in the Philadelphia bullpen while maintaining an ERA in the 2.00s. He reached double figures in saves five times over the final nine years of his career, and went 13-8 in relief in 1979 and 9-1 in 1983. He was an important cog on the Phillies teams that beat the Royals in the 1980 World Series and lost to the Orioles in the 1983 Series. He retired in 1984 at the age of forty-one. Over his nineteen seasons Reed was 146-140 with 103 saves and a 3.46 ERA. Those aren't quite Dennis Eckersley or John Smoltz numbers, but neither of those starters-turned-relievers began their big league career in another sport. For his efforts, Reed is our pick as the best baseball player who also played professionally in another sport.

THE BEST
MULTITALENTS

[5]

THE BEST-HITTING PITCHER

He Sure Knew How to Help His Own Cause

If the aim of this chapter were to coronate the best two-way player in baseball history, meaning the one who best excelled both at the plate and on the mound, then our discussion would be rather short, since, as any learned fan knows, Babe Ruth practically reinvented baseball's offensive game after he'd begun his career as an exceptional left-handed pitcher. In his first six seasons, the Bambino went 89-46 with a sparkling 2.19 ERA, helping the Red Sox to three World Championships. Then, after being traded to the Yankees in 1920, he moved to the outfield, and fifteen years later he retired with a .342 lifetime average and 714 home runs. Ruth easily trounces the field of other players who converted from pitching to hitting, or vice versa, beating out distant runners-up such as Johnny Cooney, who was 34-44 as a left-handed starter with the Boston Braves between 1922 and 1930 before switching to the outfield and batting .286 over a ten-year second career as

Rick Ankiel became a star hitter for the Cardinals after his pitching career was derailed by chronic control problems.
COURTESY OF WIKIMEDIA COMMONS

a right-handed hitter; "Smoky" Joe Wood, a staff mate of Ruth's in Boston, who was a dominant 117-57 with a 2.03 ERA before injuries limited his effectiveness and forced him to the outfield where he hit .283 with 23 homers in six seasons; and Kid Gleason, who went 138-131 on the mound in the pre–modern era before batting .261 with 1,944 hits as a second baseman. As for the more contemporary converts, Rick Ankiel didn't enjoy enough success on the mound to enter Ruth's two-way stratosphere, no matter how many home runs he may slug as an outfielder; conversely, Ron Mahay, who played briefly for the Red Sox as an outfielder in 1995, didn't do much with the bat before becoming a lefty reliever.

So if we agree that Ruth was the best two-way player ever, how is it possible that we may contend that he wasn't the best-hitting pitcher of all-time? Well, in the games in which Ruth pitched, he batted just 490 times and chalked up 149 hits. That works out to a very impressive .304 average, which ranks third all-time among pitchers with at least three hundred at-bats and helps explain why the Yankees were so eager to make him a full-time hitter. Ruth also hit fifteen homers in games in which he pitched, which ranks nineteenth all-time, tied with the lifetime totals of Mike Hampton, Don Newcombe, Early Wynn, and several others. Again, fine company, but the fact remains that eighteen hurlers hit more homers during their pitching days than Ruth did during his. And several pitchers posted nearly as impressive batting averages over pitching careers that lasted much longer than Ruth's. So let's acknowledge that Ruth was the best pitcher just waiting to have his offensive potential tapped by a mid-career position change, but let's also say that he wasn't the pitcher who performed most nobly at the plate over the course of his career on the knob. Now then, let's get to the task of determining which hurler does deserve to be called the best-hitting pitcher.

First let's give credit to the only other pitchers besides Ruth to amass as many as three hundred at-bats while maintaining a batting average north of .300. Jack Bentley rapped 109 hits in 339 at-bats for a .322 average in games in which he pitched. Meanwhile, he went 46-33 with a 4.01 ERA as a lefty pitcher for the Senators, Giants, and Phillies between 1913 and 1927. Later in his career, he played some games at first base, and as pitchers figured out his weak spots at the bat, his lifetime average declined to .291. Another unheralded two-way player, Ervin Brame, began a five-year career with the Pirates in 1928 and proceeded to collect

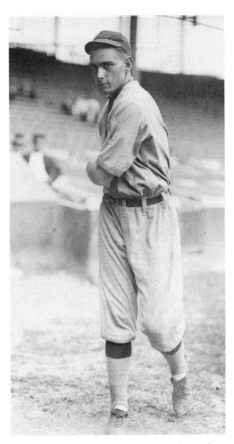

Pitcher Jack Bentley batted .322 from the pitcher's spot in the lineup. COURTESY OF THE LIBRARY OF CONGRESS

121 hits in 396 at-bats for a .306 average, while going 52-37 with a 4.76 ERA. Remarkably, in baseball's long history, Bentley, Brame, and Ruth are the only pitchers with at least three hundred career at-bats and a .300 average. And you wondered why some fans say the American League brand of ball is more exciting?

If we raise our minimum requirement to one thousand at-bats, George Uhle, who won exactly 200 games in a seventeen-year career spent mostly with the Tigers and Indians during the 1920s and 1930s, moves into the top spot among pitchers with a .289 average. Next comes Uhle's contemporary, Red Lucas, who won 157 games while batting .281 in fifteen seasons spent mostly with the Reds and Pirates. Ranked third is Wes Ferrell, who won 193 games for several teams during the same era, while batting .280.

Ferrell's power at the plate distinguished him from the other slugging hurlers of his era or of any other era, though. While Uhle and Lucas hit 9 and 3 home runs, respectively, over their long careers, Ferrell whopped a pitchers-best 37 homers (not including one hit as a pinch-hitter). Amazingly, his 38 total homers easily exceeded the 28 hit by his Hall of Fame brother Rick Ferrell, a catcher. As legend of Wes Ferrell's two-way prowess grew, his accomplishments came to include an incredible 1935 season in which the Red Sox pitcher not only led the American League with 25 wins, 31 complete games and 38 starts, but also batted .347 with 7 home runs and 32 RBIs. His 52 hits tied the single-season mark Uhle had set for pitchers thirteen years earlier, and his 32 RBIs bested the previous high of 30, which Ferrell himself had set in 1931 while pitching for the Indians. His 7 homers were two shy of his own single-season mark for pitchers, which he set in 1931. In July of 1935, Ferrell enjoyed the best two-way month any player has ever had, leading the Red Sox with 7 wins and 5 home runs. The next year, in a game against the Philadelphia A's, Ferrell hit a grand slam and a two-run homer to drive in all six runs in a 6–4 Boston win. Amazingly, that game was one of five two-homer-games in Ferrell's career.

Ferrell, who not only hit .280 but also registered a .351 on-base percentage, a .446 slugging percentage, and 208 RBIs, is the clear choice as the best-hitting pitcher ever.

But let's also give credit to some other marksmen who were also steady batsmen. Most of the heavy-hitting hurlers were all-or-nothing types who had power but didn't hit for average, while a few held their own even when they weren't touching 'em all. Bob Lemon, who started his career as a third baseman, then won 207 games for the Indians in the 1940s and 1950s, hit the second-most homers by a pitcher—35—while batting a respectable .232. Red Ruffing, who won 273 games to earn a place in Cooperstown during a career that spanned from 1924 to 1947, hit 34 home runs in the games in which he pitched, batted a solid .269, racked up 273 RBIs and tallied a pitchers-record 98 doubles. Three other top homering hurlers—all familiar baseball names—submitted sub-.200 career averages: Warren Spahn (35 home runs, .194 average), Earl Wilson (33 home runs, .195 average) and Don Drysdale (29 home runs, .187 average). Walter Johnson ranks ninth with 23 home runs to go with his .237 average and pitchers-record 41 triples. Another pitching great, Cy Young, owns many of the other cumulative batting records for pitchers, owing to his longevity in the game, even though he batted just .210. Young tops the charts with his 2,960 at-bats, 623 hits, 325 runs, and 290 RBIs.

Today, even most National League teams prefer that their pitchers focus on their primary mission and discourage extended sessions in the batting cage. American League fans who say it's boring to watch the pitchers of the Senior Circuit feebly wave and then head for the dugout are right—it is. And sacrifice bunts aren't very exciting either. That's why it's so captivating when there comes along, every so often, a pitcher who actually can tote the lumber. The Reds' Micah Owings is the latest example of this phenomenon. Owings generated tremendous interest in 2007 on his way to winning the Silver Slugger Award as a rookie pitcher with the Diamondbacks. That year, he batted .333 with 20 hits in 60 at-bats, while hitting 4 homers and driving in 15 runs. In 2008, playing for the Diamondbacks and Reds, he batted .304 with 1 homer in 56 at-bats. His success is no accident. The hulking right-hander set a Georgia schoolboy record with 69 long balls before being selected in the third round of the 2005 draft by Arizona. Then he batted .377 in parts of three minor league seasons before being called up to the majors. As for other active pitchers, Carlos Zambrano, who won the Silver Slugger in 2008 when he batted .337 with 4 home runs and 14 RBIs, and who possesses a .236 lifetime average, with 20 home runs and 58 RBIs through 2009, is one of the finest. Livan Hernandez (.227, 9 home runs, 75 RBIs) and Dontrelle Willis (.233, 8 home runs, 35 RBIs) are also respectable.

Will there ever be another pitcher who can hit for power and average like Wes Ferrell did, while pitching well enough to rack up an equally impressive lifetime body of work at the plate? And will that individual be fortunate enough to play his entire career in the National League so that he might challenge Ferrell's homer record, Johnson's triple tally, or Ruffing's two-bagger track record? Who knows, but for the current generation, Owings, who possesses a powerful right arm in addition to a sound batting eye and compact power stroke, is the best bet. In the meantime, Ferrell remains the best-hitting pitcher the game has yet known.

[6]

THE BEST-PITCHING POSITION PLAYER

He Pitched-In When Given the Chance

For as long as there have been big league hitters, there have been big league hitters who have harangued their managers to let them pitch. These sluggers, who perhaps enjoyed two-way success back in their high school or college days, want to show off their stuff to teammates and opponents alike. Usually, of course, managers quickly bristle at such pleas for an inning or two on the hill, but on occasion, usually in the later stages of blowout losses when their bullpens can stand no further bludgeoning, they have been known to relent. The obvious downside to such a move is that the pitching position player may make a mockery of the game or, worse, suffer an injury as the result of asking his body to perform a task for which it isn't properly conditioned. Do you think Rangers manager Kevin Kennedy second-guessed himself after allowing All-Star rightfielder Jose Canseco to pitch an inning in a 15–1 loss to the Red Sox in May 1993? You bet he did, and not because Canseco allowed 3 runs in the outing. One of the 90-mile-per-hour fastballs that the muscle-bound Canseco unleashed tore the ulnar collateral ligament in his right elbow, which shortly thereafter necessitated surgery and cost him the remainder of the season.

Given this obvious deterrent to letting a star hitter toe the rubber, it is somewhat surprising then that while plenty of utility infielders and fourth outfielders have taken the mound, a number of the game's best batters have as well. It should be noted though that these appearances have often come toward the end of their careers and/or toward the end of seasons in which their teams were not headed for the postseason, minimizing the risk their managers have taken. Among the Hall of Fame hitters to make cameo appearances on the bump are Ty Cobb, who pitched twice at the end of the 1918 season, when he thought he might never again have the chance to do so since he was headed off to war, and then once again in 1925 when, as Tigers player-manager, he inserted himself into a game. Cobb's lifetime line: 5 IP, 6 H, 2 ER, 2 BB, 0 SO, and a 3.60 ERA. Meanwhile, Cooperstown-bound

Cobb contemporaries Honus Wagner (8.1 IP, 7 H, 5 R, 0 ER, 6 BB, 6 SO, 0.00 ERA) and Tris Speaker (1 IP, 2 H, 1 ER, 9.00 ERA) also made like Babe Ruth—the ultimate two-way player—during their careers. A generation later, Ted Williams (2 IP, 3 H, 1 ER, 0 BB, 1 SO, 4.50 ERA) and Stan Musial—who'd been an excellent minor league hurler—tried their hands at pitching. Musial faced just one batter in the final game of the 1952 season, the Cubs Frank Baumholtz, who was already statistically guaranteed to finish runner-up to Musial in the National League batting race. After Baumholtz reached on an error, Harvey Haddix was summoned to replace Musial. More recently, Hall of Famer Wade Boggs (2$\frac{1}{3}$ IP, 3 H, 1 ER, 1 BB, 2 SO, 3.86 ERA) showed off a nasty knuckleball in two outings, one for the Yankees in 1997, and one for the Devil Rays in 1999.

While these and other big-name hitters made newspaper headlines when they took the mound, the ultimate goal of this chapter is not to identify the Hall of Fame hitter who performed most nobly in his pitching cameo, but rather to find the position player—of any skill level—who did the best when called upon to hurl at the big league level. For the purpose of truly finding the hitter who stepped out of his comfort zone to succeed on the mound, let's disqualify such early two-way players as Roger Bresnahan, Jesse Burkett, Oyster Burns, Ben Chapman, Kid Gleason, Sam Rice, and of course Ruth, all of whom are best remembered as hitters but also pitched extensively. We're not looking for the best mid-career crossover, but rather for the best "pitcher" among those who played 99 percent of their big league games at a different position.

First, let's acknowledge just how difficult it is to pitch at the big league level, a fact to which wannabes such as Manny Alexander ($\frac{2}{3}$ IP, 5 ER, 67.50 ERA), Derek Bell (1 IP, 4 ER, 36.00 ERA), Larry Biittner (1$\frac{1}{3}$ IP, 6 ER, 40.50 ERA), Dave Kingman (4 IP, 4 ER, 9.00 ERA), John Mabry (1 IP, 7 ER, 63.00 ERA), Frank Menechino (1$\frac{1}{3}$ IP, 4 ER, 27.00 ERA), Craig Reynolds (2 IP, 6 ER, 27.00 ERA) and Todd Zeile (2 IP, 5 ER, 22.50 ERA) could all surely attest.

On the other hand, usually when a position player takes the mound the score is so lopsided that many of the other team's regular batters are out of the game, which makes the task a bit more manageable. Such was the case when Brewers position players Sal Bando, Jim Gantner, and Buck Martinez combined to allow just 6 hits and 3 runs over five innings in an 18–8 loss to the Royals in 1979, after starter Jim Slaton and relievers Reggie Cleveland and Paul Mitchell had yielded 15 earned runs in three-plus innings, or when the Angels Chili Davis retired six of the seven batters he faced, allowing only Jose Canseco to reach on a hit-by-pitch, in an 18–2 loss to the Rangers in 1993. Strong-armed Indians outfielder Mark Whiten, meanwhile, faced some legitimate big league hitters in his sole pitching appearance, a 12–2 loss to the A's in 1998. Whiten allowed a run on a hit batter and a double, but also struck out the side, whiffing the red-faced Mike Blowers, Miguel Tejada, and Mike Neill. Whiten remains the only "pitcher" in big league history to throw at least one inning and record every out of his career via strikeout.

Other respectable performances in this arcane corner of baseball inquiry have included scoreless outings of at least an inning by the following, all of whom boast a career ERA of 0.00: Mike Aldrete, Matty Alou, Mike Benjamin, John Cangelosi, Rick Cerone, Jeff Cirillo, Rocky Colavito, Dave Concepcion, Steve Finley, Lew Fonseca, Jack Fournier, Terry Francona, Wayne Gross, Shane Halter, Lenny Harris, Donnie Hill, Mark Loretta, Jim Morrison, Desi Relaford, Cookie Rojas, Scott Spiezio, Jerry Terrell, Cesar Tovar, Robin Ventura, and Glenn Wilson.

In 1988 Halter pitched a scoreless frame for the Royals, and on the final day of the 2000 season, as a member of the Tigers, he faced just one Twins batter and walked him, becoming the fourth player in big league history to play all nine positions in a single game. Tovar also played all nine positions in the lone game in which he pitched, while a member of the Twins in 1968. Harris, who has more pinch-hits (212) than any other player in history, proved he could pinch-pitch too when he offered the Reds bullpen some much needed relief, working a one-two-three eighth in a 16–3 loss to the Giants in 1998.

As for the best pinch-pitcher ever, the list of very best candidates includes old-timer Jimmie Foxx, who mashed his way to Cooperstown with a .325 average and 534 home runs; the heavy-hitting Colavito, who is better remembered for his 374 long balls; and the journeyman Cangelosi, who was a fourth outfielder throughout a thirteen-year career that spanned 1985 to 1999.

Foxx was thirty-one years old and enjoying his fifteenth big league season when he stepped onto the mound for the first time and submitted a perfect inning for the Red Sox in 1939. Then, in his final season, 1945, he pitched in nine games for the Phillies, including two starts. He once again proved hard to hit, allowing just 13 hits in $22^2/_3$ innings for last-place Philadelphia, but he also walked fourteen batters. Even so, he allowed just 4 runs, good for a 1.49 ERA, and he won his only career decision on August 20, when he started the second game of a doubleheader against the Reds and submitted just 1 run over $6^2/_3$ innings in a 4–2 triumph. Foxx retired after the season with a nifty career record of 1-0, with 23²/₃ innings pitched, 13 hits, 4 earned runs, 14 walks, 11 strikeouts, and a 1.52 ERA.

Colavito was twenty-four years old and in his third season with the Indians when he was summoned to the mound in relief for the first time in 1958. He allowed only 3 walks over the final three innings of a 3–2 loss to the Tigers. He then waited ten years before being called upon to pitch again. Once again, the Tigers were Colavito's foe, but by then he was a member of the Yankees. On Sunday, August 25, 1968, Yankees starter Steve Barber allowed 5 runs in 3¹/₃ innings, prompting New York manager Ralph Houk to send Colavito to the Yankee Stadium mound with the home team trailing 5–0. The veteran slugger pitched 2²/₃ innings of one-hit relief, New York got a run in the bottom of the fourth and five more in the sixth, and Colavito earned the win. He never pitched again and retired at the end of the season with a 1-0 record, with 5²/₃ innings pitched, 1 hit, 5 walks, 2 strikeouts, and a 0.00 ERA to his credit.

Unlike Foxx and Colavito, Cangelosi was a left-hander. His pitching career began in 1988, when, as a member of the Pirates, he pitched the final two innings in a 14–6 loss to the Dodgers and allowed only one hit. Then, in 1995, as a member of the Astros, he pitched the final inning in a 13–2 loss to the Cubs, and allowed only a walk. Finally, in 1998, as a member of the Marlins, he pitched the final inning in a 10–2 loss to the Padres, and again yielded only a walk. His career line: 4 IP, 1 H, 0 R, 2 BB, 0 SO, and a 0.00 ERA. Pretty impressive. But because he never pitched in a tight game, and because he never earned a win like our other two top candidates, it doesn't seem right to declare Cangelosi the best pitching hitter. And while Foxx deserves praise for his unlikely late-career pitching prowess, our choice is Colavito, who was unscored upon in two outings, earned a legitimate win, and allowed only one hit in his entire big league career.

[7]

THE BEST BASEBALL FAMILY

Baseball's Best Bloodline

In this chapter we seek to anoint the First Family of baseball. Arriving at such a determination will surely be no easy task. After all, nearly two hundred sons of former big leaguers have followed in their fathers' footsteps to the major leagues, and more than three hundred and fifty sibling duos, trios, or—in one case—a quintet, have played big league ball.

Now, if we deferred to a strictly statistical analysis to settle this baseball argument, it would be relatively easy to narrow the field. In the best father-son division we'd have to declare the cream of the crop Bobby and Barry Bonds—they of 1,094 lifetime homers—followed by the Ken Griffeys—who became the first father-son teammates with the Mariners in 1990 on their march toward what may be 5,000 career hits by the time Junior retires. In the much deeper brothers bracket we'd have to give the nod to Lloyd and Paul Waner, who punched matching tickets to Cooperstown while patrolling the Forbes Field outfield for the Pirates in the 1920s and 1930s, while collecting a brothers-best 5,611 hits. Also ranking high on the big bro/little bro barometer would be Phil and Joe Niekro, whose knuckleballs earned 539 wins; Gaylord and Jim Perry, whose spitball and breaking ball, respectively, garnered 529 wins; and, of course, Joe, Vince, and Dom DiMaggio—the "Greatest Generation" trio of All-Stars who amassed 4,853 hits.

But sometimes the numbers don't tell the full story. In an investigation like this one, we're not just looking for the family that has produced the most statistics, but for the family tree that has the most extensive roots in the game. In other words, the questions we must ask of each family are these: For how many unique years did it have at least one member in the big leagues? Were those members any good? And just how prominent is the family name in the game's history?

According to these criteria a multigenerational tandem—such as a father-son duo—would carry more weight than a single-generational one—as in the case of brothers. Yes, the DiMaggios combined to play forty-two seasons between them, but the family name was only appearing in box scores between 1936, when Joe broke in with the Yankees, and 1953, when Dom retired from the Red Sox. That's only eighteen years. By comparison, through 2009, at least one Griffey has been playing in the bigs every season since 1973. That's thirty-seven straight years. Longevity and continuity are important in our opinion.

Quality of play counts too, of course. So, it seems reasonable to mandate that more than one family member should have been a bona fide star, or, to make such a determination less subjective, let's say an All-Star. So, with apologies to Tommie Aaron, Dale Berra, Ken Brett, Ozzie Canseco, Chris Gwynn, Mike Maddux, Billy Ripken, Pete Rose Jr., and all those squatting Molinas, we're sorry, but your relative (no pun intended) mediocrity disqualifies your family.

We'll also suspend judgment on those families for whom at least one member is still in the early stages of adding to the family legacy. Here, we're thinking of Prince Fielder, B. J. and Justin Upton, J. D. and Stephen Drew, Tony Gwynn Jr., Delmon Young, and the other up-and-comers who may yet vault their family up our list.

What's left after these subtractions is a battle between the All-Star brother combos and the All-Star father-son combos. And we might also be on the lookout for a third category: three-generation baseball families who have sent a grandfather, son(s), and grandson(s) to the big leagues. Hint: there are three such tri-generational families, two of which can count All-Stars among all three generations.

First, let's rate the bros. With a sum of sibs to nearly match the Sutter Six who skated in the NHL during the 1970s and 1980s, the most famous baseball family during the game's early era went by the surname Delahanty. The five brothers, who grew up in Cleveland, etched their first entry in the baseball annals when future-Hall-of-Famer Ed Delahanty made his debut for the Philadelphia Quakers in 1888. Next came Tom, who joined his brother in the City of Brotherly Love in 1894. Then Jim debuted with the Chicago Orphans in 1901, Frank with the New York Highlanders in 1905, and Joe with the St. Louis Cardinals in 1907.

Ed led the league in homers twice, in batting twice, and in RBIs three times, and finished his sixteen-year career with 2,596 hits and a .346 lifetime average— good for fifth-best all-time, behind only Ty Cobb, Rogers Hornsby, Joe Jackson, and Lefty O'Doul. Jim was also a star, who racked up 1,159 hits and a .283 average in thirteen seasons. But the other three Delahanty boys were fringe players. Frank lasted six seasons, hitting .226, while Joe and Tom hung around for three seasons apiece, batting .238 and .239, respectively. Nonetheless, there was at least one Delahanty in the big leagues for twenty-eight consecutive years, a stretch that didn't end until Jim hung up his spikes after the 1915 campaign. So let's give the Delahantys their due for fielding one great player and one good one. But some other family surely did better.

Paul and Lloyd Waner, known as Big Poison and Little Poison, are the only two immediate family members to share membership in the Hall of Fame. The better of the two offensively, Paul, played rightfield and collected 3,152 hits to go with a .333 average between 1926 and 1945. A centerfielder who was three years his brother's junior, Lloyd had 2,459 hits and a .316 average between 1927 and 1945. They combined for five All-Star appearances, with Lloyd making his sole trip to the Midsummer Classic in 1938 (Note: the All-Star Game wasn't introduced until 1933). Some historians have pointed to Lloyd, who was mostly a singles hitter, as one of the weaker offensive players enshrined at Cooperstown, but that doesn't diminish the duo's accomplishment. Two Hall of Famers will be hard for any other family to beat. But then again, how many of today's baseball fans have heard of the Waners? Not many. And the fact that the Waner name isn't recognizable to many of the game's fans seems like it should count for something.

The Brothers Ferrell—Rick and Wes—also submitted an impressive collective body of work. Catcher Rick earned his Cooperstown stripes during an eighteen-year career that spanned 1929 to 1947. Neither his 1,692 career hits nor his .282 batting average are eye-popping, but he played in an era when catchers distinguished themselves with their defensive acumen as much as their bats. Wes pitched fifteen seasons and was his brother's battery-mate with the Red Sox from 1934 to 1937, before they were traded together to the Washington Senators. A six-time twenty-game winner and two-time All-Star, who authored a no-hitter in 1931, Wes finished with 193 wins and a 4.04 ERA. He was also the game's greatest hitting pitcher (see Chapter 5). For their efforts, the Ferrells deserve recognition as the brothers who best succeeded on both sides of the ball.

When it comes to strictly hitting brothers, the three DiMaggios have the edge over the three Alous—Felipe, Matty, and Jesus—even if you count the second-generation contribution of Felipe's son Moises. The best baseball trio, the Brothers D appeared in at least two All-Star games apiece, combining for twenty-two trips to the Midsummer Classic. Joe won nine World Series with the Yankees, set the record for baseball's longest hitting streak, won three MVP Awards, and made thirteen All-Star teams in thirteen seasons between 1936 and 1951. Dom batted .298 and appeared in seven All-Star Games for the Red Sox between 1940 and 1953. Vince made two All-Star teams while batting a DiMaggio-low .249 between 1937 and 1946. No baseball family fascinated baseball fans during one specific moment in time quite like the Brothers D did, but the family's reign was too short-lived to claim this essay's prize. For the same reason, the Perrys and the Niekros, while remarkable in their accomplishments, also come up short.

That brings us to the best multigenerational entrants. While the accomplishments of Bobby and Barry Bonds (thirty-six seasons, seventeen All-Star teams) and Senior and Junior Griffey (forty seasons, sixteen All-Star teams) have been well documented elsewhere, neither father was a great player. In both cases the dads earned three All-Star nods, while the sons garnered the rest. Both elders were very good players, though, especially the multitalented Bobby Bonds, who amassed 332 homers and 461 steals. And in fairness, Senior Griffey was a .296 hitter, which is nothing to sneeze at. In a head-to-head match, the Bonds win out, prevailing not only over the Griffeys but every other father-son duo in such offensive categories as homers (1,094), RBIs (3,020), runs (3,485), and steals (975).

While no two family members can rival the Bonds' statistical accomplishments over two generations—1968 to 1981 for Bobby, 1986 to 2007 for Barry—we can make the case that two of the three tri-generational families accounted for longer presences in the baseball world than the thirty-six seasons of Bonds ball.

Interestingly, all three of the tri-generational baseball family trees sprouted within three years of one another. The grandfathers are Ray Boone, who began a thirteen-year career with the Cleveland Indians in 1948, Gus Bell, who began a fifteen-year career with the Pirates in 1950, and Sammy Hairston, who played the only four games of his career in 1951. All three clans consist of a grandpa, one or more son(s), and a pair of grandsons.

Let's start by disqualifying the Hairston line, and not just because Sammy was a cup-of-coffee big leaguer, but because his heirs were also unexceptional. Still, Sammy deserves credit for passing solid baseball genes on to his son Jerry, who played in the bigs from 1973 through 1989 and batted .258, and his son Johnny who played three games with the Cubs in 1969. Jerry then passed the baseball chromosome on to the still-active Jerry Jr., who has batted .260 since breaking in with the Orioles in 1998, and Scott who has batted .252 since making the Diamondbacks roster in 2004. The Hairstons are scrappy, workmanlike players who have logged a total of thirty-three big league seasons (and counting), but All-Stars they are not.

Outfielder Gus Bell was a .281 lifetime hitter and four-time All-Star. His son Buddy batted .279 and racked up five All-Star nods between 1972 and 1989. Next, grandsons David, who batted .257 between 1995 and 2006, and Mike, who batted

.222 in nineteen games for the Reds in 2000, carried on the family name. While Gus and Buddy clearly rank among the top-five father-son duos, neither David nor Mike left enough of a mark on the game to push the Bell Bunch over the top in this discussion, although it is impressive that at least one Bell took part in forty-five different seasons over a fifty-seven year period that began when Gus made his debut in 1950 and ended when David retired in 2006.

And that brings us to the Boones. Ray was a .275 hitter and two-time All-Star between 1948 and 1960. He was followed by son Bob, who played nineteen seasons (1972–1990), and grandsons Bret, who played fourteen seasons (1992–2005), and Aaron, who has played thirteen seasons (1997–2009). More than just combining to play in fifty different seasons between 1948 and 2009, and appearing on the major league diamond for seven straight decades, dating back to the 1940s, the four Boones earned at least one All-Star acknowledgment apiece. Bob, who hit .254, was the best defensive catcher of his era, winning seven Gold Gloves. Bret hit .266 with 252 home runs, and won two Silver Slugger Awards and four Gold Gloves at second base. And Aaron, who is the sole Boone to appear in only one All-Star Game, is a .263 hitter with more than 1,000 hits. In total, the four Boones have amassed more than 5,800 hits, 630 home runs, and 3,100 RBIs, totals that surpass the Bonds' marks in the hit and RBI columns, falling short only in the column for homers.

The Boones have, however, needed twenty-two more seasons than the Bondses to establish those marks. But remember, our quest was a two-pronged one, to find the baseball family that has not only provided the game with high-caliber players but also with an enduring and nearly continuous legacy. For succeeding on both fronts, the Boone family is our choice as the best baseball family. Now, if Junior Griffey or Barry Bonds someday send a son or two to the big leagues, well, then we might have to reopen the discussion.

[8]

THE WORST HOTHEADED MANAGER

Anger Management Wasn't His Strong Suit

If there were a position description on file at Major League Baseball head-quarters describing the job of big league manager, one job requirement would surely read: "Must occasionally immerse self in borderline-psychotic tantrums before stadiums full of people. Said tantrums may include dirt-kicking, base-tossing, and Gatorade-bucket-flipping, and should continue well past the point of personal embarrassment."

In all seriousness, now, while a good old-fashioned ballpark freak-out garners plenty of hits on YouTube and lots of laughs on *SportsCenter,* manager meltdowns are certainly not the type of attention the commissioner and other guardians of the "Gentleman's Game" seek to attract. But the fact is, within just about every great baseball manager there exists the capacity for absolute madness.

Before we get into the nitty-gritty of searching for the worst baseball belliger-ent of all-time, let's spend a moment reviewing the different types of manager outbursts. If you buy into the theory that baseball's players usually determine the outcomes of games, and not the aging gents filling out the lineup cards, spitting sunflower seeds, and making two or three usually predictable pitching substitu-tions toward the end of each game, then you have to admit that losing a manager midway through a game is not as great a penalty to a team as losing one of its players. This principle explains why a manager often runs onto the field to "pro-tect" one of his star players who happens to be butting heads (in the figurative sense, not the Carl Everett sense) with an umpire. Thus, serving as a proxy, the skipper unleashes a maelstrom of abuse on the ump, bringing some satisfaction to the aggrieved player as his teammates drag him away from the fracas. After taking one for the team, the ejected manager doesn't really hit the showers, of course, but only retreats to the runway between the dugout and clubhouse where he can still dictate the team's strategy. In this context, pulling up a chair in the runway is a small price to pay for keeping a star player in a game. If, on the other hand, it's a light-hitting utility player who's creating the stir, well, the manager may be less apt to come running onto the field to pick up the battle.

Of course, other times a manager isn't so much rushing to a player's defense when he goes ballistic as he is acting of his own accord, often to make a major issue of what seems like a relatively inconsequential umpiring call. Here, we're thinking of those times when the manager gets booted for arguing a bang-bang play at first base in the second inning. While the radio announcers may joke that he must have had early dinner plans, more often these ejections are calculated histrionics by managers hoping to inspire their teams. Usually these incidents are preceded by losing streaks or some lackadaisical play. The manager goes goofy, says the "magic words," and stomps around indignantly. The crowd roars. And maybe his players finally wake up.

Then there are those managers who really do become so frustrated with the poor quality of umpiring they believe they're witnessing that they truly cross that invisible line between Bobcat Goldthwait crazy and Jack Nicholson crazy. These are the more enjoyable tirades from a fan's perspective. Here, we're thinking of a beet-red Lou Piniella uprooting first base and heaving it for all he's worth into rightfield, then scurrying after it so he can throw it again, or of Billy Martin piling so much dirt on home plate that the umpires have to summon the grounds crew to fetch a Shop-Vac, or of that infamous YouTube clip of the Southern League's Mississippi Braves manager Phil Wellman crawling around the field like a soldier before biting the end off the rosin bag and hurling it at an umpire like a grenade.

So which big league skipper deserves recognition and with it, perhaps, an accompanying gift certificate to anger-management therapy, for being the biggest hothead of all-time? Let's begin by looking at the list of fearless team leaders who have racked up the most ejections. At the head of the pack is longtime Braves manager Bobby Cox, who became the most ejected baseballer ever midway through the 2007 season when he was tossed from his 132nd game. With the ejection, which transpired when Cox got the heave-ho from Ted Barrett for arguing a called third strike, Cox passed the legendary John McGraw, who had held the record for more than seven decades by virtue of his fourteen ejections as a player and 117 as manager between 1891 and 1932.

Here's the complete list of the ten most ejected managers (not counting ejections that occurred when they were players) along with the ratio of games-per-ejection during their careers.

Manager	Ejections	Total Games	Games/Ejection
Bobby Cox*	143	4,136	28.9
John McGraw	117	4,769	40.8
Earl Weaver	97	2,541	26.2
Leo Durocher	95	3,739	39.4
Frankie Frisch	82	2,246	27.3
Paul Richards	80	1,837	23.0
Tony La Russa*	75	4,561	60.8
Joe Torre*	62	4,005	64.6
Lou Piniella*	61	3,262	53.5
Clark Griffith	60	2,918	48.6

* through 2008

McGraw, one of five Hall of Famers on the list, was once ejected for throwing a cup of water in an umpire's face during the pregame exchanging of lineup cards. Another time, he was suspended for splitting the lip of umpire Bill Byron with a right hook after a game. Weaver, who's remembered particularly for his ongoing feud with umpire Ron Luciano, not once but twice got ejected from both ends of a doubleheader. Durocher's foul mouth earned him the nickname Leo the Lip. The *Sporting News* once wrote of Frisch, "Even his own players shudder at his tirades." And Griffith's uncontrollable temper contributed to his decision to move upstairs to the front office.

As for the four feisty fellows still finding new and creative ways to get thrown out of games today, the leader of the pack, Cox, was once ejected for arguing that a game shouldn't resume after a rain delay. He has also been ejected from two World Series games, in 1992 and 1996. His most recurrent offense is arguing ball and strike calls, a form of umpire intimidation that surely helped Braves Greg Maddux and Tom Glavine, who always seemed to be pitching to a home plate as wide as a turkey platter.

Cox's most bombastic season was 2001, when he was tossed eleven times, leaving him just shy of McGraw's single-season mark of thirteen, set in 1905. In May of that simmering season McGraw was ejected from a game from which he had already been suspended when, after brawling with Pittsburgh manager Fred Clarke the day before, he tracked down Pirates owner Barney Dreyfuss in the stands and accused him of bribing the boys in blue. The next season, McGraw went

The fiery John McGraw, featured on a baseball card issued by the American Tobacco Company in 1911. COURTESY OF THE LIBRARY OF CONGRESS

into the stands again, this time at Baker Bowl, to punch out a Philly fanatic. But wait, McGraw's saga gets even stranger. In 1920 police found popular actor John Slavin badly beaten in McGraw's New York City apartment, prompting a grand jury injunction that charged the manager with violating the Prohibition era's Volstead Act for possessing alcohol. These off-field incidents only added to McGraw's rap as a hothead. And, similarly, Cox's 1995 arrest on battery charges related to a dispute in which his wife alleged he had punched her and pulled her hair, lent credence to his reputation as an angry man, although the charges were later dropped.

Cox's all-time ejection record is impressive, and will no doubt continue to grow. Like McGraw, he is a strong candidate to wear our worst baseball hothead crown. As for the other current managers on the list, some of Piniella's tirades have broached legendary status, but any claim he may lay to being a "bad man" is weakened by those bottled-water commercials he did in 2008, in which he made fun of his famous temper. In our book, anyone with the self-awareness to laugh at himself is a bit too grounded to win this dubious distinction. La Russa, meanwhile, is fiery but in a lawyerly sort of way, and he's much too contemplative when interviewed after games to be taken seriously as a psychopath. Torre's longevity, more than his temper, accounts for his presence on the list. If we look at the frequency at which managers have been ejected, Richards stands out for being tossed every twenty-three games. But who can blame him? In his twelve seasons piloting the White Sox and Orioles, his clubs finished as high as second place only once.

But simply awarding our terrible-temper prize to McGraw, Cox, or Richards would neglect to recognize the contributions to the game made by another slightly-less-than-balanced group of managers: those who were ejected often but didn't stick around in baseball long enough—due to their terrible tempers, their teams' poor play, or to other factors—to crack the all-time top-ten most ejected list. After all, our search isn't for the winning manager or for the long-lasting manager who had the greatest difficulty staying on the bench, but merely for the one who had the worst temper.

Expanding our scope to include managers who didn't stick around long enough to amass top-ten credentials brings into play fellows like Larry Bowa, who spent just six years at the helm of the Padres and Phillies but was ejected twenty-six times in 853

Joe Torre entered 2009 ranked eighth all-time in manager ejections. COURTESY OF WIKIMEDIA COMMONS

games, for a 32.8 games per ejection ratio. Years later, while serving as third-base coach for Torre's Dodgers in 2008, Bowa was ejected, ironically, for refusing to stand in the third-base coach's box.

Another famous hothead who didn't crack the top-ten list but deserves mention is Billy Martin. Despite managing just 2,267 games, Martin is tied with Ralph Houk for fourteenth on the all-time list with forty-five early showers. His 50.4 games per ejection ratio is far from eye-popping, but his troubled persona and the frighteningly intense nature of his tirades made his meltdowns must-see spectacles. His off-field problems with his players and with George Steinbrenner also added to his mad-man reputation. The widely acknowledged understanding that Billy was a ticking time bomb dated back to his playing days when the second baseman once drilled incoming base runner Clint Courtney between the eyes with a throw supposedly intended for first base. Later, he was traded from the Yankees after starting a bar fight that involved several star teammates. And then there was the time he threw a bat at Cubs pitcher Jim Brewer after the hurler had pitched inside against him. As a manager, Martin proved time and again that he wasn't just fiery but combative, and he wasn't just angry with umpires but with everyone. He picked fights with Steinbrenner, with traveling secretaries, cab drivers, fans, and even his own players—most famously Reggie Jackson, with whom he brawled in the dugout one night in Boston.

From the dugout, Martin got his thrills by pushing the buttons of short-fused opponents. He turned Royals slugger George Brett into a madman when the umpires capitulated to his demand that they invalidate a home run Brett had appeared to hit off Goose Gossage because it had been struck by a bat bearing too much pine tar. He tweaked "Oil Can" Boyd by insisting that the Red Sox pitcher remove the jewelry around his neck.

When it came to dealing with the boys in blue, Martin always knew how to put on a show. He was kicked out of the final game of the 1976 World Series for throwing baseballs onto the field as his Yankees went down in defeat. But more than anything, he was known as a pioneer in the use of infield dirt. He loved to kick it onto umpires, pile it on home plate, and once, in Oakland during the 1988 season, he resorted to picking up fistfuls of infield clay and heaving them at Dale Scott. This most memorable "Billy Goes Batty" moment was prompted by a play in which Yankee second baseman Bobby Meacham appeared to catch a sinking liner off the bat of Walt Weiss, before tossing the ball around the horn. Second base umpire Rick Reed ruled that Meacham had merely trapped the ball, and that Weiss was safe at first. When Scott, the crew chief, refused to overrule the call, Billy started firing like a little boy on a beach, with two hands at a time, right into Scott's chest and face. For his antics he received a three-day suspension, which infuriated umpires throughout the league, to the point that they declared collectively that any time Martin stepped onto the field in the future, they would eject him. Ultimately, commissioner Peter Ueberroth forced Martin to apologize and the umpires retracted the one-step rule.

In summary, while McGraw deserves credit as the forefather of mad managers, and Cox as an angry iron man of sorts, when it comes to the major league manager who consistently got the most bang out of his buck, Billy Martin stands above the rest.

THE BEST
IN THE CLUTCH

[9]

THE BEST ALL-STAR GAME PERFORMER

His Star Shined Brightly in Midsummer

Baseball's first All-Star Game was played at Comiskey Park as part of the Chicago World's Fair on July 6, 1933. The exhibition drew nearly fifty thousand fans and its success made a nearly instant rite of summer out of the Midsummer Classic. In the years to follow, players, fans, and even the pundits, fell more and more deeply in love with the aesthetic delight of a midseason breather from the still-forming pennant races when the best players in the world all stepped onto the same field to showcase their talents.

In the inaugural game—a 4–2 American League win—Lefty Gomez pitched three scoreless innings to ink the first of three All-Star Game victories on his Hall of Fame résumé. Fittingly, Babe Ruth hit the first home run in All-Star competition. In the years since, the NL has amassed a 41-36 record in the game, while there have also been two ties—a 1–1 gridlock at Fenway Park in 1961 that was curtailed due to rain, and a 7–7 stalemate at Miller Park in 2002 that ended in the eleventh inning when the two teams ran out of pitchers. In 1945 there was no All-Star Game due to wartime travel restrictions, but American and National League teams paired up instead and played eight simultaneous interleague games across the country. Between 1959 and 1962 there were two All-Star Games per summer; the second to raise money for the players' pension fund. Since 2003, the game's outcome has determined which league will have home-field advantage in the World Series. But whether or not it has counted for anything so important as an edge in October, serious fans have always known that the All-Star Game is important. Not only does it provide an excuse to throw a Tuesday night party, but it also has come to possess its own lore full of unforgettable moments.

The primary goal of this chapter is to identify the player who performed most nobly over the course of his All-Star Game career. Along the way, we will also acknowledge some of the more noteworthy single-game performances in Midsummer history.

In the 1934 game, which the AL won 9–7, NL starter Carl Hubbell set a record that has been tied once but never broken. Pitching on his home mound at the Polo Grounds, the Giants star struck out five batters in succession, and not just any five, but five future Hall of Famers. After Charlie Gehringer led off with a single and Heinie Manush walked, Hubbell whiffed Babe Ruth, Lou Gehrig, and Jimmie Foxx to escape the first inning. Then he whiffed Al Simmons and Joe Cronin to start the second frame.

In 1936, Joe DiMaggio became the first rookie to start an All-Star Game. And he sure deserved the honor. The twenty-one-year-old was enjoying arguably the best rookie season the game had yet known, but he went 0 for 5 and made a costly error in a 4–3 AL loss. DiMaggio, who would make thirteen All-Star teams in his thirteen seasons, batted just .225 in forty Midsummer Classic at-bats.

One of the most historically significant All-Star Game injuries occurred in 1937 when NL pitcher Dizzy Dean was struck on the foot by an Earl Averill liner in the third inning. Neither the Cardinals nor Dean considered the broken toe he suffered too serious at the time. But Dean returned to action too soon and in adjusting his delivery to compensate for the pain in his foot, he injured his throwing arm. Prior to that fateful All-Star Game, in which the twenty-six-year-old Dean absorbed the loss, he had won 133 games in five-plus big league seasons. Afterward, he won only seventeen more games.

In 1941 Arky Vaughan became the first player to homer twice in the same All-Star Game, going deep against Sid Hudson in the seventh inning and against Eddie Smith in the eighth at Briggs Stadium in Detroit. The blasts helped the NL to a 5–3 lead after eight frames and left the Pirates shortstop, who was not known for his power, positioned to claim he'd just enjoyed the best All-Star Game yet, on the merits of his 3-for-4 day with 2 homers and 4 RBIs. Then Ted Williams, making the second of his sixteen All-Star appearances, stole Vaughan's thunder. Williams came to bat with two outs in the bottom of the ninth with the AL trailing 5–4. With two men on, he unloaded on a Claude Passeau fastball and sent it into the rightfield upper deck for a three-run walk-off homer.

For Williams, who hit .304 in forty-six All-Star Game at-bats with 10 runs, 4 home runs, and 12 RBIs, the best was yet to come. But first, he and several other stars of the era suspended their careers to serve in the military. Thus, when the first nighttime All-Star Game took place in 1943 at Shibe Park in Philadelphia, Williams, DiMaggio, Johnny Mize, and several other prominent players were overseas. The same was true of the next All-Star Game, and after that, the 1945

Game was cancelled. Williams returned with a bang in 1946, though, at a game appropriately played at Fenway Park. In a 12–0 blowout, Teddy Ballgame set or tied several records that still stand. He went 4 for 4 with home runs against Kirby Higbe and Rip Sewell—whose famous Eephus pitch was said to be the most difficult pitch in either league to take deep, owing to its looping arc. Williams also scored 4 runs and drove in 5. He still shares the record for most home runs with Vaughan and three other players; for RBIs with Al Rosen, who drove home 5 teammates in the 1954 Game; and for most hits with Joe Medwick and Carl Yastrzemski. Meanwhile, Williams's 10 total bases and 4 runs have never been equaled. As we continue our review, his will be a difficult single-game performance for any player to beat, and his career accomplishments in the game may prove equally unsurpassable.

The 1950 game was less rosy for Williams. Not only did the NL win 4–3 on a fourteenth-inning home run by the Cardinals Red Schoendienst, who had entered the game as a defensive replacement for Jackie Robinson in the tenth, but Williams also broke his elbow crashing into the Comiskey Park fence to make a leaping catch. The stubborn slugger stayed in the game, but later required surgery that sidelined him until September.

Stan Musial, another Cardinal, was an extra-inning hero in 1955. His shot off Frank Sullivan in the bottom of the twelfth gave the NL a 6–5 win at County Stadium. The next year, Musial homered again to help the NL to a 7–3 win in Washington. Over twenty-two seasons Musial played in twenty-four Midsummer Classics, a statistical anomaly made possible by the four years—1959 through 1962—when he played in two All-Star Games per season. Musial's twenty-four games match the totals submitted by Hank Aaron and Willie Mays, who both also benefited from the two-game era. In all, Musial batted .317 in 63 at-bats. He holds records with his 6 home runs, 10 at-bats as a pinch-hitter, and 3 pinch-hits. His 40 total bases tie him with Mays for the most ever.

The 1957 game was notable for Cincinnati fans stuffing the ballot boxes and selecting Reds to start at seven of the NL's eight positions. Everyone but Cincinnati first baseman George Crowe benefited from the fans' overexuberance. It's worth noting that the Reds were a respectable, but certainly unremarkable, 44-36 through the first half of the season. And so, Ford Frick invoked his best-interests-of-the-game powers and removed two of the Reds—Gus Bell and Wally Post—from the lineup. The AL won 6–5, and the next year the players and managers picked the rosters.

In 1960 Mays stole the show, going 6 for 8 in the two games, hitting for the cycle between them. Played at Kaufman Stadium in Kansas City and Yankee Stadium in New York, the games were separated by a single travel day. Batting leadoff, Mays went 3 for 4 in each contest. He led off the first game with a triple off Bill Monbouquette and the second with a single against Whitey Ford. He also homered off Ford in the third inning. Mays's career numbers reflect a .299 average in a record 75 at-bats with 3 home runs and 9 RBIs. He also holds records with 20 runs and 23 hits, marks attributable to his longevity, frequent placement atop the NL batting order, and, of course, his immense talent.

In 1962 baseball named an All-Star MVP for the first time: Maury Wills was the unlikely first winner after entering as a pinch runner for the forty-one-year-old Musial in the sixth inning. Wills promptly stole second base and then scored on a single by Dick Groat to knot the game 1–1. In the eighth, Wills led off with a single, raced all the way to third base on a single to leftfield, and then scored on a shallow pop foul to right. His 1 for 1 effort with 2 runs and a steal was good enough to earn MVP honors in the 3–1 NL win.

In 1968 the game was played indoors for the first time at the Astrodome, which didn't sit well with some purists. Mays led off the bottom of the first with a single against Luis Tiant and came around to score on a Willie McCovey double play. That was all the scoring in a 1–0 NL win, and Mays, who was 1 for 4, was named the MVP.

In 1969 McCovey took home the top-player trophy, homering twice and driving in three runs in a 9–3 NL win at Memorial Stadium in Washington. But in six career All-Star appearances, McCovey was just 3 for 16 at the plate.

The 1970 game is remembered for Pete Rose bowling over catcher Ray Fosse in the twelfth inning as he scored from second base on a single to extend the NL's winning streak to eight in a row with a 5–4 victory. On the play, which took place before Rose's hometown fans at Riverfront Stadium, the popular Fosse suffered a fractured shoulder, which raised questions about whether Charlie Hustle had hustled too much, since the game was, after all, an exhibition. Despite the NL victory, Yastrzemski earned MVP honors by virtue of his 4-for-6 night at the plate.

Six future Hall of Famers hit home runs in the 1971 game, as the AL ended its losing streak with a 6–4 win at Tiger Stadium. The Cooperstown-bound sextet included Junior Circuit sluggers Frank Robinson, Reggie Jackson, and Harmon Killebrew, and Senior Circuit icons Johnny Bench, Hank Aaron, and Roberto Clemente.

For their careers: Robinson played in twelve All-Star Games and hit .240 in 25 at-bats with 2 home runs and 3 RBIs; Jackson played in twelve games and hit .269 in 26 at-bats with 3 home runs and 4 RBIs; Killebrew played in eleven games and hit .308 in 26 at-bats with 3 home runs and 6 RBIs; Bench played in twelve games and hit .357 in 28 at-bats with 3 home runs and 6 RBIs; Aaron played in twenty-four games and hit .196 in 67 at-bats with 2 home runs and 8 RBIs; and Clemente played in fourteen games and hit .323 in 31 at-bats with a homer and 4 RBIs.

Triples were wild at the 1978 game in San Diego. AL first baseman Rod Carew led off both the first and third innings with three-baggers, but eventual MVP Steve Garvey, the NL first baseman, hit the triple that mattered most, a leadoff trey against Goose Gossage in the eighth to start a four-run rally and propel the NL to a 7–3 win. Garvey, who was 2 for 3 with 2 RBIs in that All-Star Game, played in ten Midsummer Classics, hitting .393 in 28 at-bats with 2 triples, 2 home runs, and 7 RBIs.

The 1980s are remembered for the great pitchers who shined in All-Star competition. Bruce Sutter started his four-year run of All-Star dominance in the late 1970s, in fact. After earning wins in both the 1978 and 1979 games, Sutter notched saves in 1980 and 1981. In those four games, his only All-Star appearances, the future Hall of Famer pitched $6\frac{2}{3}$ innings, surrendering just 2 hits, and no runs.

A hitter, Fred Lynn, had himself a day at Comiskey Park in 1983. The Angels outfielder hit the first grand slam in All-Star history. The blast—which put the exclamation point on a seven-run third inning—came after NL manager Whitey Herzog had ordered Atlee Hammaker to intentionally walk Robin Yount. The 13–3 AL win snapped a string of eleven straight NL wins and ended a stretch in which the NL had won 19 of 20. Lynn's All-Star career is an interesting one. He never had more than one hit in any of his nine games through the first nine years of his major league career, but through those nine games and his first twenty All-Star at-bats he hit .300 with 4 home runs and 10 RBIs. At thirty-one he seemed poised to challenge Williams's record of 12 RBIs and Musial's record of 6 home runs. But he struggled with injuries in the latter half of his career and never played in another All-Star Game after his big night in 1983.

Hurlers Fernando Valenzuela, Dwight Gooden, and Roger Clemens also left their mark on the 1980s. In 1984, Valenzuela struck out three future Hall of Famers in a row in the third inning—Dave Winfield, Jackson, and George Brett. Then, the very next inning, the nineteen-year-old Gooden whiffed the less impressive trio of Larry Parrish, Chet Lemon, and Alvin Davis. There were a record 21 Ks in the 3–1 NL win.

Valenzuela was at it again in 1986, matching Hubbell's three-decade-old record by striking out five in a row. But Clemens stole the show. Pitching in front of his home-state fans at the Astrodome, the Rocket pitched three perfect innings to set the tone in a 3–2 AL win. In five All-Star appearances, Valenzuela pitched $7^2/_3$ innings, allowing 5 hits and no runs, and striking out 9. Clemens appeared in a pitchers-record ten games, throwing thirteen innings and going 1-1 with a 4.15 ERA.

Oakland reliever Dennis Eckersley earned saves in 1989, 1990, and 1991, then Boston's Pedro Martinez turned in the best All-Star pitching performance of the 1990s when he electrified a Fenway Park crowd by striking out five of the six batters he faced in the first two innings of the 1999 game. The diminutive right-hander whiffed Barry Larkin, Larry Walker, and Sammy Sosa consecutively in the first inning, then started the second by punching out Mark McGwire. After the fifth batter, Matt Williams, reached on an error, Martinez struck out Jeff Bagwell as Williams was thrown out trying to steal. For his effort, Martinez was named the MVP of a 4–1 AL win. In three career All-Star Games, Martinez was 1-0 in four innings, allowing 2 hits and no runs, and striking out 8.

The 2001 game featured Cal Ripken Jr. making what everyone knew would be the last of his eighteen All-Star appearances. Fittingly, Ripken claimed MVP honors in a 4–1 AL win at Safeco Field. The aging iron man trotted out to third base in the top of the first inning, but was soon convinced by starting shortstop Alex Rodriguez to swap positions, so that he could play one final game at the position he occupied during his glory days. When Ripken came to bat in the bottom of the third, he was greeted by a thunderous standing ovation as fans paid their respects to one of the era's heroes. After doffing his cap and finally stepping into the batter's box, Ripken swung at the first pitch from Chan Ho Park and sent it over the leftfield fence. In total, Ripken batted .265 in 49 All-Star at-bats with 2 home runs and 8 RBIs.

Prior to the tie of 2002, Major League Baseball had announced that forever hence the MVP Award would be known as the Ted Williams Award. Unfortunately, no MVP was named for the embarrassing tie. The next year, the Angels Garrett Anderson became the first Williams Award winner, thanks to a 3-for-4 effort in a 7–6 AL win.

We agree with MLB that Williams deserves such an honor and that his prodigious 1946 Midsummer Classic represents the best single-game All-Star performance ever submitted. However, our choice for best lifetime All-Star goes to Mays, who did not rack up quite the power totals that Williams did, but was such a fixture in the game for two decades that his lifetime records for at-bats, hits, and runs will never be broken.

Finally, we offer a quick tip of the cap to the best All-Star among today's players, Derek Jeter, who through ten games has gone 9 for 21 at the plate (through 2009).

[10]

THE BEST WORLD SERIES PERFORMER

He Starred on the Game's Grandest Stage

In our current era of expanded playoffs, baseball's postseason records have become severely distorted. The heroes of the game's yesteryears built their postseason portfolios solely in the World Series, of course, while latter-day stars have been afforded Championship Series and, more recently, Divisional Series opportunities as well to pad their October résumés. Today's players may participate in as many as nineteen games each October should their team play the full slate of games in all three postseason tiers. Consequently, the old record book has been rewritten to reflect the statistical bounty more modern stars have harvested thanks to all those extra games. Derek Jeter played in twenty-eight October series between 1996 and 2009, for example, enabling him to set records for postseason hits with 175 and runs with 99, while his former Yankee teammate Bernie Williams, who played in twenty-five series himself between 1995 and 2006, put his name atop three different postseason record columns with 29 doubles, 22 homers, and 80 runs batted in. The updated list of standout October hurlers reflects a similarly modern bent, as the all-time wins list reads: Andy Pettitte (18), John Smoltz (15), Tom Glavine (14), Roger Clemens (12), and Greg Maddux (11).

Hence, this chapter's task is not to identify the best *postseason* performer, which time and playoff expansion have made practically impossible to judge, but instead we seek to crown the player who best excelled in *World Series* competition. During the course of our investigation we'll acknowledge particularly dominant single-series performances, but in the end our goal is to isolate the best lifetime World Series achiever. We will consider not only each player's production at the plate or on the mound, but also how his teams fared when the games mattered most. For the sake of narrowing the field, let's stipulate that to be considered for this distinction a player must have appeared in at least three World Series. This provision will exclude players like Randy Johnson, who went 3-0 with a 1.04 ERA in two starts and one relief appearance for the 2001 Diamondbacks in his only

Series, and Billy Hatcher, who went 9 for 12 at the plate for the Reds in 1990 in his only Series. Likewise, Paul Molitor will be left out, despite batting .418 with a .475 on-base percentage in thirteen games over two Series.

To begin, let's review the hitters who have dominated in World Series play. Yankee-haters, be warned: Thanks to the Bombers' forty October Classic appearances this chapter is something of a Pinstripe parade. And chief among the many Yankees in the fray is Yogi Berra, who holds several World Series records, including the most important one of all. The Yankees backstop is the only player to earn a championship ring for every one of his fingers and both thumbs. He played in fourteen World Series and his Yankees won ten of them. Along the way he set records by appearing in seventy-five games, accruing 259 at-bats, and racking up 71 hits. His 12 home runs rank third all-time. Now, obviously the hit record is a reflection of the expanded opportunities Berra's great teams afforded him. It seems likely that if Johnny Bench or another Hall of Fame catcher had played in three-score and fifteen games, he might hold the same records and might even have exceeded Berra's solid, but unspectacular, .274 batting average, .359 on-base percentage, and .452 slugging percentage. For the record Berra, who batted above .300 in five of fourteen Series, was particularly dominant in 1953, 1955, and 1956, all against Brooklyn, when he batted .429, .417, and .360, racking up 28 hits in twenty games. In 1956, he had 3 homers and drove in 10 runs in seven games, while slugging .800. So, let's give Yogi credit for earning ten rings and submitting some great efforts along the way.

Another New Yorker of the same era who benefited from the same bevy of World Series appearances was Mickey Mantle, whose teams won seven of his twelve Series. He holds records with 42 runs, 26 extra-base hits, 18 homers, 40 runs batted in, 123 total bases, 43 walks, and 54 strikeouts. On three occasions, he slugged 3 homers in a Series—1956, 1960, and 1964—but he batted .300 or higher only three times, and his .257/.374/.535 ratio stats are respectable, but not as impressive as those that have been submitted by some of the game's other diamond kings. Nonetheless, because Mantle benefited from playing in sixty-five Series games—a total that modern players are unlikely to approach due to the extra playoff rounds and to the parity that now exists in the game—his records appear unbreakable. Interestingly, Mantle never won a World Series MVP Award, a nuance introduced in 1955 when he played in his fourth October Classic.

A third Yankee of the same period, Bobby Richardson, set the single-series mark for RBIs in 1960 when he drove in 12 runs, and for hits in 1964 when he wrapped 13 safeties. But the Pinstripes lost both series—to the Pirates and Cardinals—and Richardson's teams won just three of his seven Series despite his .305/.331/.405 performance at the plate in thirty-six games.

Looking back further into Yankee chronology, Lou Gehrig's October exploits stand out. After the Yankees lost to the Cardinals in Gehrig's first World Series in 1926, they won the final six of his career, four by sweeping their opposition. The Iron Horse batted a robust .361 with an all-time-best .477 on-base percentage and a .731 slugging percentage in 119 at-bats. He twice exceeded a .500 batting average in a Series—hitting .545 with 4 home runs and 9 RBIs in a sweep of the Cardinals in 1928, and .529 with 3 home runs and 8 RBIs in a sweep of the Cubs in 1932. He finished with 30 runs, 10 homers and 35 runs batted in over thirty-four games.

Gehrig's teammate Babe Ruth was also a perennial second-season force. First, he won three rings in three tries with the Red Sox in the early part of his career when he was a left-handed pitcher, going 2-0 with a 0.87 ERA in three World Series starts for Boston, including a fourteen-inning 2–1 win against Brooklyn in 1916. Then he batted .300 or higher in six of his seven October series with the Yankees, with whom he won four more rings. Ruth homered at least twice in each of his final five Series, including in 1932 against the Cubs when he hit his legendary "Called Shot." Still, over forty-one games and 129 at-bats, Ruth racked up 37 runs, 15 homers, and 33 runs batted in, while batting .326/.467/.744.

The best World Series hitter in recent decades is Mr. October, Reggie Jackson, who won four championships in five tries with the A's, Orioles, and Yankees, while piling up an impressive twenty-seven-game stat line that includes 35 hits, 10 homers, and 24 runs batted in, to go with a .357 batting average, .457 on-base percentage, and .755 slugging

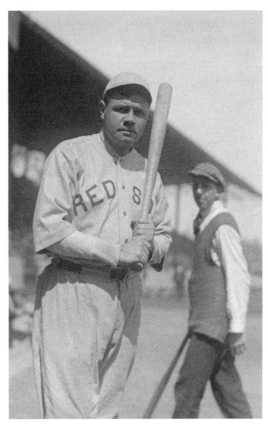

Babe Ruth earned his first three World Series rings with the Boston Red Sox.
COURTESY OF THE LIBRARY OF CONGRESS

percentage. Jackson won two MVPs, the first with the A's in 1973 when he followed a regular season in which he also won the MVP with a solid Series against the Mets that included a homer in Game Seven. His second MVP came in 1977 with the Yankees when he hit a record 5 homers, including 3 on successive swings in the decisive sixth game against the Dodgers. Counting his eighth-inning shot against Don Sutton the game before, Jackson actually homered on four consecutive swings. His impressive power display should not be viewed as too surprising—after all, he hit 563 regular-season long balls—but his batting average in Series play truly was. In his five Series, Jackson's batting averages were .310, .286, .450, .391, and .333—this from a man who hit .262 for his career in the regular season.

When it comes to best October pitchers, a number of Yankee hurlers quickly come to the forefront. Whitey Ford, whose Pinstripes were 6-5 in the eleven Series in which he participated, wasn't the best Series starter ever, but owing to his wealth of opportunities he holds several records, including those for 22 games started, 8 series-opening starts, 146 innings, 10 wins, 8 losses, and 94 strikeouts. His 2.71 ERA was certainly respectable too.

Ford's contemporary Don Larsen, famous for his perfect game against the Dodgers in Game Five of the 1956 Series, was 4-2 with a 2.75 ERA in six starts spread over five Series, only two of which were won by the Bronx Bombers.

Two earlier Yankees pitchers, who like Ford earned enshrinement in Cooperstown, also deserve mention. Red Ruffing and Lefty Gomez pitched for the 1930s Yankees juggernaut and both consistently rose to the occasion when the bell tolled in October. Ruffing went 7-2 with a 2.63 ERA, with eight complete games in ten starts, as the Yankees won six of his seven Series. He also won all four Series openers he pitched. Gomez, meanwhile, went 6-0 in seven starts, while the Yankees won all five of his October Classics.

Three non-Yankee pitchers also stand out for their heroics in October: Christy Mathewson, Bob Gibson, and Sandy Koufax. Mathewson's Giants won just one of the four Series in which he pitched between 1905 and 1913 and his win-loss record in eleven starts was just 5-5. But his 0.97 ERA and 10 complete games speak volumes about how dominant he was. His first Series was his best, when he pitched 3 shutouts against the Philadelphia A's in 1905 to lead the Giants to victory. In 1912 against the Red Sox, he again submitted 3 complete games, including a 6–6 eleven-inning tie in Game Two when all 5 runs against him were unearned. He allowed just 3 earned runs in 28²/₃ October innings that year, despite going 0-2. Because he wasn't a bigger winner in October, we can't crown "Matty" the best World Series marksman, but his consistency and durability are admirable.

Koufax and Gibson both won a pair of World Series MVP Awards in the 1960s, and remain the only pitchers to win the award more than once. Koufax's Dodgers won their first three trips to the Series while he anchored their rotation, before they bowed to the Orioles in his final season, 1966. After getting his first taste of October baseball in 1959 and losing his only start against the White Sox, the introspective lefty seized the spotlight in 1963 against the Yankees when he pitched a pair of complete-game victories—including the opener and the clincher—allowing just three runs. He won his second MVP Award in 1965 when he held the Twins to 1 earned run in twenty-four innings, going 2-1 in three starts, and spinning a 3-hit shutout in Game Seven. In seven Series starts, Koufax was 4-3 with a 0.95 ERA.

Christy Mathewson's 5-5 record in World Series games belies how well he pitched. COURTESY OF THE LIBRARY OF CONGRESS

Gibson's Cardinals won the first two World Series of his career—in 1964 against the Yankees and in 1967 against the Red Sox—and both times he claimed the MVP trophy. Against the Yankees, he was 2-1 with a 3.00 ERA and 2 complete games, the first a ten-inning victory in the pivotal fifth game, the second, a nine-inning win on two days' rest in Game Seven. In 1967, Gibson dominated the Red Sox to the tune of a 3-0 record and 1.00 ERA in three complete game efforts. His 7–2 win over Jim Lonborg in Game Seven was punctuated by his own fifth-inning home run. Gibson homered again during the 1968 Series against the Tigers and pitched three more complete games, going 2-1 with a 1.67 ERA, but was outpitched by Mickey Lolich who beat him 4–1 in Game Seven. In all, Gibson's October line reads 9 games, a 7-2 record, a 1.89 ERA, and 8 complete games. In eighty-one innings, he struck out 92 batters.

In conclusion, our nod to the best World Series performer of all-time goes to Ruth, who narrowly edges Gehrig, Jackson, and Gibson, thanks to his consistency, remarkable production at the plate, and the added value of his early-career pitching heroics. As for the best single Series, Gibson's 1967 trio of wins narrowly trumps Jackson's quintet of homers in 1977.

[11]

THE BEST HOME RUN

Long Gone, but Not Forgotten

Ask most fans and they'll agree that a home run is the most important play that can happen in the course of a baseball game. Sure, a steal of home, a triple play, or even a bang-bang triple is more electrifying, but these plays happen too infrequently to regularly impact a typical day at the ballpark. But any family heading to the local yard stands a good chance of seeing a dinger or two, and chances are those long balls are what they'll be talking about at work or school the next day—"We saw Braun hit one out!" or "Pujols sure socked one!"

The home run captivates fans and players alike. It represents a hitter's ultimate triumph over a pitcher. The play begins at regular baseball speed and finishes—except in the rare case of inside-the-park home runs—in slow motion, with the hitter suddenly pulling up as the ball disappears over the fence and breaking into a leisurely trot while the pitcher shakes his head, raises his glove for a new ball, and tries to figure out what went wrong. During this victory lap around the bases, fans cheer or boo, depending on whether one of their own or one of the bad guys has "gone yard." Then, finally, the game resumes.

Not surprisingly, baseball lore is steeped with stories of famous home runs that have shaped the outcomes of important games, or put the proverbial exclamation points on Hall of Fame careers. This chapter seeks to identify the big fly that was most dramatic in its time and which has proved to be the most memorable through the years, making it the best four-bagger of them all.

To tackle this broad topic, let's segment the better baseball belts into three categories: milestone moon shots, clinching clouts, and World Series whammies. One thing the ding-dongs we'll discuss have in common is that they all came at defining moments in the game's history, when the nation's eyes were focused squarely on the baseball world. But while fans were just waiting for some of these cookies to be clocked, others caught them completely by surprise.

BEST MILESTONE MOON SHOTS

The most famous homer in our milestone bracket is Hank Aaron's 715th tater, which broke Babe Ruth's lifetime mark while simultaneously shattering the notion that the country's remaining bigots could prevent the advancement of an African American in achieving his dream. In the face of a public embarrassingly divided over whether it wanted to see a black man claim the national pastime's most cherished prize, Aaron soldiered on with unwavering resolve and grace. And on a damp April night in 1974, he stepped to the plate at Atlanta–Fulton County Stadium and knocked an Al Downing fastball over the leftfield fence and into the record books. Watching the now-famous footage of Aaron rounding the bases with his head down—as two college students raced onto the field to pat him on the back between second and third base—one notices not so much the joy in Aaron's gait as the relief.

Just as Aaron's pursuit of baseball's most coveted lifetime record was bittersweet owing to the racism of the day, Roger Maris's conquest of the game's most hallowed single-season prize—Ruth's mark of 60 homers—was also controversial and achieved under less than glorious circumstances. Maris succeeded in walloping 61 big flies in 1961, but not before many Yankees fans had stated their preference to see his teammate Mickey Mantle, who was also making a play for the mark, supplant The Babe. Further detracting from Maris's moment, commissioner Ford Frick, who'd been a friend of Ruth, decreed that because Maris had hit only fifty-nine homers through the season's first 154 games—the number in a season in the days when Ruth played—the feat should be differentiated in record books as a sort-of record but not *the* record. Thus, the metaphoric "asterisk" entered baseball's lexicon even before Maris stepped to the plate in the fourth inning of the regular-season finale with a sparse Yankee Stadium crowd on hand and sent a Tracy Stallard offering into the rightfield stands.

BEST CLINCHING CLOUTS

While Aaron and Maris earn our congratulations as owners of the best home runs to punctuate personal accomplishments, another especially resonant rounder type is the kind that propels a team to victory when the outcome of an especially significant game hangs in the balance. Fans and players nervously grit their teeth and then suddenly, as a ball flies out of the yard, find themselves flooded with delirium, or, on the other side of the field, disappointment. Our list of the best homers to clinch games that really mattered must begin with Bobby Thomson's

"Shot Heard 'Round the World," which, in the blink of an eye, turned a 4–2 Dodgers lead into a 5–4 Giants win and sent the Giants into the 1951 World Series. To set the stage for Thomson's heroics, the Giants had battled back from a 13½ game deficit in August to tie the Dodgers at 96-58 at season's end. Then they bounced back after a 10–0 loss in the second game of the three-game playoff to decide the NL pennant. As the third playoff game entered the bottom of the ninth, the Dodgers led 4–1 behind Don Newcombe and appeared headed to the World Series. Three hits and one out later, Newcombe was hitting the showers and Ralph Branca was coming on to face Thomson with runners on second and third. The rest, as they say, is history. Thomson yanked Branca's second pitch down the leftfield line to ignite mass pandemonium at the Polo Grounds. The moment was immortalized by Giants radio broadcaster Russ Hodges's now-familiar call, "The Giants Win the Pennant! The Giants Win the Pennant!"

What is often forgotten is that the Giants lost to the Yankees in the World Series that followed, which suggests that a similarly dramatic home run to seal a World Series would carry even greater importance. But first, let's tip our caps to three other clinching dingers that vaulted teams into, or deeper into, October. All three were struck by Yankees.

After the Royals George Brett had hit a three-run homer to forge a 6–6 tie in the fifth and deciding game of the 1976 American League Championship Series, New York's Chris Chambliss hit a walk-off shot that brought a flood of fans onto the Yankee Stadium turf. The fans were so quick in barreling out of the stands that Chambliss couldn't even reach home plate. Fearful of the throng, he fought his way from second base to the Yankees dugout, and only later emerged once the crowd had been subdued, to touch home plate and officially end the game. The Yankees went on to lose to the Reds in the World Series.

Bucky Dent's fly ball over Fenway Park's fabled Green Monster in the one-game playoff that decided the AL East title in 1978 has also gone down as one of baseball's more memorable game-changing jacks, even if it didn't occur in the final inning. The shot's mythic stature can be traced to three factors: the vitriol in the Red Sox–Yankees rivalry, which had reached a crescendo by 1978; Dent being such an unlikely hero; and the stakes being so high. After the light-hitting Dent put the Yankees ahead with his three-run poke off Mike Torrez in the seventh, the Yankees beat the Royals in the ALCS and the Dodgers in the World Series.

Staying with the Yankees-Red Sox theme, Aaron Boone's eleventh-inning long ball down the leftfield line at Yankee Stadium gave New York a 6–5 win over Boston in Game Seven of the 2003 ALCS, while prolonging the Red Sox's championship drought for another year. But the Yankees lost to the Marlins in the World Series.

BEST WORLD SERIES WHAMMIES

Now let's turn our attention to those home runs hit when the stakes were at their absolute highest. In more than a century of World Series play, only twelve homers have instantly ended games, and of those, only two ended series. As you might expect, one of the two deserves to be rightly called the most dramatic, most memorable and, in our book, the best home run ever hit. First, though, let's acknowledge some other famous long balls that occurred in October action.

According to baseball lore, Ruth's "Called Shot," which came off Charlie Root in Game Three of the 1932 World Series, came moments after Ruth had pointed to the Wrigley Field bleachers into which, on the very next pitch, he deposited the ball. Historians have debated whether Ruth was actually predicting a homer, or just gesturing toward the Cubs dugout, since he'd been bantering with several Cubs all series long, but the fact remains that the alleged Called Shot is one of the most famous homers in hardball history.

Another long ball that has engendered a legend all its own is Carlton Fisk's twelfth-inning yank against the Reds' Pat Darcy, which came in Game Six of the 1975 Series. The solo shot gave the Red Sox a 7–6 win and kept their hopes alive for another day. Because the Series was one of the most exciting ever, because the homer struck Fenway's leftfield foul pole, and because a television camera captured the image of Fisk waving the ball fair as he shuffled toward first base, the shot remains one of baseball's best-known and most revered, even though the Red Sox lost Game Seven.

Kirk Gibson's pinch-hit homer against the A's Dennis Eckersley at Dodger Stadium in Game One of the 1988 World Series also ascended to mythic stature seemingly before it had touched down. Gibson was the heart and soul of the underdog Dodgers, but he limped into the World Series on two bum legs and was not expected to play. Indeed, he made only one plate appearance in the five-game Dodgers' romp, but he sure made it count. The heavily favored A's seemed on their way to an opening-night win when Tommy Lasorda sent Gibson to the plate against the premier closer of the era with two outs, a runner on first, and the Dodgers trailing 4–3. Gibson fell behind 0-2 in the count, then worked the count full before flicking—entirely with his upper body—an Eckersley slider into the rightfield pavilion. Having thus delivered an improbable victory, Gibson hobbled around the bases like a determined gladiator.

In 1991 Kirby Puckett hit a walk-off shot in Game Six against the Braves to ensure that the Twins would live another day. Puckett, who earlier in the game had reached over the Metrodome fence to rob Ron Gant of a homer, dug in against Charlie Leibrandt to lead off the bottom of the eleventh and blasted a 2–1 changeup into the leftfield seats for a 4–3 win. And unlike Fisk's Red Sox, the Twins won the next game, taking a 1–0 thriller in ten innings to claim Minnesota's second championship in four years.

Joe Carter hit an even more gratifying big-game big fly in Game Six of the 1993 Series, blasting a ninth-inning Mitch Williams offering over the SkyDome fence for a three-run romp around the sacks that turned a 6–5 Phillies lead into an 8–6 Blue Jays win and delivered Toronto's second consecutive championship. While the Blue Jays were not in immediate danger of losing the series, they were two outs away from having to play a seventh game, and who knows what would have happened then. As for Carter, he leapt up and down like the picture of pure joy before touching 'em all.

The only other player to end a World Series with a bang, the Pirates' Bill Mazeroski, did so when the stakes were higher still, in Game Seven of the 1960 Classic. In a glaring statistical anomaly, the Yankees outscored the Pirates 55–27 in the Series, but the Pirates prevailed when Mazeroski stepped to the plate against Ralph Terry and sent the Forbes Field throng into happy hysterics with a game-ending clout that flew over leftfielder Yogi Berra's head into the branches beyond the wall. The shot snapped a 9–9 tie and sent Pittsburgh's first championship champagne bottles popping since 1925.

Although he was just a .260 career hitter who hit only 138 home runs in his career, Mazeroski eventually earned enshrinement in Cooperstown, in part, no doubt, because he will be forever linked to one magical moment in time when he seized his team's fate like no other player before or since and delivered baseball nirvana unto his city.

As for Forbes Field, though it has long since been razed, the stretch of outfield fence over which Maz's legendary homer sailed still stands, preserved like a monument on the University of Pittsburgh campus. Every year on October 13 devoted Pirates fans gather and celebrate the anniversary of the most dramatic World Series home run—and our choice for the best home run ever hit—by listening to the radio broadcast of the game, shucking a few peanuts, and tipping back a few beverages in Mazeroski's honor.

[12]

THE BEST END TO A HALL OF FAME CAREER

Immortal Even at the Closing Curtain

As a baseball icon approaches the end of his career a familiar ritual usually plays out. First there are the retrospectives in the local newspapers that recount his heroics through the years, including photos that cause fans to pause and remark, "Look how thin he was," or "Remember when he had that much hair?" Then comes a long string of "lasts." His last Opening Day, his last All-Star Game, his last trip to New York, or to St. Louis, or to some other city especially significant to his career. Then comes the bittersweet final series of the season, and finally, the heartrending final game when fans turn out to say goodbye, the player says a few words on the field before the game, his teammates present him with some keepsakes, and his final nine innings play out. The crowd stands and cheers every time he comes to bat and applauds even the routine plays he makes in the field. But by the time the later frames roll around and with them the inevitable specter of the fading star's last at-bat, the mood turns melancholy. Fans old enough to remember when the player was still green, just up from the minors with his whole baseball life ahead of him, begin to mark the passage of time in their own lives by the shell of the once great player before them rubbing down his bat with pine tar one last time in the on-deck circle, walking slowly to the batter's box as the crowd rises, tipping his helmet, and then stepping to the plate one more time before the last embers of his career flicker out.

Usually by the time this moment arrives, everyone knows that it is time for the player to bid the game adieu. Either his skills have diminished to the point where he can no longer perform at the level he once did, or he can still hit or pitch reasonably well, but his body keeps breaking down. There is another phenomenon that has often played out as well. More often than fans may care to remember, great players have had difficulty accepting that their talents have eroded, or have loved the game too much to walk away from it, even when they've become sad foils for the young bucks they once were. They stick around too long, subjecting fans to performances that begin to tarnish our memories of what they could do in their prime. In some special cases, though, star players have left the game while still very near the top of their game. And this chapter is devoted to celebrating the Hall of Famers who have left the game in blazes of glory.

Our goal is to identify the Cooperstown inductee who had the best final season. But first, let's devote a few paragraphs to those Hall of Famers who, more typically, have departed after some mighty struggles. Doing so will demonstrate why the focal characters of this essay's exploration deserve our praise and admiration.

Older fans still lament the two seasons a washed-up Willie Mays played for the Mets after being traded from the Giants early in the 1972 season. Sure, it was nice to see the "Say Hey Kid" back in the city where his career began, but he batted just .250 in 1972 and .211 in 1973, with little pop in his bat and little tread left on his wheels. Thus ended a long decline for a career .302 hitter who batted below .300 in each of his final eight seasons. Similarly, Ernie Banks, who had endured a subpar season in 1970, came back and batted .193 in thirty-nine games for the Cubs in 1971, before accepting it was time to hang up his spikes. Gary Carter batted .218 in his return to the Expos in 1992. Orlando Cepeda batted .215 for the Royals in 1974. Joe DiMaggio submitted just his second sub-.300 season in his final campaign, batting .261 with a career-low 12 home runs in 116 games in 1951. Carlton Fisk batted .241, .229, and .189 for the White Sox over the final three years of his long career. Harmon Killebrew, who slugged 573 home runs and batted .256 lifetime, hit just .242, .222, and .199 in his final three seasons for the Twins and Royals, adding only 32 long balls to his résumé over his final 297 games. Willie McCovey hit .204 in forty-eight games for the Giants in 1980, adding just 1 homer to his lifetime tally of 521. Fellow Giants legend Mel Ott hit .069 over his final 72 at-bats between 1946 and 1947, adding only 1 homer to his total of 511. Brooks Robinson batted .201, .211, and .149 in his final three seasons with the Orioles. Enos Slaughter hit .171 for the Yankees and Braves in 1959. Dave Winfield batted .191 in forty-six games for the Indians in 1995.

Even the greatest player ever, Babe Ruth, couldn't see the writing on the wall as early as his Yankees could. New York released the forty-year-old Bambino before the 1935 season, freeing him to play for the Boston Braves. The .342 life-time hitter batted .181 in twenty-eight games for the Braves before accepting it was over. He did have one last moment in the sun though, hitting the final 3 homers of his career in a game at Forbes Field in May, five days before he retired.

As for the swan song of the game's biggest star before Ruth, Honus Wagner—owner of a .327 lifetime average—batted below .300 in each of his final four seasons with the Pirates.

Pitchers, though they tend to bow out more quickly once they've lost their stuff, are no exception to the swan-song blues. Thirty-nine-year-old Steve Carlton posted a very respectable 13-7 record for the Phillies in 1984, but then hung around for four more years, going 16-37 for five different teams, while his ERA ballooned into the 5.00s and 6.00s. Bob Gibson went 3-10 with a 5.04 ERA for the Cardinals in 1975. Catfish Hunter went 2-9 with a 5.31 ERA for the Yankees in 1979. Jim Bunning went 5-12 with a 5.48 ERA for the Phillies in 1971. Juan Marichal went 22-33 over his final four seasons. Rube Marquard went 2-8 with a 5.75 ERA for the Boston Braves in 1925.

Indeed, a Hall of Fame hitter is more apt to post a batting average in the .100s in his final season than in the .300s. And a Hall of Fame pitcher is more apt to have an ERA over 5.00 than in the 3.00s. And this is why we must congratulate those lifetime .300 hitters who retained their hand-eye-coordination throughout their final campaign, even if other parts of their games and their bodies had begun to fail, and those hurlers who maintained their stuff right to the finish line.

The list of notable Hall hitters is highlighted by career .366 hitter Ty Cobb, who finished above .300 for the twenty-third consecutive season in his final campaign, batting .323 for the Philadelphia A's in 1928. Ed Delahanty, a career .346 hitter, batted .333 in limited action for the Washington Senators in 1903. Career .341 hitter Bill Terry hit .310 for the Giants in 1936. Zack Wheat hit seven points better than his lifetime average, batting .324 for the A's in 1927. Career .320 hitter Mickey Cochrane batted .306 in twenty-seven games for the Tigers in 1937 and homered in his final plate appearance. More recently, Wade Boggs, who batted .328 over his career, hit .301 for the Devil Rays in 1999, and Tony Gwynn, a career .338 hitter, exceeded .300 for the nineteenth straight year when he batted .324 for the Padres in 2001. Like Cobb, Gwynn batted below .300 in his first season, and then never again.

Ted Williams joined Cochrane as the only other future Cooperstown inductee to homer in his final at-bat. Williams, who retired with a .344 lifetime average, batted below .300 for the only time in his nineteen-year career in 1959 when he hit a paltry .254. After that woeful season, during which he suffered the ignominy of being benched by Red Sox manager Pinky Higgins, many thought The Kid was finished. But the Boston icon returned for one final season in 1960 and hit .316 at age forty-two. In 113 games, he hit 29 home runs in just 310 at-bats, drove in 72 runs, and had a .451 on-base percentage and .645 slugging percentage. He even registered a hit in the All-Star Game. On the final home date of the season, after he'd already decided not to accompany the Red Sox to New York for the final series, Williams came to bat in the eighth inning against the Orioles' Jack Fisher and socked a pitch

Ted Williams is one of two Hall of Famers to homer in his final at-bat. COURTESY OF THE BOSTON PUBLIC LIBRARY, PRINT DIVISION

out of the deepest part of Fenway Park, the right-centerfield triangle. He circled the bases with his head down to end his career.

As for the Hall of Fame hitters whose careers ended abruptly and unexpectedly, Lou Gehrig comes to mind first and foremost. The Iron Horse batted .340 over his career, but played just eight games for the Yankees in 1939, getting 4 hits in 28 at-bats, before a mysterious illness forced him to tearfully retire. In 1938, his final full season, Gehrig had batted below .300 for the first time since his rookie year, hitting .295 with 29 home runs and 114 RBIs. Another tragic figure, Roberto Clemente, wound up his career as a .317 hitter after batting .312 in his eighteenth and final year with the Pirates in 1972. Clemente, who finished with exactly 3,000 hits, perished in a plane crash on December 31, 1972, while trying to deliver emergency relief supplies to earthquake-ravaged Nicaragua. Career .318 hitter Kirby Puckett had his career cut short by glaucoma, but not before batting .314 in his twelfth and final season with the Twins in 1995, collecting 39 doubles, 23 homers, and 99 runs batted in.

As for the better swan songs by Hall of Fame pitchers, there aren't too many that stand out. The fact is, most pitchers take their lumps or battle injuries when the end is near. Tim Keefe went 10-7 with a 4.40 ERA for the Phillies in 1893. Eddie Plank went 5-6 with a spiffy 1.79 ERA for the St. Louis Browns in 1917. Eppa Rixey went 6-3 with a 3.15 ERA for the Reds in 1933. Bruce Sutter had fourteen saves and a 4.76 ERA for the Braves in 1988. Despite the dearth of highly successful final seasons submitted by Hall of Fame pitchers, the most successful swan song in the game's history was indeed submitted by a pitcher, who like Gehrig, Clemente, and Puckett saw his career end quite abruptly, and before anyone could have imagined it would.

In 1966, thirty-year-old Sandy Koufax went 27-9 with a 1.73 ERA and struck out 317 batters in 323 innings. Of the forty-one games the Dodgers lefty started, he completed 27, including 5 shutouts. For his efforts he earned his fifth-straight ERA crown and third Cy Young Award and finished a close second to Clemente in the National League MVP balloting. But as he put the finishing touches on the 1966 regular season to complete a five-year reign in which he had gone 111-34, Koufax knew he was nearing the end. He started the second game of the 1966 World Series against the Orioles, already suspecting that it would be his final appearance on the Dodger Stadium mound. He allowed 4 runs (1 earned) in six innings, in a 6–0 loss to Jim Palmer. The Orioles proceeded to sweep the Dodgers and a few weeks later, the young southpaw shocked the baseball world by announcing he had decided to retire while, as he said, he could still comb his hair. Arthritis in his prized left arm, he explained, made continuing unfathomable. Thus, in 1972 at the tender age of thirty-six, Koufax became the youngest former player ever inducted into the halls of Cooperstown. His success over his final five seasons earns his closing salvo our praise as the best the game has yet seen.

THE BEST
OF THE BEST

THE BEST BASEBALL RECORD

It Will Never Be Broken

For years, baseball observers considered Roger Maris's 61 home runs in a season and Hank Aaron's 755 home runs over his career among the game's most unbreakable records. Then Mark McGwire and Barry Bonds came along, and the rest, as they say, is history. The similarly "unapproachable" 257 hits George Sisler rapped out in 1920 stood for more than eight decades before Ichiro Suzuki collected 262 safeties in 2004. Lou Gehrig's 2,130 consecutive games played once appeared insurmountable, as did Don Drysdale's 58 consecutive scoreless innings pitched, before Cal Ripken Jr. and Orel Hershiser came along. Baseball's records truly are made to be broken. Yet, as the game evolves, countless variables that are forever shifting in one direction or another, cause us to define and then redefine what is possible for a human being to accomplish between the two white lines. Thus, to accurately rank baseball's records according to their potential breakability, or unbreakability, one would need a crystal ball to foresee the changes in technology or human evolution that might occur. With that being said, there are certain records that would seem less breakable than others and the very best of these comprise this chapter's field of inquiry.

For the purposes of our discussion, we will categorize baseball's records into three broad categories: the most noteworthy streaks, the most remarkable single-season marks, and the most impressive career marks. After reviewing the better candidates in each subsection of baseball idolatry, we'll pick the most unbreakable and therefore best baseball record of them all.

THE STREAKS

Ask baseball fans outside of Baltimore County what the most hallowed streak in baseball history is and they'll tell you it's Joe DiMaggio's 56-game hit streak, which captivated the nation between May 15 and July 16 of 1941. During the streak Joltin' Joe batted .409, while racking up 91 hits, 15 homers, 56 runs, and 55 runs batted in. He struck out only 7 times. Remarkably, after going 0 for 3 against the Indians on July 17, DiMaggio began another 16-gamer the very next day. So if not for two sparkling defensive plays by Indians infielders Ken Keltner and Lou Boudreau who helped snub him on July 16, he might very well have hit in seventy-three straight games. Even so, a 56-gamer is pretty remarkable, especially when viewed in light of how much it exceeded the previous record and in light of the fact that it's never been seriously challenged in the seven decades since it was set. Prior to DiMaggio's eight-week binge, Sisler's 41 straight games with a hit had stood since 1922. Since DiMaggio raised the bar, only Pete Rose—who had a 44-gamer in 1978—and Paul Molitor—who hit in 39 games in a row in 1987—have come within shouting distance, and then just barely. The greatest argument for this feat as the most unbreakable baseball record is the intense fan and media scrutiny any serious assault on it would incur, which would no doubt wear on the psyche of the would-be challenger. Then again, people once pointed to the same factor to suggest Maris's home run mark would stand forever.

Ripken's 2,632 consecutive games between May 30, 1982, and September 20, 1998, equates to more than sixteen seasons without a day off. Not only did the Baltimore infielder keep showing up, but he was a star. He won a Rookie of the Year Award, two MVPs, and made sixteen All-Star appearances during the streak. The previous record holder, Gehrig, played just 81 percent as many consecutive games as Ripken, while Everett Scott, owner of the third-longest streak, a 1,307-gamer, played just under 50 percent as many games in a row. To supplant Ripken, a player would need incredible mental stamina, the good fortune to avoid injuries, the strength to play through injuries, and the talent to justify his place on the field year after year. Although it does not have quite the cachet as DiMaggio's streak, it's hard to disagree with those rabid Orioles rooters who say Ripken's mark is the most unbreakable baseball streak.

Hershiser's 59 consecutive scoreless innings over the closing weeks of the 1988 season also deserves mention, but the previous record holder, fellow Dodger legend Don Drysdale, had held opponents scoreless for nearly as long in 1968, whereas DiMaggio and Ripken raised the bar in their categories into previously uncharted territories.

Another impressive pitching record that might be termed a streak is Johnny Vander Meer's two no-hitters in a row, which he authored four days apart in 1938. The Reds hurler blanked the Braves 3–0 on June 11, and the Dodgers 6–0 on June 15. This, from a pitcher who eventually finished his thirteen-year career with a 119-121 record. Although it seems possible that Vander Meer's record may be matched one day by some red-hot hurler, a pitcher would have to submit three straight no-hitters in order to break the record, which seems unfathomable. After all, there have been fewer than three hundred no-hitters in history, and only twenty-three pitchers have thrown more than one.

THE SINGLE-SEASON MARKS

In 2001 Bonds made a further mockery of what was once the most glamorous single-season record in baseball when he hit 73 presumably steroid-fueled home runs to surpass the total of 70, which a similarly bulked-up Mark McGwire had hit just three years before. Because only two men—Ruth and Maris—reached 60 long balls without chemical help, it is tempting to call Bonds's mark the most unbreakable record in this category. But that assumes baseball will be able to keep its players clean in the years ahead and to stay on the cutting edge of the research necessary to safeguard itself from new approaches in performance enhancement. And frankly, given baseball's track record, that seems less than likely. In other words, to state one's faith in the staying power of Bonds's bogus record is to declare one's faith in the game's ability to keep its players clean, which we're not prepared to do.

Records similarly vulnerable to another artificially enhanced offensive era would include Hack Wilson's 191 RBIs in 1930 and Ruth's 177 runs in 1921, but it is worth noting that neither was challenged during the steroid era.

Among the other single-season marks that appear secure are Rickey Henderson's 130 stolen bases in 1982, Chief Wilson's 36 triples in 1912, and Ray Chapman's 67 sacrifice bunts in 1917. Even with teams placing a greater premium on small ball in the post-BALCO era, it seems unlikely that some future player will ever hoist the second-base bag up over his head and proclaim himself the greatest ever upon stealing Number 131. And no matter how far the balance swings back toward pitching, it's hard to imagine anyone approaching Chapman's 67 sacrifices. Bert Campaneris, who ranks thirty-sixth all-time in the category, had 40 sacrifice bunts in 1977, and that's the closest any player has come in the lively ball era. As for the triples mark, changes in ballpark design may someday affect the likelihood of some fleet-footed gap-hitting slasher challenging it, even if only three players have hit as many as 26 in the near century since Wilson set the mark, even after the advent of Astroturf playing surfaces.

The two most unbreakable single-season records, though, are probably Nap Lajoie's modern-era-best .426 batting average in 1901 and Jack Chesbro's 41 wins in

1904. Although the runners-up in each category—Rogers Hornsby, who hit .424 in 1924, and Ed Walsh, who had 40 wins in 1908—came pretty close to duplicating these feats, both assaults were long ago when the game was very different. To put things in perspective, no one has batted .400 or better since Ted Williams hit .406 in 1941. And if the greatest hitter who ever lived couldn't get within 20 points, no one's ever going to do it. As for the wins record, Dizzy Dean, Lefty Grove, and Denny McLain are the only pitchers to reach 30

Barry Bonds holds the all-time record with 762 home runs and the single-season record with 73 home runs. PHOTO BY KEVIN RUSHFORTH, COURTESY OF WIKIMEDIA COMMONS

wins in a season during the last eight decades. Dean had exactly 30 in 1930, Grove had 31 in 1931, and McLain had 31 in 1968. Even if the four-man rotation one day becomes the norm again, and starters resume routinely throwing 150 pitches per start, it's hard to imagine Chesbro's win total being challenged.

THE CAREER RECORDS

For reasons to which we've already alluded, most fans today don't view Bonds's 762 lifetime home runs with the reverence with which they once regarded Aaron's 755 or Ruth's 714. Nor do they expect Bonds's mark to stand very long, as conservative forecasts project admitted-steroids-user Alex Rodriguez will sail past the mark sometime around 2014 on his way to what will surely be 800-plus homers before he's finished. There are plenty of other career statistics, however, that still retain their original meaning. The most widely known and highly regarded of baseball's lifetime numbers are Cy Young's 511 victories, Pete Rose's 4,256 hits, and Ty Cobb's .366 lifetime batting average. Young's record seems the least approachable, in part because it's not truly a "modern" record, since the great hurler racked up 72 of his wins from a pre-1893 mound just fifty feet from home plate. And 267 of his W's came before the turn of the century, when other important rules familiar to the modern game were finally adopted. More impressive, but less well known, is the win tally of the second-winningest pitcher ever, Walter Johnson, who claimed all 417 of his victories in the modern era. Although Young can boast that he completed an all-time best 749 games in 815 starts, Johnson registered a record 110 shutouts—34 more than the fourth-place Young—in 666 starts, which should be viewed as an equally unbreakable record.

Rose hung around for four years past his last truly productive season, which was 1982, so that he could wrest baseball's hit crown from the ghost of Cobb. In the end Charlie Hustle surpassed the Georgia Peach by 67 hits, 4,256 to 4,189. Third best on the list is Aaron at 3,771, followed by Stan Musial at 3,630, and Tris Speaker at 3,514. No other player has reached 3,500 safeties. What makes this record seem breakable is the fact that Rose was a very good hitter, year in and year out, but never a great one, as his .303 lifetime average attests. Now, I know it sounds silly to call a lifetime .300-hitter who had more hits than any other player to ever play the game anything less than a great hitter. But consider this: Among players with at least 3,000 plate appearances, Rose is tied with Buddy Myer and Mike Greenwell for 170th all-time in batting average, placing just behind such good, but not great, players as Moises Alou, Will Clark, Mark Grace, Hal Morris, and Al Oliver. So, if Rose's accomplishment is as much a testament to his longevity—see eighteen seasons with at least 170 hits, including ten seasons with at least 200—as to his steady bat handling, it seems plausible that some other swell-swinging iron man will one day venture onto a path that eventually surpasses his, especially

Ty Cobb owns the best lifetime batting average of all time: .366.
COURTESY OF THE LIBRARY OF CONGRESS

in the era of the designated hitter and of superior athletic conditioning. Still, our mythic challenger would have to average 170 hits for twenty-five years, which, when put in those terms, seems unlikely.

As for the players with the best lifetime batting averages over at least three thousand plate appearances, Cobb tops the chart with a .366 mark, followed by Hornsby (.359), Joe Jackson (.356), Lefty O'Doul (.349), and Ed Delahanty (.346). Since Williams (.344) retired with the seventh-best average of all-time in 1960, the best anyone has done is the .338 Tony Gwynn carried from the game in 2001.

Rose's hit total, in our judgment, is more breakable than Cobb's .366 lifetime average and Johnson's 417 modern-era wins, but none of these marks seems apt to fall any time soon.

To sum up, Vander Meer's back-to-back no-hitters, Lajoie's .426 single-season average, Chesbro's 41-win season, and Cobb's .366 lifetime average are the most unbreakable records. As for the best record of all, our choice is Lajoie's mark. It seems more likely that the four-man rotation will one-day return, thus making an assault on Chesbro's mark remotely plausible, or that a hurler will come along dominant and lucky enough to pitch three straight no-hitters, or that a speedy line-drive-hitting machine will emerge to perennially hit in the .360s and .370s to challenge Cobb over the course of what would have to be a relatively short career, than it seems possible that the balance between hitting and pitching will ever tilt so dramatically toward hitters to allow a batter to top .426 in a season. But then again, you never know.

[14]

THE BEST STATISTICAL CLUB

Pretenders Need Not Apply

For more than a century, America's young males have entertained the common dream of becoming big league ballplayers. And as baseball has welcomed an increasing number of foreign players into its ranks, the past several decades have allowed for the transfer of this dream to millions of youngsters growing up overseas. But only a minuscule percentage of big-league-dreamers ever succeed in wriggling through the siphon designed to filter out the best players at each amateur and minor league level. In fact, since 1871, when the National Association of Professional Base Ball Players was formed, only about seventeen thousand men have ascended to the Major Leagues.

Meanwhile, as the children have dreamt, the select few players who have reached the bigs have dreamt too, of winning championships, claiming batting titles, and making All-Star teams. And since the 1930s the loftiest individual goal to which these players have aspired has been to one day be regarded one of the best players who have ever played their position, so as to earn enshrinement in the National Baseball Hall of Fame. Of the more than seventeen thousand players who have made it to The Show, only 202 (through 2009) have been so honored (not counting the thirty players posthumously inducted on the basis of their Negro Leagues careers). That means only 1.1 percent of big leaguers make the Hall of Fame.

But there is still a more prestigious pantheon to which players may ascend. Among the players in Cooperstown, fewer than one-third may claim additional membership in one of three informal, but widely celebrated, statistical clubs. These are the 500 Home Run Club, the 3,000 Hit Club, and the 300 Win Club. The aim of this chapter is to determine which of these extra-special fraternities should be regarded as the most prestigious. In other words, we seek to figure out which of these statistical milestones represents the greater baseball accomplishment. First, we'll offer a quick overview of each group's membership, and then we'll get to the nitty-gritty of measuring the clubs against one another.

In 2009, Randy Johnson became the twenty-fourth pitcher to reach 300 victories, which bodes well for his Hall of Fame chances, considering that twenty of the twenty-three pitchers to previously accomplish the feat already have plaques bearing their likenesses in Cooperstown, while the other three—Tom Glavine, Roger Clemens, and Greg Maddux—have not yet been retired the mandatory five years so that their names may appear on Hall ballots.

Meanwhile, Gary Sheffield connected for his 500th home run in 2009, becoming the twenty-fifth player to reach the milestone. In doing so, he too bolstered his Cooperstown credentials. Every Hall-eligible slugger in this stratosphere has gained entry except for Mark McGwire, whose suspected steroid use has resulted in his failure to achieve the 75 percent of votes required. In the coming decades Barry Bonds, Sammy Sosa, Rafael Palmeiro, Jim Thome, Frank Thomas, Alex Rodriguez, Ken Griffey Jr., Manny Ramirez, and Sheffield will eventually become eligible, and it will be interesting to see how history and the Baseball Writers Association of America will judge them considering their generation's ties to rampant steroid use throughout the game. Surely some of these players benefited from the illegal substances that inflated their power numbers during the 1990s and 2000s, but some of them (surely, presumably, hopefully?) reached the milestone the clean and honest way. It is impossible to predict how Hall voters will separate the legitimate sluggers from the dirty ones, but either way, this is one club that has expanded rapidly in the past few years, which has diminished the grandeur once associated with it markedly.

Likewise, the 3,000 Hit Club has seen its numbers swell, even if its expansion has not drawn the media scrutiny that the ballooning of the 500 Home Run Club has. Eleven new members have joined the 3,000 Hit Club since 1992, while eleven have joined the 500 Home Run Club. The most recent tri-millennial hitter, Craig Biggio, accomplished the feat in 2007 when he became the twenty-seventh member of the club and joined a group that has seen all its members enshrined except for Palmeiro, whose name will first appear on Hall ballots in 2010, and the ineligible Pete Rose.

So what's the most telling statistical marker of greatness? Racking up all those wins, smacking all those dingers, or connecting for all those safeties? Let's see . . .

THE 300 WIN CLUB

This feat was first accomplished in 1888 when Pud Galvin of the Pittsburgh Alleghenys beat the Indianapolis Hoosiers for Number 300. Galvin, who was just thirty-one years old at the time, went on to post a 364-310 record in fifteen seasons, while completing 646 of his 689 starts. Of course, the game was very different in Galvin's day. To begin, most teams featured just three starting pitchers, which allowed Galvin to average nearly fifty starts per year. He made seventy-five starts, in fact, for the Buffalo Bisons in 1883 when he registered 46 wins, then the next year he made seventy-two starts and won another 46 games. Galvin's gaudy start totals help explain why he is one of the seven 300 game winners who turned the trick by 1901. There were other factors aiding pitchers in his time too. For example, prior to 1893 the pitching rubber was just 50 feet from home plate. The switch to 60 feet 6 inches occurred only after the old configuration had benefited eventual 300 game winners like Tim Keefe (342-225 career record, 300th win in 1890), Mickey Welch (307-210, 1890), Charley Radbourn (309-195, 1891), John Clarkson (328-178, 1892), Kid Nichols (361-208, 1900), and Cy Young (511-316, 1901). As for Galvin, he claimed all 364 of his wins pitching from the short mound.

Christy Mathewson (373-188, 1912) and Eddie Plank (326-194, 1915) were the first members of the 300 Win Club to gain all of their W's without the benefit of those fifty-start seasons and 50-foot tosses from the rubber to the plate. Then Walter Johnson (417-279, 1920) and Grover Cleveland Alexander (373-208, 1924) both reached their 300th in the 1920s, at the dawn of what would be a long hitter's era. Over the next fifty-eight years, the 300 Win Club admitted only three new members: Lefty Grove (300-141, 1941), whose .680 winning percentage is the best among club members; Warren Spahn (363-245, 1961), who is the winningest southpaw in history; and Early Wynn (300-244, 1963), who stuck around long enough to reach the milestone and then hung up his spikes. How do we explain the admission of only three newbies in nearly six decades? Well, in addition to the advent of the lively ball in the 1920s, which diminished win totals, several star pitchers also lost important years from the middle parts of their careers due to war service. Bob Feller, who finished with 266 wins, despite missing the entire 1942, 1943, and 1944 seasons, as well as most of the 1945 season, while ages twenty-two to twenty-six, is a prime example of a hurler who would have surely joined this exclusive fraternity if he hadn't heeded the call of a greater duty.

Today, despite recurrent rumors that the 300 game winner is a dying breed, this rare bird seems far from extinction. In fact, eight new members, or 35 percent of the club's members, have joined since 1982, when spitballing Gaylord Perry (314-265) blazed a path for Steve Carlton (329-244, 1983), the second-winningest southpaw ever; Tom Seaver (311-205, 1985); Phil Niekro (318-274, 1985), who had only 31 wins upon turning thirty years old; Don Sutton (324-256, 1986), who never missed a turn in the rotation and only once reached 20 wins in twenty-three seasons; Nolan Ryan (324-292, 1990), who tallied more losses than any other modern pitcher; Clemens (354-184, 2003); Maddux (355-227, 2004); and Glavine (305-203, 2007).

Despite having been spoiled by so many pitchers reaching the milestone in recent decades, today's pundits have pointed to the five-man rotation and the death of the complete game as reasons why current and future hurlers will fail to accomplish this feat. What these observers fail to recognize, however, is that today's game also offers certain benefits to stellar pitchers that may aid them in their pursuit of this magical milestone. By pitching every fifth day and keeping their pitch counts in the 100-per-game range, quality pitchers are apt to extend their careers by three or four healthy seasons. Additionally, advances in sports medicine and the increased financial incentive good players have to keep playing for as long as possible will also extend their careers. Furthermore, a fire-balling closer actually stands

Christy Mathewson won 373 big league games—372 with the Giants and 1 with the Reds.
COURTESY OF THE LIBRARY OF CONGRESS

a better chance of protecting a one-run lead than a tiring starter, no matter how great his pedigree. And further still, free agency results in the game's better pitchers playing for the game's better teams, which ensures elite pitchers don't waste too many of their prime years on clubs that don't support them. Winning 300 games is obviously an extraordinary feat, but the long-term trend points to an increase in the club's membership, not a leveling off.

THE 500 HOME RUN CLUB

It would be an understatement to say the 500 Home Run Club also figures to grow in coming years. Once upon a time, hitting 500 long balls established a hitter's dominance beyond any measure of doubt and guaranteed his place in the Hall of Fame. The stain of the steroid era has already changed this perception. It's hard to believe that as recently as 1984 there were only twelve residents of this baseball frat house. That season Reggie Jackson (who would finish with 563 homers) connected against Bud Black for his 500th. Since then, the club has doubled in size. Using the fifteenth member, Eddie Murray (504 lifetime), who reached the stratosphere in 1996, as a dividing line, we might subcategorize this club into the old guard, and the new.

First, the oldies. After practically inventing the long ball, Babe Ruth (714) became the first man to reach 500 taters in 1929. Five years after the Bambino retired, Jimmie Foxx (534) crossed the still mythic threshold in 1940, then Mel Ott (511) joined in 1945. Fifteen years later, forty-one-year-old Ted Williams (521) became the fourth member. Before the 1960s were through, the club had doubled in size, as Willie Mays (660), Mickey Mantle (536), Eddie Mathews (512), and Hank Aaron (755) joined. The 1970s ushered in Ernie Banks (512), Frank Robinson (586), Harmon Killebrew (573), and Willie McCovey (521), and the 1980s welcomed Jackson and Mike Schmidt (548).

In 1996, Murray connected with a Felipe Lira offering to guarantee his place in Cooperstown by becoming the fifteenth member. It took Murray 2,950 games and 11,095 at-bats to reach the milestone, longer in both categories than any other player. What's striking is that of the first fifteen players to swat 500 big flies, only three stuck around long enough to reach 600. Most often, a player hit his 500th as a sort of exclamation point at the end of his career. Then the great home run chase of 1998 changed everything. The comfortable pattern that had been established whereby two, or three, or four players per decade might ascend to such a lofty baseball pedestal was shattered shortly after McGwire and Sosa took center stage in pursuit of Roger Maris, and both handily passed his record 61 homers in a season. McGwire hit his 400th that season, then sailed past 500 the very next year, becoming the first player to pass two homer centuries in consecutive seasons. A previously unfathomable 10 players—and counting—have joined the 500 Home Run Club since 1999, including McGwire (583), Bonds (762), Sosa (609), Palmeiro (569), Thomas (521), and the still-active Griffey Jr. (630), Rodriguez (583), Thome (564), and Ramirez (546).

Rodriguez, who became the youngest player to ever reach 500, did so eight days after his thirty-second birthday in 2007 and appears on pace not only to break

Bonds's record of 762 but also to surpass 800. Once, Rodriguez was billed as baseball's savior, as the media trumpeted his ascendancy on the home run ledger as a chance to return the game's most coveted lifetime record to a player who had not cheated to achieve greatness like Bonds, but then, of course, the Yankees star admitted in 2009 to his own personal steroids use. Cranking 500 homers clearly doesn't signify what it used to. And we have players like Rodriguez, Bonds, Palmeiro, and McGwire to blame for that. This fact will become even more obvious as several of McGwire's pumped-up contemporaries join him as 500 Home Run Club members who will need to purchase admission tickets in the years ahead if they'd like to enter the hallowed halls of Cooperstown.

Gary Sheffield joined the 500 Home Run Club in 2009. COURTESY OF WIKIMEDIA COMMONS

THE 3,000 HIT CLUB

Long considered the greatest measure of superior bat handling, the 3,000 Hit Club has also been quickly expanding in recent decades to the point where it now counts twenty-seven members. The first player to reach the mark was Cap Anson (3,055 lifetime hits) in 1897. He retired a short while later, becoming the first of nine club members to retire with fewer than 3,100 hits. The fact that fully one-third of this club's members came up short of adding another 3 percent more hits to their career total speaks volumes to the fact that most players who reach 3,000 hits do so at the very near end of their baseball lives. Indeed, many a fine hitter has hung on past his prime to reach 3,000 due to the prestige associated with the accomplishment.

By 1925 six players had reached the tri-millennial mark, as Anson was followed by Honus Wagner (3,415) and Nap Lajoie (3,242) in 1914, Ty Cobb (4,189) in 1921, and Tris Speaker (3,514) and Eddie Collins (3,315) in 1925. After Paul Waner (3,152) joined in 1942, and Stan Musial (3,630) in 1958, the group had eight members. With hits in scarce supply in the 1950s and early 1960s, not a single player reached 3,000 hits during the 1960s. Then the 1970s saw the club pick up seven new members, thanks to milestone hits by Hank Aaron (3,771) and Willie Mays (3,283) in 1970, Roberto Clemente (3,000) in 1972, Al Kaline (3,007) in 1974, Pete Rose (4,256) in 1978, and Lou Brock (3,023) and Carl Yastrzemski (3,419) in 1979.

The group welcomed just one member in the 1980s—Rod Carew (3,053) in 1985. Then the 1990s matched the 1970s as the most bountiful decade to date, adding Robin Yount (3,142) and George Brett (3,154) in 1992, Dave Winfield (3,110) in 1993, Murray (3,255) in 1995, Paul Molitor (3,319) in 1996, and Tony Gwynn (3,141) and Wade Boggs (3,010) in 1999. The first decade of the 2000s added Cal Ripken Jr. (3,184) in 2000, Rickey Henderson (3,055) in 2001, Palmeiro (3,020) in 2005, and Biggio (3,060) in 2007.

The fact that fourteen of the 3,000 Hit Club's twenty-seven members have joined since 1979 may be attributed to the lowering of the mound in 1969, the gradual expansion in the number of the league's teams from twenty to thirty-two—which has diluted pitching talent—and to improvements in ballpark lighting, all of which have tilted the game's balance in the offensive direction. Still, amassing three grand in the hits column is a triumph of endurance that should not be regarded lightly, and indeed every eligible member of this club currently possesses a plaque bearing his likeness in Cooperstown.

So, which celebrated club is the most prestigious? Our choice is the 300 Win Club. Only sixteen players have reached the mark in the modern era—compared to the twenty-five who have joined the 500 Home Run Club and the twenty-six who have joined the 3,000 Hit Club in that time. Contrary to what the doomsayers proclaim, there will surely be new 300-game winners to celebrate in the years ahead, but the current offensive era will produce far more 500-homer sluggers and 3,000-hit batters.

Note: For active players, statistical totals listed are through 2009.

[15]

THE BEST MANAGER

His Players Were Pretty Good Too

It has been said that a manager is only as good as the players on his roster, and, seeing as we tend to agree with that, our review of the best baseball skippers of all time must begin with a healthy disclaimer to that effect. To cite a current manager as a case in point, let's look at Joe Torre, who ranks fifth all-time in managerial wins with his 2,246-1,915 record (through 2009), behind Connie Mack (3,731-3,948), John McGraw (2,763-1,948), Tony La Russa (2,552-2,217) and Bobby Cox (2,413-1,930). During his twelve years with the Yankees, Torre won ten division titles, six AL pennants, and four World Championships. Thanks to two wild-card berths, he managed to take New York to the playoffs in all twelve of his seasons in the Bronx, while his Yankees averaged 97.75 wins per season and a .605 winning percentage. Clearly, Torre was an integral part of the Yankees' success, owing to his adept handling of the ego-driven veterans George Steinbrenner's millions attracted, his ability to integrate talented younger players into the mix, and his resilience to withstand the pressure of managing in the nation's largest media market under the scrutiny of the game's most meddlesome owner. However, there is no discounting that Torre had, in New York, the most highly paid roster in baseball year after year. And if we examine his lengthy record over fourteen seasons with three teams prior to his landing in the Bronx, we see that his current stature as a surefire Hall of Fame manager was greatly bolstered by his having been in the right place at the right time. In his fourteen pre-pinstriped seasons with the Mets, Braves, and Cardinals, Torre never led a team to more than eighty-nine wins. He chalked up just one first-place finish—with the 1982 Braves, who promptly lost three straight games to the Cardinals in the National League Championship Series. He had a winning record in just five of those fourteen seasons. He finished in last place four times. And his teams had a .470 winning percentage.

Our point is not that Torre hasn't defined himself as an excellent manager in the years since his career was resurrected in the Bronx. Rather, it is that if one of

Torre's contemporaries, like Jim Leyland or Lou Piniella, for example, had become the Yankees field general in 1996, we might now be talking about that person as a can't miss Hall of Famer. The truth is, there's no way to determine how a manager's contributions—in filling out the lineup card, setting up the pitching rotation, utilizing the bullpen, directing game strategy, and managing the diverse personalities in a big league clubhouse—translate into more wins or fewer than his roster should have otherwise delivered based on its talent. So, let's begin our discussion by clarifying that we are seeking the manager who has enjoyed the most success over the course of his career, through his own talent as well as the good fortune to have been surrounded by talented players.

Of the more than 660 men who have managed at least one game in the big leagues, only seventy-two have maintained a winning record while sticking around long enough to manage one thousand games, and only nineteen have been inducted into the Hall of Fame on the basis of their managing (Note: This total does not include Rube Foster who gained posthumous entry to Cooperstown in 1981 on the basis of his career as a player, manager, owner, and commissioner in the Negro Leagues). If we rank the Hall of Fame skippers by winning percentage, Joe McCarthy (2,125-1,333) heads the list with a .615 clip over his twenty-four seasons. After winning one NL crown in five seasons with the Cubs, McCarthy joined the Yankees in 1931 and proceeded to win eight pennants and seven World Series, while enjoying six 100-win campaigns in sixteen seasons. He had an even temperament and low-key approach—not unlike Torre—which proved especially useful in handling an aging Babe Ruth, and in bringing along youngsters like Joe DiMaggio, Joe Gordon, and Charlie Keller. McCarthy left the Yankees midway through the 1946 season due to failing health, then returned to the game with the Red Sox in 1948, where he enjoyed two second-place finishes, winning 96 games each season, and losing a one-game playoff against the Indians in 1948. He retired midway through 1950, again due to poor health. In twenty-four years, McCarthy's teams never had a losing record. His seven World Championships tie Casey Stengel (1,905-1,842, .508) for the most all-time.

Stengel took over the Yankees two and a half seasons after McCarthy's departure, joining the team in 1949 after having guided the Dodgers and Braves to nine consecutive second-division finishes in his nine previous years managing in the bigs. He inherited holdovers like DiMaggio and Phil Rizzuto from the McCarthy regime, and in his first five seasons he guided New York to five World Championships, with Yogi Berra, Whitey Ford, and Mickey Mantle helping to form the backbone of a new dynasty. After accruing just a .436 winning percentage in his pre-Yankee days, Stengel posted a .623 percentage in twelve seasons with the Yankees, winning ten pennants and those seven World Series. Ironically, his only 100-win season came in 1954, when the Yankees finished second to the Indians despite winning 103 games.

Later, Stengel moved across town to join the fledgling Mets, and his career wound down with three and a half dreadful seasons, in which he guided a team that finished last in the National League four straight years. Although Stengel's seven rings are impressive, McCarthy's résumé is superior, based on his success prior to, during, and even after his time with the juggernaut in New York. For the same reasons, a stronger argument can be made for McCarthy as the "best" manager than for Torre, even though Torre moved ahead of him on the all-time wins list in 2008 when he guided his new team, the Dodgers, to 84 wins and a first-place finish in the mediocre NL West division.

Another New Yorker who deserves consideration is McGraw, who piloted the Giants from 1902 to 1932 after starting his career with two-and-a-half unremark-able seasons as player-manager in Baltimore. After being released by the Orioles and signing with the Giants midway through 1902, McGraw went on to win 2,763 games and finish with a .586 winning percentage—seventh best all-time. The Giants finished second in his first full season, then in 1904 they won the first of ten pennants and enjoyed the first of four 100-win seasons to which the fiery skipper would lead them. After that first league title, McGraw refused to play the AL champion Red Sox in the World Series, though, owing to his disdain for the Junior Circuit. When his team finished atop the NL again in 1905, however, he had a change of heart and consented to play Mack's Philadelphia A's. That was the first of three World Series McGraw's teams won. In all, his clubs finished above .500 in twenty-nine of thirty-three seasons. He is also often credited for inventing the Baltimore Chop, the hit-and-run, and the hand signals managers use to instruct pitchers and catchers regarding pitch selection.

When the year-old Hall of Fame decided to open its doors to managers in 1937, McGraw and Mack were the first two inductees. By then McGraw had been dead three years. Mack, meanwhile, was still managing. One of two Hall of Fame managers with a losing record, Mack amassed more wins and more losses than any manager in history during his record fifty-three years in the big leagues. He couldn't have provided a greater contrast to McGraw. While the unapologetically uncouth McGraw heckled umpires and picked fights with fans and players, the gentlemanly Mack sat in the dugout in a full-suit and with a fedora atop his head. He demanded that his players call him Mr. Mack. His career began inauspiciously, though. He was a twenty-seven-year-old journeyman catcher when he signed with and invested in the Buffalo Bisons of the ill-fated Federal League in 1890. When that league went out of business after just one season, Mack was left penniless and without a team. His comeback began as player-manager for the Pittsburgh Pirates from 1894 to 1896. Then he spent four years as a minor league manager in Milwaukee. Then with help from AL founder Ban Johnson, Mack became the first manager of the Philadelphia A's in 1901. He held the post for the next half century, not retiring until the conclusion of the 1950 season at age eighty-seven. In the five decades in between, he assembled and disassembled two dynasties—the first spanning 1910 through 1914 when Eddie Collins, Frank Baker, and Eddie Plank led teams that won four pennants and three World Series, the second spanning 1927 through 1932 when Mickey Cochrane, Jimmie Foxx, Al Simmons, and Lefty Grove formed the nucleus of a three-peat pennant winner that won back-to-back World Series in 1929 and 1930. Facing the unique pressure of being a club owner as well as manager, Mack subscribed to a business model that resulted in his teams being either very good or very bad but rarely mediocre. He would develop a core of young stars, ride them for a few years, and then sell them off one at a time to the highest bidders. In this way, he kept the fans interested and also turned a profit. In addition to his

Bucky Harris (at left) and Connie Mack guided their teams to 2,157 and 3,731 wins, respectively.
COURTESY OF THE LIBRARY OF CONGRESS

five championship rings and nine pennants, he had five 100-win seasons and ten 100-loss seasons. His teams finished above .500 in twenty-five of his fifty years in Philadelphia, and his lifetime winning percentage was .486.

Four skippers who saw game action as late as the 1980s have been since selected for enshrinement at Cooperstown. They are Earl Weaver (1,480-1,060), Tommy Lasorda (1,599-1,493), Sparky Anderson (2,194-1,834), and Dick Williams (1,571-1,451). Weaver won four pennants in his seventeen seasons in Baltimore and a World Championship in 1970. Five times his teams topped 100 wins. As for Lasorda, his teams won five pennants and three World Championships in his twenty full seasons with the Dodgers. Although his teams won eight division titles, nary a one reached 100 wins. Anderson ranks fifth all-time in wins and twenty-fourth in winning percentage at .545. He won five pennants and three World Series in twenty-six years. He was the first manager to guide teams from both leagues to World Championships (a feat since duplicated by La Russa). His Reds and Tigers combined for six division titles and four 100-win seasons. And Williams won pennants with three of the five different teams he managed—the Red Sox, A's, and Padres—and back-to-back World Championships with the A's in 1972 and 1973.

Mike Scioscia began 2010 with the best winning percentage among active managers.

As for today's active managers, they account for eleven of the seventy-two game strategists with winning records over careers that have spanned at least 1,000 games. Through 2009, they include Cox, who has a .556 winning percentage; Mike Scioscia (.556); Ron Gardenhire (.546); Charlie Manuel (.547); Torre (.540); La Russa (.535); Dusty Baker (.520); Cito Gaston (.516); Jerry Manuel (.510); Piniella (.521); and Terry Francona (.525).

With apologies to Cox—whose Braves finished first fourteen times during a span of fifteen seasons (failing to do so only in the prematurely curtailed 1994 season) but won just five pennants and one World Championship—and to Torre, whom we've already discussed, La Russa, who ranks third all-time with his 2,552 wins is the best of this bunch. And indeed, by the time he's through managing, he may deserve acclaim as the best ever, especially if he passes McGraw and moves into second place on the all-time wins list. An innovator who has been known to bat his pitcher eighth to increase RBI opportunities for his Number Three hitter, and who is credited with inventing the modern specialized bullpen, La Russa began his managing career with the White Sox in 1979 at the tender age of thirty-four. Since then, his astute maneuvering has translated into steady success with three organizations. His 1983 White Sox won a league-best 99 games before falling to the Orioles in the ALCS. His A's won three consecutive pennants and a World Series between 1988 and 1990. His Cardinals won three division titles, two pennants, and a World Series between 2004 and 2006. His teams have finished .500 or better in twenty-two of his first thirty-one seasons, winning twelve division titles, five pennants and two World Series. He has guided teams to 100 or more wins four times and his teams have suffered only two 90-loss campaigns. At age sixty-five as the 2010 season began, he was on pace to pass McGraw's 2,763 wins well before his seventieth birthday.

Finally, it's time to pick this chapter's winner. In the game's early era, McGraw gets the nod over Mack, for being a consistent winner as well as an innovator. Later, McCarthy distinguished himself as a steady hand with three different clubs—not just the Yankees as was the case with Stengel. In twenty-four seasons, McCarthy's teams always had a winning record and always finished in the first division. He is the only manager in the modern era to maintain a .600 winning percentage over 1,000 games, and he didn't just do it, he did it to the tune of a robust .615 clip. Thus, he is our pick for the most successful manager in baseball history . . . but he sure had some help from those talented players he had at his disposal.

Note: For active managers, totals are through 2009.

[16]

THE BEST COMMISSIONER

He's Done a Thankless Job Well

If this chapter were entitled "The Worst Commissioner," we might begin by piling criticism upon the withered shoulders of that goofy baseball whipping-boy Bud Selig for, among other things, canceling the 1994 World Series, ruining the 2002 All-Star Game, and allowing the steroid scourge to metastasize into an epidemic. And yet, we begin what is in fact a chapter dedicated to the game's best commissioner with the shocking revelation that Bud Selig enters the discussion as a strong contender—perhaps even the front-runner—for this prestigious distinction.

Now, before you accuse your humble author of taking kickbacks in the form of bratwursts with secret sauce and Milwaukee's Best, let's state plainly that the nine men who have sat in baseball's highest chair since its creation in 1920 have all submitted tenures flawed in one way or another. Hence, in picking the best commish, we must weigh the foibles that seem inherent to holders of the position against the positive decisions and innovations baseball's commissioners have contributed. Ultimately, we will judge each man based on the degree to which he strengthened the game and its place as the nation's premier sport over the course of his reign.

We should begin by noting that the commissioner's position was created in the wake of the Black Sox Scandal, in which eight members of the Chicago White Sox conspired with gamblers to fix the 1919 World Series. At the time of the fraudulent series, which the Cincinnati Reds "won," the game's oversight was in the hands of the National Commission, a three-man panel of unapologetically self-interested baseball men that included the American and National League presidents and Reds president Garry Herrmann. And you probably thought Mr. Selig was the first guardian of the game to serve amid a rather glaring conflict of interest, when he was "interim commissioner" as well as de facto owner of the Brewers. It is hard to imagine that Mr. Herrmann was very eager to confirm the widespread suspicions that his Reds had been handed their first championship on a silver platter.

Not surprisingly then, the National Commission disbanded after the controversial World Series, and baseball operated without a governing body in 1920. Meanwhile, Joe Jackson and his co-conspirators continued to play. And allegations of other "dirty" players cast an ever-darkening shadow over ballparks throughout the country. Baseball was spiraling into crisis when the team owners turned to a federal judge from Illinois to restore public faith in the game. Kenesaw Mountain Landis, baseball's first commissioner, made it clear from the outset that, though the owners had hired him, he would not answer to them. As one of his first acts he required all sixteen team owners to sign a pledge of loyalty stating, "Each of us will acquiesce in [the commissioner's] decisions even when we believe them mistaken, and we will not discredit the sport by public criticisms of him or one another."

Landis was hired to clean up baseball, and he didn't waste much time before doing just that. Although the eight Black Sox were acquitted in a court of law after the mysterious disappearance of three signed confessions, Landis acted swiftly and without mercy, banning them from the game in 1921. Then he banned another known gambler, Hal Chase of the Giants, then another, minor league infielder Joe Gideon, then another, Claude Hendrix of the Cubs. In all, he banished nineteen players during his first four years, including Benny Kauff, another Giant, who wasn't even a gambler. Kauff was acquitted in a New York court on charges that he'd stolen a car, but he didn't receive the benefit of the doubt when he reported to the Avenging Angel. Landis banned him for dishonoring the game. With the players, owners, and even umpires walking scared, Landis presided over a record twenty-four-year term, wielding an unquestioned power that no other man has ever enjoyed in the game. He left office at age seventy-eight, and, only then, because he had died.

After the initial shock of Landis's censures, the growing national pastime settled into a period of relative tranquility. For cleaning up the sport and helping it take root as America's Game, Landis might at first glance appear an obvious choice as best commissioner. But there was a dark side to his legacy too. He was one of the principals in upholding the so-called Gentlemen's Agreement that kept blacks out of baseball for decades. In the early 1940s, when a small but persistent chorus of voices in favor of integrating began to rise up, Landis refused to hear the melody. He stood in the way of an attempt by the Pirates to sign Negro Leagues star Josh Gibson, then he and NL president Ford Frick prevented Bill Veeck from buying the Philadelphia Phillies and stocking the club with Negro

Kenesaw Mountain Landis cleaned up the game in the wake of the Chicago "Black Sox" scandal of 1919. COURTESY OF THE LIBRARY OF CONGRESS

Leaguers. Clearly, Landis did not act in the best interests of baseball or social progress when he made these decisions.

Landis's successor, a jovial politician from Kentucky named Happy Chandler, confirmed that the Avenging Angel had actively blocked the path of blacks to the major leagues. In his autobiography, *Heroes, Plain Folks, and Skunks*, Chandler wrote, "For twenty-four years Judge Landis wouldn't let a black man play. I had his records, and I read them, and for twenty-four years Landis consistently blocked any attempts to put blacks and whites together on a big league field." In the book, Chandler details how he, Happy Chandler, was the one who gave Branch Rickey the encouragement needed to recall Jackie Robinson from the minors in 1947, remembering a conversation prior to the start of the season when a conflicted Rickey expressed second thoughts about the "great experiment." Chandler recalls telling Rickey, "Branch, I'm going to have to meet my Maker some day and if He asks me why I didn't let this boy play and I say it's because he's black that might not be a satisfactory answer. If the Lord made some people black and some white, and some red or yellow, He must have had a pretty good reason. It's my job to see the game is fairly played and that everybody has an equal chance. Bring him up. I'll sign the transfer." While Chandler comes off as the champion of baseball integration in this account, historians more commonly have portrayed him as having played a passive role in the movement. He was neither an outspoken critic of nor advocate for integration, but simply chose not to impede Robinson's progress. For that, Chandler deserves credit, but certainly not as much as Rickey and, most of all, Robinson.

Aside from his dealings in the Robinson triumph, Chandler enjoyed a reputation as a "player's commissioner" by creating a pension fund for retirees and granting amnesty to eighteen big leaguers banned for trying to join the upstart Mexican League. He also caused a flap by handing a one-year suspension to Dodgers manager Leo Durocher for incidents that reflected poorly on the game. Chandler also levied fines against several teams for bending rules that pertained to signing amateur players. Before long, the owners, three-quarters of whom would need to vote for Chandler in order for him to begin a second six-year term, became discontented. Realizing he was a lame duck, Chandler resigned midway through the 1951 season.

Next came Frick, a former baseball writer who'd spent seventeen years at the NL helm. He lasted fourteen years in the commissioner's office, third longest behind Landis and Selig. The knock on Frick is that, according to most accounts, he didn't do very much of anything. For better or worse, he stood idly by while teams like the Giants, Dodgers, and Braves relocated. He added the metaphoric asterisk to Roger Maris's 61st home run because it occurred after the Yankees' 154th game of the season, making it a different accomplishment, so his argument went, than the 60-homer season submitted by Babe Ruth, with whom Frick had once co-written a book. To his credit, Frick helped found the Hall of Fame, but that occurred in the 1930s when he was still NL president.

The short and forgettable tenure of General Spike Eckert began in November 1965 and concluded in December 1968. Eckert, who knew embarrassingly little about baseball—he was once shocked to learn that the Dodgers had ever played in Brooklyn—was hired for his reputation as a businessman. Before long, the owners realized that only a quarter of them needed to voice their dissent to prompt his removal from office, and they did just that. At the time of his ouster, he was portrayed by the media as a sympathetic figure who tried against impossible circumstances to uphold the auspices of an obsolete position. The owners had simply grown too strong under Frick to go back to answering to a single, all-powerful, guardian of the game.

Bowie Kuhn's stewardship proved more memorable than his predecessor's. The lawyer presided over the game from 1969 to 1984 and oversaw the expansion from twenty to twenty-six teams, the advent of free agency, and a changing of the guard as owners like Veeck and Charlie Finley yielded to newer blood. Kuhn is best remembered for invoking his best-interests-of-the-game powers to thwart Finley's sale of Vida Blue, Rollie Fingers, and Joe Rudi at the 1976 trading deadline on the grounds that the fire sale would upset competitive balance. He then fended off a challenge by Finley in court. He is also remembered for taking a tough stance on drugs and suspending several star players. On gambling, too, he toed a hard line, ruling that icons Willie Mays and Mickey Mantle could no longer serve the game in any official capacities so long as they were lending their names to casinos with which they'd signed endorsement deals. Hypocritically, though, Kuhn did not reprimand Yankees owner George Steinbrenner, who owned a racetrack in Florida. But this inconsistency was just one of many troubling aspects of his commissionership. He also chose not to attend Fulton County Stadium on the night Hank Aaron surpassed Babe Ruth's all-time home run record. This slight shocked and saddened many people within the game. To his credit, Kuhn proposed the long-overdue induction of Negro Leagues stars into the Hall of Fame, but then he undermined the gesture by crassly arguing that their plaques should hang in a separate—dare we say "segregated"—wing of the gallery. Later, when the players went on strike in 1981, Kuhn made little effort to bridge the gap between Marvin Miller's union and management. Rather, he waited out the stoppage in play, then endorsed a ridiculous split season that awarded first-half and second-half crowns in each of the four divisions.

The next commissioner, Peter Ueberroth, arrived fresh off his success as CEO of the 1984 Olympics in Los Angeles. He took office with a reputation as a problem solver and unifier. And when the owners complained that escalating player salaries were eating into their profits, he suggested a way for them to work together to solve their problem. He encouraged them to secretly agree to stop bidding on free agents, and the resulting collusion had the desired effect of deflating player salaries. Unfortunately, the maneuver was illegal and led to a series of shameful losses for the owners in court. In 1988, shortly before the courts awarded the Players Association hundreds of millions of dollars, Ueberroth stepped down. His tenure as commissioner is widely considered the worst ever.

The next commissioner, former Yale University president A. Bartlett Giamatti, loved the game intensely but left a controversial stamp on it by banning all-time hit-king Pete Rose for gambling. Giamatti issued the Rose ruling on his 145th day in office, and died on his 154th, September 1, 1989, of a heart attack. His premature departure leaves behind too thin a body of evidence upon which to judge him. The same could be said of his successor, Fay Vincent, who served for less than three years before resigning in 1992 after a vote of no-confidence from owners discontented with his decisions related to the game's national TV contract, the work stoppage of 1990, and the divvying of new revenue from the expansion that created the Florida Marlins and Colorado Rockies.

And that brings us to Mr. Selig, a man many of today's fans view about as fondly as a rainout. The former Milwaukee car dealer served as interim commissioner from 1992 through 1998, while continuing to own the Milwaukee Brewers. Rightly, this conflict left many fans scratching their heads. And rightly, many still blame Selig for the lost World Series of 1994, and for affronts to tradition such as interleague play and the wild card. The steroid epidemic too has been rightly laid at Selig's doorstep. As much as purists hate to admit it, though, each of these departures from tradition put the game on sounder financial footing than it had been previously. Yes, even the steroid scandal, as much as it pains this writer to admit it. To begin, the work stoppage of 1994-1995 laid the groundwork for the subsequent collective bargaining agreements that have led to the revenue sharing that has leveled the playing field for smaller market teams. Interleague play, the wild card, and the realignment from four to six divisions have resulted in more interesting pennant races, giving more fans reason to remain interested in the game into September. These changes have also translated into more revenue for owners and players to share, making them less likely to stage another work stoppage. As for the steroid-fueled home run binge of 1998, it put baseball on the front pages of newspapers across the land and attracted millions of new fans. Even in the wake of recurrent steroid revelations, MLB set attendance records for four straight seasons from 2004 through 2007, before suffering only a 1.1 percent decline in attendance in 2008, despite the overall crashing of the rest of the American economy.

Furthermore, whether you agree with the public-financing model he's advocated or not, Selig has shepherded the construction of the many new ballparks we now enjoy. They're a big reason why attendance has skyrocketed from fifty-five million fans per season when the Reign of Bud began in 1992 to nearly eighty million today. In short, the owners are making more money than ever, the players are making more money, the ballparks are more comfortable and welcoming, and the game has more fans than at any previous time. And let's face it, as much as we fans grouse about steroids use, we're still watching the games and turning out at the ballpark and tending to our fantasy baseball teams and following the game as intently as ever. With the state of the game such as it is, we must acknowledge that despite his flaws, Bud Selig has done more to further the best interests of the game than any other commissioner. That doesn't mean we shouldn't still be bitter about 1994, or that we shouldn't blame the commissioner for that Barry Bonds or Mark McGwire jersey hanging shamefully in our closet, or that we should hold our tongue when those November World Series games don't reach their final innings until after midnight on the East Coast. It just means that along with the game's current warts, baseball as it exists today is healthier than it's ever been. And for that, the eccentric fellow from Milwaukee deserves a toast come Opening Day.

THE WORST OF THE BEST AND BEST OF THE WORST

[17]

THE WORST HALL OF FAMER

The Most Mortal "Immortal"

Each year, select members of the Baseball Writers' Association of America are charged with the task of deciding which recently retired players will be enshrined in the National Baseball Hall of Fame. Former players become eligible in the writers' ballot as soon as they've been retired for five seasons, upon which time they must receive 75 percent of the vote in any one of their first fifteen years of eligibility in order to gain induction. Those who fail to gain admittance to Cooperstown via this means must pin their hopes on a second process, whereby a Veterans Committee consisting of all living Hall of Famers selects the individuals whom it believes have been overlooked by the scribes.

The criterion for judging aspirants in both processes is rather vague. The Hall of Fame charter instructs, "Voting shall be based upon the player's record, playing ability, integrity, sportsmanship, character, and contributions to the team(s) on which the player played." If we interpret a player's *record* to be his statistics, then it is difficult to define exactly what *playing ability* means. After all, a player with a lot of ability who doesn't amass much of a record is usually considered an underachiever. So perhaps this just means that the Hall is looking for talented players who played well over long enough periods of time to build substantial statistical bodies of work. As for *integrity*, *sportsmanship*, and *character*, these words all seem to hint at the same inherently subjective question: Was the player a decent fellow?

While the matter of whether these so-called "personal conduct" qualifiers should be relevant to Hall voters is another argument for another day, this chapter aims to identify the enshrinees whose accomplishments afield don't quite seem to measure up to those of the other best players ever at their position. We'll take a position-by-position approach to the lightweights for whom plaques hang in the Hall's gallery, starting with the pitchers. And for the purposes of this discussion, we'll confine our ruminations to only those 202 players inducted to the Hall on the merits of their major league service, as there is too little comparable statistical evidence available for us to fairly evaluate the thirty players who were inducted on the basis of their Negro Leagues careers.

Three hundred wins is usually thought of as the unofficial magic number that delineates starting pitching immortals from the rest of the schlubs who have made a living on the mound, but the fact is only twenty of the sixty-three pitchers in the Hall of Fame reached that total, including Lefty Grove and Early Wynn who finished with exactly 300. The majority of Cooperstown hurlers finished with win totals in the 200s, and several didn't even reach the 200 plateau, including Dizzy Dean who won 150 games over a twelve-year career shortened by injury and Sandy Koufax who won 165 over a similarly shortened twelve-year sprint. Reliever Rollie Fingers—who made the Hall by virtue of his 341 career saves—didn't even have a winning record, finishing with a win-loss mark of 114-118. And many of the immortals who surpassed 200 wins did so with less than remarkable winning percentages and/or unspectacular ERAs. To wit, Waite Hoyt was 237-182 with a 3.59 ERA in twenty-one seasons and reached 20 wins in a season only twice. Jesse Haines was 210-158 with a 3.64 ERA in nineteen seasons and had three 20-win campaigns. Ted Lyons was 260-230 with a 3.67 ERA in twenty-one seasons, including three 20-win efforts and two 20-loss efforts. And Red Ruffing was 273-225 with a Hall-high 3.80 ERA in twenty-two seasons that included a string of four 20-win years for the Yankees in the late 1930s after a string of five straight losing seasons with the Red Sox in the 1920s. For their relatively lofty ERAs and several seasons apiece in which they lost more games than they won, Lyons and Ruffing are the weakest pitchers in the Hall in our opinion. That's not to say they weren't very good pitchers. They were. But their *records* don't reflect the same level of dominance most other Cooperstown hurlers achieved.

The second most common position among Hall of Famers is outfielder. Through 2009, sixty men who patrolled the grassy pastures have been inducted, and only four failed to achieve either a lifetime batting average of .300, 350 home runs, or 3,000 hits. The four who fall short of satisfying any one of these markers by which we normally determine batting excellence include pre-modern star Tommy McCarthy, who batted .294 with 44 homers, 1,496 hits, and an unknown number of steals for several teams between 1884 and 1896; Max Carey, who batted .285, with 70 homers, 2,665 hits, and 738 stolen bases for Pittsburgh and Brooklyn between 1910 and 1929; Harry Hooper, who batted .281 with 75 homers, 2,466 hits, and 375 stolen bases for the Red Sox and White Sox between 1909 and 1925; and Larry Doby, who batted .283 with 253 homers and 1,515 hits for the Indians and White

Sox between 1947 and 1959. The first three on this list get extra-credit points for having been spectacular defensive outfielders, while Doby's résumé is enhanced by his trailblazing role in integrating the American League in 1947. Now, it's obviously too simplistic to conclude that just because an outfielder didn't hit many home runs, he isn't Hall-worthy, especially considering that the first three players in this grouping played all or most of their seasons in the dead-ball era. However, there were plenty of batters who maintained .300 averages when these men were failing to do so, and there were plenty who racked up more hits. Nonetheless, all four of our least statistically impressive outfielders were widely considered very good players in their day. Appearing more suspect is a player who did manage to hit .300 but without much thump in his lumber: Lloyd Waner. In eighteen seasons spent mostly playing alongside his Hall of Fame brother Paul on the Pirates lawn, Little Poison batted .316 and led the National League in singles four times. But he never had more than 28 doubles or 5 home runs. He stole 14 bases in his rookie campaign of 1927 but never reached double figures again, tallying just 67 career steals. He finished with 2,459 hits, a respectable .353 on-base percentage, a middling .393 slugging percentage, 27 homers, and 598 RBIs. These totals are similar to those of fellow Hall of Fame outfielder Richie Ashburn who batted .308/.396/.382, while racking up 2,574 hits, 29 homers, and 586 RBIs in a fifteen-year career spent mostly with the Phillies. Ashburn needed three fewer seasons to surpass Waner in hits and to steal 234 bases, though, and his on-base percentage was exceptional. In our book, Lloyd Waner is the weakest link in the Cooperstown outfield.

There are only twenty-nine corner infielders in the Hall, compared to forty middle infielders.

Frank Chance, pictured here at the Polo Grounds, had only 1,273 hits in his Hall of Fame career. COURTESY OF THE LIBRARY OF CONGRESS

Of the third and first sackers, two first basemen stand out as less than stellar. Both were admitted by the Veterans Committee—or Old Timer's Committee, as it was then called—in the mid-1940s. And they were admitted at a time when the committee was charged with a mandate to add at least ten golden oldies to the Hall each year. Former Cubs first-sacker Frank Chance is immortalized in the famous Tinker-to-Evers-to-Chance refrain from a poem that ran in the *New York Evening Mail* in 1910 celebrating the trio's defensive acumen. Chance, who played seventeen seasons, including a couple before the turn of the last century ushered in the modern era, batted .296/.394/.394, while collecting only 1,273 hits and 596 RBIs. As player-manager, he guided the Cubs to four NL pennants, which seems like it should count for something. And in fairness, he played in an era when players just didn't hit for much power or drive in many runs. He was also reputed to be a fine-fielding first baseman. A more suspect first base selection would appear to be George Kelly, who played at the dawn of the lively ball era but achieved neither eye-popping power totals nor an exceptional batting average. He played sixteen seasons for five NL teams between 1915 and 1932, batting .297/.342/.452 with 1,778 hits, 148 home runs, and 1,020 RBIs. During a seven-year stretch with the Giants in his prime, he averaged 17 home runs and 106 RBIs, while leading the NL with 23 home runs in 1921 and 94 RBIs in 1920 and with 136 RBIs in 1924. Then his numbers tailed off dramatically over his final six seasons. Kelly's lifetime totals don't even compare to those of such latter day non–Hall of Famers as John Olerud, Will Clark, and Mark Grace. And even in his own time, Kelly failed to achieve batting averages approaching the gaudy figures that were being turned in by his peers, who accounted for seven .400 or better seasons during the years in which Kelly, who topped out at a career high of .324 in 1924, was playing.

That brings us to the middle infielders. Let us first establish that although second base and shortstop are often referred to as defense-first positions, it is historically inaccurate to assume that there were not batting savants among the middle infielders of the game's early days. We need look no further than to slugging Hall of Famers like Nap Lajoie, Honus Wagner, Rogers Hornsby, Travis Jackson, Charlie Gehringer, Bobby Doerr, and Tony Lazzeri to disprove this assumption. Nonetheless, the long list of offensively challenged second sackers and shortstops includes many "good glove men" who managed to gain entry into this most elite baseball fraternity despite eminently mortal offensive output. The five most notable examples of this phenomenon are:

Player	Seasons	AVG/OBP/SL	Hits	Home Runs	Stolen Bases
Johnny Evers (2B)	18	.270/.356/.334	1,659	12	324
Rabbit Maranville (SS)	23	.258/.318/.340	2,605	28	291
Bill Mazeroski (2B)	17	.260/.299/.367	2,016	138	27
Joe Tinker (SS)	15	.262/.308/.353	1,687	31	336
Phil Rizzuto (SS)	13	.273/.351/.355	1,588	38	149

Among this quintet of slick fielders, Mazeroski had the most power. He also hit one of the most dramatic home runs in baseball history and won eight Gold Gloves. But in our opinion he is the least deserving of the keystone enshrinees. He usually batted eighth in the Pirates order, and he never hit better than .283 in any season. In fact, he only topped .270 in five of his seventeen seasons. And he never had more than 167 hits, scored more than 71 runs, or had more than 82 runs batted in. He was not fleet afoot and did not reach base frequently via walk. He is the only position player in the Hall of Fame who failed to reach base at least 30 percent of the time and his lifetime ratio statistics (batting average, on-base percentage, slugging percentage) don't compare favorably to those of other middle infielders like Dave Concepcion, Garry Templeton, Jim Fregosi, Jim Gantner, and Jose Offerman, none of whom are, or deserve to be, in the Hall. Mazeroski is not, however, our choice as the least credentialed Cooperstowner. That distinction goes to one of the thirteen catchers in the Hall.

Hall of Famer Ray Schalk batted .253 in his eighteen-year career. COURTESY OF THE LIBRARY OF CONGRESS

Ray Schalk was an honest fellow who didn't take the bait that eight of his White Sox teammates did when gamblers came calling with a scheme to fix the 1919 World Series. He was also an outstanding defensive backstop who led the AL in fielding percentage in eight of his eighteen seasons. And he possessed good speed for a catcher as evidenced by his 30 stolen bases in 1916, which set a single-season record for catchers that stood until John Wathan had 36 in 1982. But over a career that spanned 1912 to 1929, Schalk batted only .253/.340/.316 with just 1,345 hits, 579 runs, and 594 RBIs. His lifetime batting average is the lowest of any Hall of Fame position player and his 11 homers and 259 extra-base hits are the fewest. Sure, he called a good game, but the same can be said of a lot of .250-hitting catchers who are not in the Hall. Thus, Schalk edges out runner-up Mazeroski to claim this chapter's ignominious title.

THE BEST PLAYER NOT IN THE HALL OF FAME

He's Still Waiting for the Call from Cooperstown

Usually when fans discuss the players who have been slighted by the Hall of Fame's selection process, we tend to favor the ones who toiled for our favorite teams. It's nearly impossible to be unmoved by our rooting interests. Furthermore, the era to which a player belonged has the capacity to sway opinions, especially considering the variance between league-wide pitching and hitting balance during different generations of the game's history. Thus, we state plainly at the outset of this baseball argument that the challenge facing Cooperstown's two selection caucuses—the one for recent retirees consisting of the better baseball writers, and the other for veteran retirees consisting of the living Hall of Famers—is immense. And for the most part, we believe, the voters have done an exceptional job. But a case can be made for the addition of several excellent players not yet enshrined. This chapter is devoted to identifying the player with the biggest beef of all.

To begin, let's state plainly at the outset that none of the players we'll be discussing was a hands-down, no-brainer pick for Cooperstown upon his retirement. If he was, the writers would have voted him in. And perhaps that is the best argument against any of these players' worthiness. But at the same time, a case can be made that many recurrent All-Stars and statistical leaders who find themselves on the outside of the plaque gallery looking in deserve another look.

To clarify our pursuit, let's put aside Joe Jackson and Pete Rose—two obviously credentialed non-members who are ineligible for enshrinement due to their off-field indiscretions. And let's also remove from the discussion all the recently retired players who haven't yet sat out the mandatory five seasons to become eligible. And let's also set aside Mark McGwire and the others who belong to the first wave of steroid-era stat hogs, whose worthiness the writers are still trying to determine. Most of the candidates that remain fit broadly into one of two categories: Either they were dominant during their heyday but for too short a time period to amass the gaudy lifetime statistics expected of "immortals," or they were never truly dominant, but played a very long time, allowing them to accumulate a statistical body of work that appears to overstate their playing ability.

The poster child for the too-briefly brilliant big leaguer is Lefty O'Doul, owner of a .349 lifetime batting average—fourth highest all-time among players with at least 3,000 plate appearances. O'Doul also won two batting titles and set the NL record for most hits in a season, 254, which was later matched by Hall of Famer Bill Terry. O'Doul played eleven big league seasons—enough to satisfy the Hall's requirement that a player take part in at least ten, but his first four years were spent as a pitcher with the Yankees and the Red Sox between 1919 and 1923. It was not until he returned from the minor leagues as a slugging left-fielder in 1928 that his career really took off. He was thirty-one years old when he resurfaced with the Giants to begin a seven-year binge in which he hit for both power and average, accounting for his robust career batting average, his .413 on-base percentage, and his .532 slugging percentage. He collected 1,140 hits, 113 home runs, and 542 RBIs. Then, after batting .316 in 1934, he retired at age thirty-seven and returned to the Pacific Coast League to manage the San Francisco Seals, with whom he mentored a young Joe DiMaggio and led several barnstorming tours to Japan.

Lefty O'Doul struggled as a pitcher for the Yankees and Red Sox before leaving New York and blossoming as a hitter.
COURTESY OF THE LIBRARY OF CONGRESS

The Best Player Not in the Hall of Fame

On the other end of the not-quite-worthy-of-Cooperstown continuum are the players who racked up impressive stats due more to longevity in the game than to dominant skills. In this group we find players like Tommy John whose 288 wins were testament to his twenty-six seasons between 1963 and 1989. Although he did reach the 20-win plateau three times, he only reached 15 wins on five occasions. He made four All-Star teams and twice finished second in the Cy Young Award balloting. He didn't overpower hitters, striking out just 4 per nine innings, and in ten different seasons he lost more games than he won. He ranks twenty-sixth all-time with those 288 wins, and fifty-third with 760 games pitched. But he averaged only 11 wins per season and his 3.34 career ERA ranks just 314th best all-time (tied, ironically, with Hall of Famers Lefty Gomez and Fergie Jenkins).

While O'Doul and John represent examples of players who, for very different reasons, have piqued debate among Hall voters and observers, there are plenty of other players for or against whom similar arguments may be made. With apologies in advance to such good but not great players as Maury Wills, Harold Baines, Dale Murphy, Dave Parker, Bill Buckner, Jim Kaat, and Lee Smith, as well as to franchise icons like Gil Hodges, Tony Oliva, Ron Santo, and Steve Garvey, who had better careers than some of the suspect Hall of Famers at their positions—as detailed in the previous chapter—but are still not quite deserving themselves, here are the players for whom we believe the strongest cases may be made.

THE PITCHERS

The three most justifiably grumpy pitchers still waiting for the call from Cooperstown are Luis Tiant, Jack Morris, and Bert Blyleven. Of the three, Tiant was the most dominant in his prime—but his prime was the shortest among the trio. Over nineteen seasons, he twice led the AL in ERA, posting a minuscule 1.60 ERA for the Indians in 1968 and a similarly microscopic 1.91 ERA for the Red Sox in 1972 during an era when the balance between pitching and hitting league-wide was clearly favoring pitchers. He reached 20 wins four times and led the AL in shutouts on three occasions. His 49 career shutouts—in just 484 career starts—rank twenty-first all-time, tied with Hall of Famers Don Drysdale, Early Wynn, and Jenkins. And nineteen of the twenty pitchers ahead of Tiant on the all-time shutout list are in the Hall of Fame, with the lone exception being Blyleven. Tiant was also a big-game pitcher who went 3-0 with a 2.86 ERA in four postseason starts. Those arguing against his credentials might point out, however, that his 229-172 lifetime record and 3.30 ERA are good but less than eye-popping, and that he only reached the 15-win plateau six times. His portfolio compares favorably, nonetheless, to those belonging to Cooperstown clubbers like Jim Bunning (224-184, 3.27 ERA), Waite Hoyt (237-182, 3.59 ERA), Jesse Haines (210-158, 3.64 ERA), and Herb Pennock (240-162, 3.60 ERA).

Like Tiant, Jack Morris struck an imposing presence on the mound and was regarded as one of the game's best during his peak years in the 1980s. He was a bulldog who almost always gave his team a chance to win. Over an eighteen-year career, he reached 20 wins three times and 15 wins on twelve occasions, which doesn't even include the strike-shortened 1981 season when he led the AL with 14 W's despite making only twenty-five starts. Morris won three World Series with three different teams—the 1984 Tigers, 1991 Twins, and 1992 Blue Jays—while going 7-4 with a 3.80 ERA in thirteen postseason starts. He won the World Series MVP in 1991, pitching a ten-inning shutout against the Braves to give Minnesota a 1–0 victory in Game Seven. His 254-186 record is certainly good enough for Cooperstown, but the knock against him is his 3.90 ERA, which is higher than any Hall of Famer's.

Bert Blyleven had a handful of dominant seasons for the Twins early in his career in the 1970s, then spent the latter three-quarters of his career as a very good pitcher who played for some mediocre teams and a few good ones, before finishing 287-250 with a 3.31 ERA. That win total ranks twenty-seventh best all-time, leaving Blyleven to commiserate with John and his 288 wins, and Bobby Mathews—who won 297 games in the 1870s and 1880s—as the winningest pitchers excluded from the Hall. The knocks on Blyleven are that he needed twenty-two seasons to amass his robust win total and that he reached 20 wins only once—when he went 20-17 as a twenty-two-year-old for the Twins in 1973. Despite winning 15 games on nine occasions, Blyleven made just two All-Star teams. On the other hand, his 3,701 strikeouts rank fifth all-time and his 60 shutouts in 685 games started rank ninth. And he was 5-1 with a 2.47 ERA in the postseason. He won World Series with the Pirates in 1979 and Twins in 1987.

Among pitchers, the choice comes down to Tiant, who was the most dominant but over a relatively short period; Morris, who was never as dominant but was one of the best top-of-the-rotation starters in the game between 1979 and 1992; and Blyleven, who was the least dominant but was consistently very good for the longest time. The choice here is for Morris, despite his high ERA, for racking up those twelve seasons with 15 wins or more and for being a clutch performer in the postseason. Blyleven places a close second.

THE HITTERS

The best offensive players not yet admitted into the Hall's glorious gallery include Bob Johnson, Dick Allen, and Andre Dawson. All three were prodigious run-producers who were also perennial threats to bat .300. Let's begin with the least-well-known player, Johnson, who was one of the lone bright spots on some awful Philadelphia A's teams during the 1930s and 1940s before he spent his final two seasons with the Red Sox. After batting .290 with 21 home runs and 93 RBIs as a rookie in 1933, Johnson went on to become just the fifth player to reach 20 home runs in nine consecutive seasons. The leftfielder reached 100 RBIs seven straight times during that span. And over his thirteen-year career, he reached 100 RBIs eight times, and topped the 100-run mark six times, while making eight All-Star squads. When he retired in 1945, he ranked eighth all-time with 288 home runs. The knock on him is that he played only thirteen seasons because he broke into the big leagues at age twenty-seven. Nonetheless, he hit .296/.393/.506 with 2,051 hits, 1,239 runs, and 1,283 RBIs, which probably would have earned a plaque in Cooperstown had he played for a higher-profile team.

Dick Allen was also a dominant force at the bat, who excelled in a career that, like Johnson's, was too brief to convince Hall voters. Allen was widely regarded, however, as a below-average defensive player. And he wasn't the world's friendliest fellow. He feuded with teammates and coaches, engendering a reputation as a negative factor in the clubhouse. He hit for power and average, though, at a time when both were in short supply. He won the NL Rookie of the Year Award and finished seventh in the MVP balloting in 1964 when he batted .318, while collecting 201 hits, 125 runs, 29 home runs and 91 RBIs. Allen went on to reach 20 homers in nine straight years, and surpassed the mark ten times over his entire career. He hit a personal best 40 home runs in 1966, and then, after joining the White Sox, led the AL with 37 home runs in 1972 and with 32 home runs in 1974. He won the 1972 AL MVP, was a member of seven All-Star teams, led his league in slugging and extra-base hits three times, in on-base percentage twice, and in runs and triples once each. He retired in 1977 at age thirty-five, having hit .292/.378/.534, with 1,099 runs, 1,848 hits, 351 home runs, and 1,119 RBIs. His slugging percentage ranks forty-first all-time. The knocks on him are that even though he amassed impressive power numbers during a pitcher's era, he didn't play long enough to rack up gaudy lifetime totals, and he led his league in errors four times—twice at third base and twice at first.

When it comes to the best hitter excluded from the Hall, though, the most convincing case can be made for Andre Dawson. A five-tool-player, Dawson was a solid hitter for average, a very good hitter for power, a spectacular defensive outfielder, and a great base runner before several knee injuries slowed him down later in his career. The Hawk broke into the bigs with the Expos in 1977, when he batted .282 with 19 home runs and 65 RBIs to win NL Rookie of the Year honors. Over the next decade, his power numbers steadily increased, culminating in a 49–home-run, 137-RBI MVP season for the last-place Cubs in 1987. This came after he had finished runner-up for the Award in 1981 and 1983 while still a member of the Expos. Dawson hit 20 homers or more thirteen times, and exceeded 20 stolen bases seven times. He started for seven of the eight All-Star teams he made, four times in centerfield and three in rightfield. He covered a lot of ground in the outfield and had a cannon for an arm, enabling him to win eight Gold Gloves, including six in a row as a centerfielder between 1980 and 1985, and two as a rightfielder. He won four Silver Slugger Awards, and racked up 4,787 total bases, which ranks twenty-fifth all-time. He struggled through four sub-par seasons at the tail end of his twenty-one-year career, before retiring in 1996, having batted .279/.323/.482 with 1,373 runs, 2,774 hits, 438 home runs (thirty-sixth most all-time), 1,591 RBIs (thirty-fourth most all-time), and 314 stolen bases. And he played before the steroid era, making his power totals all the more impressive. The knocks against him would be that he reached 100 RBIs just four times, hit .300 or better only five times, and had good but not great ratio statistics. Still, he is one of only three players to hit 400 homers and steal 300 bases—joining Willie Mays and Barry Bonds in this elite company—and he was a defensive standout who wielded a very productive bat for a prime that lasted from 1977 until 1992.

In 2009 Dawson received 67 percent of the Baseball Writers' vote, leaving him, for the time being, the best player not in the Hall of Fame. When his induction day inevitably arrives, he will pass that unwanted mantle on to our runners-up Jack Morris and Bert Blyleven.

[19]

THE WORST START TO A HALL OF FAME CAREER

Before Immortality There Were Some Mortifying Moments

In this chapter we'll explore a Cooperstown query that hasn't been investigated as exhaustively as some of the other Hall of Fame debates that tend to arise. Simply stated, our goal is to determine which Hall of Famer endured the rockiest start to his career, the "immortal" who looked the most glaringly mortal during his first few seasons.

To begin, let's run down some of the inglorious debuts experienced by some of the sport's more illustrious stars. Would you believe Ty Cobb, who owns the record for the highest lifetime batting average at .366, only managed to hit .240 as a rookie? The Georgia Peach collected just 36 safeties in 150 at-bats for the Tigers in 1905, before proceeding to bat .316 or higher in every one of his remaining twenty-three seasons. But we'll cut Cobb some slack for that lackluster start. He was, after all, just eighteen years old at the time.

Willie Mays narrowly missed breaking into the bigs as a teenager himself. The Giants called up the Say Hey Kid just two weeks after his twentieth birthday, fresh off his bludgeoning American Association pitching to the tune of a .477 average with the Minneapolis Millers. But Mays went 0 for 12 to start his major league career. Then he broke through for a homer against no less a hurler than Warren Spahn on May 28, 1951, for his first hit, and he proceeded to win the 1951 NL Rookie of the Year Award with a .274 average and 20 home runs. The next season he batted .236 with 4 homers in thirty-four games before shipping out to serve his country in the Korean War. His military service cost him the entire 1953 season as well. Finally, he returned from the Army in 1954 and jump-started his career by hitting .345 with 41 homers during the regular season, before making the most famous catch in World Series history as the Giants swept the Indians in October.

As Mays was blossoming in New York, another future star was taking his lumps in Pittsburgh. Twenty-year-old Roberto Clemente batted .255 in his first campaign for the Pirates in 1955 with just 5 homers in 124 games. His sophomore season was a big improvement, as he batted .311 and hit 7 long balls. But then he slipped to just a .253 average with 4 home runs in 1957. By the end of the 1959 season, Clemente had five big league seasons under his belt and had a .281 average and 26 career homers. Then, as his body filled out, he found his batting eye and power stroke, enabling him to have a breakout season that yielded a .314 average with 16 home runs in 1960. The next year, he hit .351 with 23 homers. And he was on his way to batting better than .300 in twelve of his final thirteen seasons, while reaching double figures in homers every year.

Unlike Clemente, who is remembered as a great pure hitter but not so much as a slugger, the hard-hitting Al Kaline made his name as a masher, blasting 399 dingers in his career. Would you believe the Tigers slugger hit just 5 homers and had just 45 RBIs in his first 532 at-bats though? Those were Kaline's totals after 28 at-bats as an eighteen-year-old in 1953 and 504 as a nineteen-year-old in 1954. He batted .274 over those first two seasons, before breaking out in 1955 to hit .340 with 27 home runs and 102 RBIs.

Likewise, Duke Snider, who hit 407 lifetime long balls, hit just 5 in 243 at-bats and ninety-three games over his first two seasons, and Harmon Killebrew, who belted 573 big flies, hit just 11 homers over his first five fragmentary big league seasons while bouncing back and forth between the Washington Senators and the minor leagues, prior to smacking 42 long balls for Washington in 1959.

Of course legendary pitchers also have sometimes gotten off to shaky starts before amassing Hall of Fame credentials. A young Hal Newhouser was 34-52 over his first five seasons in Detroit, before going 29-9 with a 2.22 ERA for the Tigers as a twenty-three-year-old in 1944 en route to a 207-150 career record. Similarly, Sandy Koufax bounced between the Dodgers bullpen and rotation throughout his first six seasons while accruing just a 36-40 record. Then he joined the rotation to stay in 1961 and went 18-13 on his way to a 165-87 lifetime mark. As for Gaylord Perry, he had a 24-30 record through four seasons, before going 21-8 at age twenty-eight in 1966 and finishing his twenty-two-year career with a 314-265 record.

While a young Tom Seaver found immediate success for the Mets in the late 1960s, teammate Nolan Ryan struggled with his control. Seaver made his debut in 1967, and in his first five seasons he posted a 95-54 record. Ryan had a cup of coffee with the Mets in 1966 and then didn't resurface in the bigs for good until 1968. By the time his five seasons with the Mets reached their end in 1971, he had a 29-38 mark. Then, after the Mets traded him to the California Angels, he went 19-16 with a 2.28 ERA and 329 strikeouts in 1972. And what did the Mets receive in return for Ryan and a trio of other fringe players? Jim Fregosi, who batted .232 in 1972 and .234 in 1973, before being sold to the Rangers. For the record, Seaver finished with 311 wins, Ryan with 324.

To this point we've touched upon several Hall of Famers whose careers got off to starts that, in retrospect, offered little to suggest greatness would follow. In the cases of the pitchers especially, we might go so far as to say their debuts were worse than merely mediocre—that is to say, poor. Our goal is to do worse than poor, however. We want to single out the Hall of Famer who flat-out stunk up the joint in his early years. There are two candidates whose entrées into the big leagues qualify.

Before Mike Schmidt won three NL MVP Awards and ten Gold Gloves, made twelve All-Star teams, led the Phillies to six postseason berths, and became the thirteenth member of the 500 Home Run Club, the Philadelphia third baseman suffered through a rookie campaign that must have made even Mario Mendoza cringe. As a twenty-three-year-old coming off a 26-homer season at Triple-A Eugene, where he'd also hit a respectable .291, Schmidt struck out nearly twice as frequently as he reached base via a hit for the Phillies in 1973. In 132 games he collected just 72 safeties in 367 at-bats while whiffing 136 times. His .196 batting average was the lowest in either league among players with 300 at-bats, and his strikeout ratio of once every 2.7 at-bats was the highest. As the lone bright spot in a dismal debut, Schmidt hit 18 home runs. The next season, he wasted little time in turning around his career trajectory, blasting a walk-off homer against Tug McGraw on Opening Day to give the Phillies a dramatic win over the Mets. Having turned the Veterans Stadium boos to cheers with one prodigious whack, Schmidt batted .282 with 36 home runs and 116 RBIs as a sophomore and lowered his strikeout ratio to once every 4.2 at-bats. Eighteen seasons later, he put the finishing touches on a career that garnered a resounding 96.5 percent of the vote from the baseball writers when he first became eligible for Cooperstown.

While Schmidt quickly rebounded from a disastrous debut, our other seriously slow starter, Red Ruffing, took much longer to blossom into Cooperstown material. The right-hander weathered no fewer than five dismal seasons as a Red Sox starter in the 1920s before a trade to greener baseball pastures breathed new life into his career. It's true that Ruffing played for some horrendous teams in Boston, which surely contributed to his 39-96 career win-loss record through the first four games of his 1930 season. But he also had a 4.61 ERA up to that point. At the time of his trade to the Yankees—for Cedric Durst—on May 6, 1930, the twenty-five-year-old Ruffing was 0-3 with a 6.38 ERA. Surely, his opportunity in New York represented one final chance to chisel out a place in the game, and if he failed to do so he'd no doubt be returning to Illinois to work the mines with his father. Upon switching jerseys, however, everything clicked for Ruffing. With solid run support and a better defense behind him, he went 15-5 with a 4.14 ERA over the final five months of 1930. He also batted .374 for the Pinstripes, banging out 37 hits in 99 at-bats, including 4 homers and 21 runs batted in. Having turned the corner, he won 16 games the next year, and then 18 the year after that. Over a twenty-two-year career that did not end until 1947, he went 273-225 with a 3.80 ERA. At the plate, meanwhile, he cranked 36 homers and collected a pitchers-best 273 RBIs. And to think, he was *that* close to returning to those mines. For hanging in there through five dreadful seasons before answering the door when opportunity knocked, and for carrying a sub-.500 career record over his first fourteen seasons, Ruffing is our pick as the slowest-starting Hall of Famer.

Finally, here are some stats from three recent players who will certainly warrant Cooperstown consideration someday but haven't yet been retired long enough to see their names appear on the ballot. Greg Maddux was 8-18 with a 5.58 ERA over his first two seasons with the Cubs, before going 18-8 as a twenty-two-year-old in 1988. Tom Glavine was 9-21 with a 4.76 ERA over his first two seasons with the Braves, before going 14-8 as a twenty-three-year-old in 1989. And Craig Biggio batted .211 over fifty games with the Astros in 1988, before boosting his average to a still-mediocre .257 in 1989, and didn't top .300 for the first time until batting .318 as a twenty-eight-year-old in 1994 along his way to more than 3,000 lifetime hits.

20

THE BEST TEAM THAT DIDN'T WIN THE WORLD SERIES

Its Loss Shocked the Baseball World

Discussions concerning the best baseball teams ever usually devolve rather quickly into dissections of the different Yankee dynasties. The Murderer's Row club of 1927 is one of the first squads that fans usually bring up, and for good reason, seeing as that Pinstripe edition outscored its opponents by 376 runs on the way to a 110-44 record and .714 winning percentage. Then it swept the Pirates in the World Series, all the while fielding six future Cooperstowners—Earle Combs, Lou Gehrig, Waite Hoyt, Tony Lazzeri, Herb Pennock, and Babe Ruth. Other Yankee teams that commonly appear on best-of-the-best lists include: the 1932 squad that went 107-47 (.695) before sweeping the Cubs in the World Series; the 1939 club that went 106-45 (.702) while outscoring opponents by 411 runs, before a sweep of the Reds; the 1961 team of Mantle and Maris that went 109-53 (.673) and beat the Reds in five games in October; and the 1998 Yankees, who were 114-48 (.704) before an 11-2 postseason that culminated with a sweep of the Padres. When other franchises are admitted into the discussion, Cincinnati's Big Red Machine gets props for its back-to-back championships in 1975 and 1976 when the Reds won 108 and 102 regular season games respectively. Other powerhouses like the 1986 Mets (108-54, .667), 1970 Orioles (108-54, .667), and Philadelphia A's of 1929 through 1931, who surpassed 100 wins three years running, also receive their due.

As interesting as this debate concerning the best team ever is, the subject has been well exhausted by fans and writers through the years. To offer a different approach, this chapter instead seeks to identify the greatest team that fell short of tasting World Series champagne. We're looking for the best team to ever end its season with a loss, baseball's equivalent, if you will, of the NFL's 2007 New England Patriots—who won 18 straight regular-season and playoff games before bowing to the Giants in the Super Bowl.

The most recent example of a baseball team that thoroughly dominated its foes in the regular season before disappointing fans in October is the 2001 Seattle

Mariners. The M's had lost their star shortstop, Alex Rodriguez, to free agency during the off-season, but regrouped by importing Ichiro Suzuki, who batted .350 and collected a remarkable 242 hits and 56 stolen bases on his way to winning Silver Slugger, Gold Glove, Rookie of the Year, and MVP honors. The Mariners also featured newcomer Bret Boone, who batted .331 with 37 home runs and 141 RBIs, and returnees John Olerud (.302, 21 home runs, 95 RBIs), Edgar Martinez (.306, 23 home runs, 116 RBIs), and Mike Cameron (.267, 25 home runs, 110 RBIs, 34 stolen bases). Heading into the All-Star break, manager Lou Piniella's team carried a 63-24 record. Over the second half of the season the M's went 53-22 on their way to setting the AL record for most wins in a season, finishing a remarkable seventy games above .500, at 116-46 (.716). They led the league in runs scored and allowed the fewest runs, clubbing opponents 927–627. But despite their league-best 3.54 ERA, they didn't have a bona fide stopper in a rotation that consisted of Freddy Garcia (18-6, 3.05 ERA), Jamie Moyer (20-6, 3.43), Aaron Sele (15-5, 3.60), Paul Abbott (17-4, 4.25), and John Halama (10-7, 4.73). Nonetheless, as the Mariners entered a Division Series tilt against the Indians, pundits were already debating where they ranked among the most elite teams in history. Then they lost two of their first three games against Cleveland before bouncing back to win the final two and advance to play the Yankees in the American League Championship Series. The Mariners lost three close games—including the pivotal fourth game, which New York won on a walk-off homer by Alfonso Soriano—and then dropped a 12–3 blowout in New York to lose the series in five games. It will be hard for us to find another team that so dominated baseball's spring and summer only to wither in the autumn.

Another recent regular season powerhouse that collapsed like a house of cards in October can be found in reviewing the Braves dynasty that made fourteen playoff appearances between 1991 and 2005 but only once won the World Series. During the Braves' amazing run, Bobby Cox guided six different teams that surpassed 100 wins and every one of them fell short of World Series glory. Ironically, the club's lone World Series triumph came in 1995, when the Braves accumulated a paltry 90 wins in a 144-game regular season. The 1998 Braves had the most regular-season success of any Atlanta club during the team's long playoff run, going 106-56 (.654) and outscoring opponents by 245 runs. That lineup mashed 215 long balls, led by Andres Galarraga (.305, 44 home runs, 121 RBIs), Chipper Jones (.313, 34 home runs, 107 RBIs), Andruw Jones (.271, 31 home runs, 90 RBIs), and Javy Lopez (.284, 34 home runs, 106 RBIs). Meanwhile, Atlanta's pitchers led the NL with a 3.25

ERA, with five starters—Greg Maddux, Tom Glavine, John Smoltz, Kevin Millwood, and Denny Neagle—claiming at least 16 wins apiece. The Braves were 59-29 prior to the All-Star break, before coasting to the finish eighteen games ahead of second-place New York. They swept the Cubs in the Division Series as Smoltz, Glavine, and Maddux allowed just 4 runs over 21⅔ innings pitched. But the NLCS was a different story. The Padres won three straight close games to take a commanding 3-0 lead before the Braves bounced back to win Games Four and Five, then the Braves' vaunted offense managed just two hits against a quintet of San Diego pitchers in Game Six, as the Padres prevailed 5–0 to end the series.

Cleveland fans likely found perverse satisfaction in watching those 1998 Braves morph from team of destiny into team of despair. After all, a few years earlier it had been the Braves who spoiled the Tribe's sensational 1995 season. That year, the second-winningest Indians team ever went 100-44, while outscoring opponents by 233 runs over the work-stoppage-shortened schedule. Had the season consisted of the usual 162 games, the Indians' .694 winning percentage projects that they would have claimed 112 wins, but Clevelanders were content just the same to see their team emerge from the abbreviated slate as baseball's prohibitive postseason favorite. Although they led the league with a 3.83 ERA, the Indians' greatest strength was a lineup that boasted three (future) members of baseball's 500 Home Run Club in Eddie Murray (.323, 21 home runs, 82 RBIs), Manny Ramirez (.308, 31 home runs, 107 RBIs), and Jim Thome (.314, 25 home runs, 73 RBIs), in addition to Albert Belle (.317, 50 home runs, 126 RBIs), Carlos Baerga (.314, 15 home runs, 90 RBIs), and Kenny Lofton (.310, 54 stolen bases). Cleveland led the league in virtually every offensive category, including batting average, on-base percentage, slugging percentage, runs, doubles, homers, and steals. In hindsight, the team's rotation was eminently mortal, though. Charles Nagy (16-6, 4.55 ERA) and the aging duo of Orel Hershiser (16-6, 3.87) and Dennis Martinez (12-5, 3.08) were the only starters to reach double figures in wins. But the bullpen, led by Jose Mesa, who had 46 saves and a 1.13 ERA, and Julian Tavarez, who was 10-2 with a 2.44 ERA, was an area of strength. After sweeping the Red Sox in the ALDS and beating the Mariners in six games in the ALCS, the Indians lost the first two World Series games in Atlanta. Then they won Game Three on a walk-off hit by Murray. After dropping Game Four, and winning Game Five, their lineup was held to just one hit—a sixth-inning single by Tony Pena—in a series-clinching 1–0 loss to Glavine and reliever Mark Wohlers in Game Six. Glavine, who paced a staff that held the Indians to a .179 batting average, was named MVP. And the Indians and their fans were left to wallow in a special kind of self-pity that reminded many Tribal elders of a similar heartbreak in 1954.

We'll get to those 1954 Indians shortly, but for the sake of continuing our review in reverse chronological order, let's first touch upon the 1969 Baltimore Orioles. The O's began a run of three straight World Series appearances in 1969, which also happened to be the first year of divisional play and of the League Championship Series. During a 109-53 (.717) regular season, Earl Weaver's lineup boasted a pair of future Hall of Famers in Brooks Robinson (.234, 23 home runs, 84 RBIs) and Frank Robinson (.308, 32 home runs, 100 RBIs), as well as hard-hitting Boog Powell (.304, 37 home runs, 121 RBIs) and Paul Blair (.285, 26 home runs, 86 RBIs). With their help, the O's smacked 175 home runs and scored 779 runs—only 11 fewer than the league-leading Twins. The team's hallmark, though, was its pitching, which led the AL with a 2.83 ERA and 20 shutouts, while limiting opponents to 517 runs. Twenty-three-year-old Jim Palmer (14-4, 2.34 ERA) was the club's fourth starter, behind Dave McNally (20-7, 3.22 ERA), Mike Cuellar (23-11, 2.38 ERA), and Tom Phoebus (14-7, 3.52 ERA). And in the bullpen four relievers had sub-2.50 ERAs. The Birds finished nineteen games ahead of the Tigers in the AL East. They then swept the Twins in the first-ever ALCS to set up a showdown with the Miracle Mets in the World Series. Baltimore won 4–1 in the opener, as Cuellar beat Tom Seaver. Then the Orioles' bats went silent. The O's scored just five runs over the next four games to lose the series. To this day, many people consider this series the greatest shocker in October history. As for the Orioles and their fans, they no doubt found some solace the next season, when Baltimore went 108-54 and beat the Reds in the World Series.

Now, let's look at those 1954 Indians who went 111-43 (.721) and outscored opponents by 242 runs to edge the talented Yankees by eight games for the AL pennant. Cleveland was led by a pitching staff that included three future Hall of Famers—Early Wynn (23-7, 2.73 ERA), Bob Lemon (23-11, 2.72 ERA), and Bob Feller (13-3, 3.09 ERA)—as well as by Mike Garcia (19-8, 2.64 ERA) and Art Houtteman (15-7, 3.35 ERA). The quintet helped Cleveland to a league-best 2.78 ERA. Meanwhile, big bats Larry Doby (.276, 32 home runs, 126 RBIs), Al Rosen (.300, 24 home runs, 102 RBIs), and Bobby Avila (.341, 15 home runs, 67 RBIs) paced the league's second-highest scoring offense. After staving off the Yankees in the regular season, the Indians found another New York team standing between themselves and baseball immortality: the Giants. In Game One, Willie Mays made The Catch, nullifying a potentially game-changing Vic Wertz drive with two runners

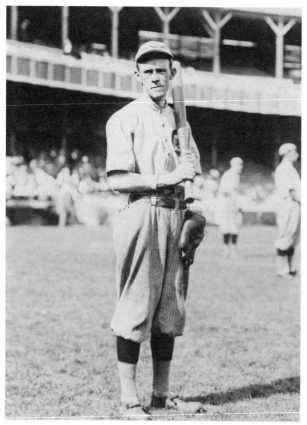

Johnny Evers played second base for the star-crossed 1906 Cubs. COURTESY OF THE LIBRARY OF CONGRESS

on base in a 2–2 game in the eighth inning, as the Giants went on to win 5–2 in ten innings, courtesy of a Dusty Rhodes walk-off homer. Leo Durocher's underdogs then won the next three games to sweep the shell-shocked Tribe.

Finally, we arrive at the most star-crossed incarnation of baseball's most star-crossed franchise: the 1906 Chicago Cubs, who went 116-36 to account for a best-ever .763 winning percentage, while outscoring opponents 705–381. Yes, the 2001 Mariners tied the 1906 Cubs win total, but the M's had the benefit of a 162-game schedule. The Northsiders started the season winning just 6 of their first twelve games, then picked up their pace to stand at 56-24 by midsummer. Buoyed by a 14-game win streak in August, they went 60-12 down the stretch. While today's fans are more familiar with the trio of Hall of Famers who patrolled the infield for these early Chicagoans—shortstop Joe Tinker, second baseman Johnny Evers, and first baseman Frank Chance—the club's leading hitter was newly acquired third-baseman Harry Steinfeldt, who batted .327 with 83 RBIs. Five Cubs starters, meanwhile, finished the regular season with sub-2.00 ERAs, highlighted by future Hall of Famer Mordecai "Three Finger" Brown, who went 26-6 with a 1.04 ERA. The Cubs scored 80 more runs than the Giants, and allowed 89 fewer than the Pirates. They tossed 31 shutouts. And as if being the league's best-hitting and best-pitching team wasn't enough, they made 30 fewer errors than the NL's next slickest-fielding club. After finishing 20 games ahead of the Giants in the NL pennant race, the

Cubs headed into the World Series against their crosstown rivals, the White Sox, as heavy favorites. A week later, the "Hitless Wonder" White Sox, who had managed to win the AL pennant despite batting just .230 and hitting only 7 home runs all season, were the new World Champions despite batting a paltry .198 in the Series, and the Cubs were wondering how the heck their magical season had gone up in smoke so quickly. The vanquished Cubbies needed look no further than their dormant bats for an answer. In the six-game tilt, they batted an anemic .196. Tinker, Evers, and Chance combined to go 11 for 59 with just 2 RBIs. The saga had a somewhat happy ending, though, as the Cubs bounced back to win World Series in both 1907 and 1908, both times against the Tigers. Here, however, we choose to honor the 1906 Cubs as the best team ever to lose in baseball's postseason.

21

THE WORST NO-HITTER

No Hits, No Wonder

Few moments of a baseball season are as exciting as those rare times when a stadium holds its collective breath as a pitcher bears down to put the finishing touches on a no-hitter. The drama begins to grow sometime around the sixth inning, then heightens with each new out that the hurler records. Teammates suddenly refuse to sit near the flawless pitcher in the dugout. The pitching coach and catcher refrain from speaking to him. And the team clown stops spitting sunflower seeds in his direction. All this, in deference to the age-old axiom that says to acknowledge a no-no in the making is to surely seal its doom. Fans and play-by-play announcers, too, refuse to articulate the word *no-hitter* for fear of invoking the dreaded jinx. They instead make oblique references to the scoreboard in an effort to alert less-observant friends that something historic just might be unfolding before their very eyes. In the later innings, the tension mounts with every pitch, hanging palpably in the air above the stadium like the scent of so many delicious ballpark hot dogs. The crowd cheers with each out, finally reaching a crescendo when, with two down in the ninth, the pitcher stands alone in the middle of the diamond and knocks on the door to baseball immortality, hoping that Lady Luck will answer and not her ugly stepsister.

Perhaps the most mystifying thing about the no-hitter is that although it is a rare phenomenon, virtually any major league pitcher has the talent necessary to throw one. Whether he happens to find himself graced by the ample portion of luck that is often also required, is another matter entirely, however. Roger Clemens, for example, won 354 big league games but never authored a no-hitter, while inarguably unspectacular pitchers like Jose Jimenez (24-44 lifetime record), Bud Smith (7-8), Tommy Greene (38-25), Juan Nieves (32-25), Joe Cowley (33-25), and Mike Warren (9-13) all commanded the respect of the baseball world for one special day and earned a place among the immortals in the no-hitter exhibit at Cooperstown. Mind you, this sextet of no-name no-no throwers comprises only the least-impressive pitchers to accomplish the feat since 1983. And there are scores more like them if we expand our search to include all 262 of the pitchers who have thrown nine-inning no-hitters (not including rain-shortened official games) since 1876.

The purpose of this chapter is not to determine the worst pitcher ever to toss a no-hitter—if it were, we'd likely crown Bumpus Jones, owner of a 2-4 career record and 7.99 ERA with that distinction—but rather we seek the no-hit game that was least impressive. In other words, we're looking for the no-no in which the vanquishing pitcher (or pitchers) proved least dominant, even if the opposing team failed to record a hit.

The truth is, spinning a no-no isn't always the storybook experience we might assume. And pitching nine hitless innings doesn't even guarantee that a pitcher will be credited with an official no-hitter. Just ask Pirates southpaw Harvey Haddix who held the Braves without a base runner for twelve innings in 1959, before surrendering a hit and losing the game in the thirteenth. Likewise, the Yankees Tom Hughes carried a no-hitter into the tenth against the Indians in 1910, only to yield a hit and five runs in a hard-luck loss. But these efforts can hardly be classified as failures, or games in which the pitchers were not at their masterful best, even if MLB chooses not to recognize them with official no-hit accreditation. After all, it wasn't the pitchers' fault that their teams didn't score them any runs.

What we're more interested in are the no-hitters in which pitchers surrendered base runners aplenty and perhaps some runs along the way too. Believe it or not, thirty-three of the teams that have been no-hit have scored at least one run. And seven of them actually managed to win the game despite failing to record a safety. Before we review the worst-pitched efforts among these unusual games, let's define our parameters. Although Major League Baseball changed the official definition of a no-hitter in 1991 to read, "An official no-hit game occurs when a pitcher (or pitchers) allows no hits during the entire course of a game, which consists of at least nine innings," for our purposes we will still include the four games in which pitchers accomplished the feat in visiting ballparks where they didn't have the opportunity to pitch the bottom of the ninth because their teams had already lost. As a concession to MLB's no-hitter definition, though, we will ignore the thirty-seven weather-shortened no-nos.

Now let's see what lackluster "gems" remain. Recent play provides a few less than stellar no-hitters to consider, most memorably one turned in by a young Marlins flamethrower. A. J. Burnett shut out the Padres 3–0 to earn his 8th big league win with a no-hitter on May 12, 2001, but he walked nine batters, hit one, threw a wild pitch, and found the strike zone with just 65 of 129 pitches. He had just 7 strikeouts, and set the record for most walks in a nine-inning no-hitter. He enjoyed just three one-two-three innings.

At least Burnett preserved his shutout, though, something famously erratic southpaw Matt Young failed to accomplish when he became just the third big leaguer to lose despite holding his opponent hitless in a nine-inning game. Young spun his "beauty" on a rainy April day in 1992 when the Red Sox fell to the Indians 2–1. He walked seven batters and allowed six runners to steal bases in a game that prompted the *Boston Globe* to run the memorable headline, "No Hits, No Win, No No-Hitter," the latter clause in reference to MLB's new rule that stipulated only pitchers who pitched the ninth inning should be regarded as bona fide no-no authors. As for the Hall of Fame, it accepted a signed ball from Young. And Young himself viewed his effort as a no-hitter, telling reporters afterward, "They didn't get any hits. The game's over. People can make rules all they want. It doesn't matter to me." He also expressed the kind of loser's remorse we're looking for in a chapter like this, telling the *Globe*, "I thought when you throw a no-hitter, you're supposed to strike out the last guy and the catcher comes out and you jump around. When you have to go back in the dugout and see if your team can score another run, it's kind of anticlimactic."

Another nine-inning complete-game no-hitter that Major League Baseball refuses to officially recognize belongs to Andy Hawkins, whose Yankees lost 4–0 to the White Sox on his "special day" in Chicago in 1990. After walking 5, striking out 3, and watching his teammates commit 3 errors behind him in the bottom of the eighth inning—including a Jim Leyritz hack job on a fly ball that allowed the first three runs to score—Hawkins said, "I'm stunned. This is not the way I envisioned a no-hitter. I always dreamed of getting the last out and jumping up and down. Everybody congratulated me, but I gave up four runs and lost. I'm stunned that I threw a no-hitter, and I'm stunned that I got beat. I'll have to sleep on this." Here's betting he actually lost sleep over it. But at least things couldn't get any worse for unlucky Andy. Or could they? In his very next start he carried a shutout into the twelfth inning against Minnesota before losing 2–0. Now that's one heck of a hard-luck story, but Hawkins can't be blamed for either loss. His teammates let him down on both occasions, especially in his no-hitter when their nonexistent offense and lousy defense tainted what should have been one of his finest moments.

As for the first pitcher to ever know this special kind of agony, it was the prematurely gray-haired Silver King, who in 1890 became the first pitcher to lose a nine-inning no-hitter. Brooklyn scored the lone run of the Players League contest when Chicago shortstop Dell Darling booted a ground ball. King didn't have to pitch the ninth because his team was on the road. This may be small consolation for Andy Hawkins, but at least it shows he's not the only pitcher who ever brought his A-game to the park only to see his teammates fail to hold up their end of the bargain.

More than half a century after King's loss, Houston Colt .45s right-hander Ken Johnson tossed a no-no to no avail in 1964 when he and second baseman Nellie Fox both made ninth-inning errors that enabled the Reds to win 1–0. John-

Silver King was the first big league pitcher to lose despite pitching a no-hitter.
COURTESY OF THE LIBRARY OF CONGRESS

son issued just 2 walks, and two runners reached via error, but at least he shared the blame with his teammates since he botched a Pete Rose bunt to start the Reds' winning rally.

Three years later, a pair of pitchers turned in an effort that we deem here the least dazzling no-hitter of all. The story goes something like this: Steve Barber was a wild lefty who had just enough control to be a passable big league pitcher, at least for a while. He enjoyed his best season in 1961 when he went 18-12 for the Orioles despite walking 130 batters in 248 innings. But by 1967 batters had figured out that the key to beating Barber was to simply wait for his wildness to be his undoing. Before that season concluded, Barber would wear out his welcome in Baltimore and be traded to the ninth-place Yankees. But first, he flirted with baseball immortality and in so doing co-authored the worst no-hitter ever pitched.

While still pitching for the Orioles, Barber carried a no-hitter and 1–0 lead into the ninth inning of an April game against the Tigers. Through eight frames he'd surrendered 7 walks, hit 2 batters, and allowed a batter to reach in every inning but the fifth. He'd struck out just 3. True to form, he walked the first two batters of the top of the ninth, then, after a sacrifice bunt moved the runners to second and third, he induced a pop-out that brought the Memorial Stadium crowd to its feet. Barber got ahead of Mickey Stanley, a ball and two strikes, then threw a wild pitch past catcher Andy Etchebarren to enable the tying run to trot home. Frazzled, Barber proceeded to walk Stanley, for his tenth base on balls allowed in the game. And that was as many as Orioles manager Hank Bauer could stomach. The skipper walked to the mound and summoned reliever Stu Miller, who entered a tie game with the no-hitter still intact. Miller induced the next batter to hit a routine ground ball to shortstop, but normally sure-handed Orioles second baseman Mark Belanger dropped the throw from short to second for the force out, and the error allowed the go-ahead run to score. Miller then got the final out of the inning to preserve the no-no. But the Orioles failed to score in the bottom of the ninth, handing a loss to Barber, who'd allowed one earned run, and one unearned run. Because Barber was one strike away from winning a no-hit shutout, his game ranks as the most heartbreaking no-no ever pitched, as well as the worst, since he allowed those ten walks, hit two batters, and threw two wild pitches—including the errant toss that determined his unusual fate.

THE BEST AND WORST
BASEBALL SURPRISES

22

THE BEST LATE-ROUND DRAFT PICK

This Diamond in the Rough Sure Cleaned up Nicely

Since baseball's first annual amateur draft in 1965 there have been plenty of first-round busts and just as many late-round bargains, proving time and again that forecasting the big league success of eighteen- to twenty-two-year-old prospects is something of a crapshoot. How else can you explain the phenomenon of all twenty big league teams passing on the chance to draft schoolboy Nolan Ryan, over and over again, until the Mets finally selected him in the twelfth round (226th overall) of that very first draft? The Mets finally chose Ryan at the behest of a scout who claimed the Alvin Yellowjackets pitcher had the best arm he'd ever seen. And Ryan responded by going 17-2 with a 2.51 ERA at Class A Greenville the next year before making a late-season start in the big leagues. After struggling with his control early in his career, he won 324 career games, pitched a record 7 no-hitters, and struck out a record 5,714 batters. Not bad for a kid who was drafted immediately after Richard Koslick, Craig Scoggings, and Donald Cook, picks 223, 224, and 225, respectively, in 1965.

Ryan's selection in the later rounds of that inaugural draft makes him the answer to the trivia question: Who was the first eventual Hall of Famer that every team passed on in the draft at least ten times? But in the years since, plenty more eventual superstars have slipped through the talent evaluators' cracks. Many have fallen even lower than Ryan, some because they were late bloomers who developed their power strokes or added miles per hour to their fastballs later than usual, others because their draft stature was diminished by injuries or questions regarding their likelihood of foregoing college to sign with a big league team. Still others played for remote high schools or small-time colleges, prompting scouts to conclude they'd flounder against better competition.

For whatever reasons, all of the star players we'll be tipping our caps to in this chapter proved the experts wrong and excelled beyond the baseball intelligentsia's wildest expectations. Ultimately, our goal is to crown the player who enjoyed the most major league success after being drafted the lowest.

Five years after the Mets nabbed Ryan as the steal of that very first draft, the White Sox chose Colorado Springs high schooler Rich Gossage in the ninth round (198th overall) in 1970. Gossage went 18-2 with a 1.83 ERA for Appleton in the Midwest League as a nineteen-year-old the next season, and was in Chicago by 1972. After a few trades and a switch to the bullpen, The Goose emerged as one of the best relievers ever and punched his ticket to Cooperstown.

The next year, the Cardinals took Keith Hernandez in the forty-second round (776th overall) in 1971. The first baseman from San Bruno, California's, Capuchino High School gradually improved his game over parts of four seasons at Double-A Tulsa, then established himself as a starter with the Cardinals in 1976 and went on to rack up 2,182 hits, eleven Gold Gloves, a batting title, an MVP Award, and five trips to the All-Star Game. Those may not be Hall of Fame numbers, but considering that 775 players were picked before him in his draft class, they're pretty good.

Another solid big leaguer Mike Hargrove (twenty-fifth round, 572nd overall), was the steal of the 1972 draft, then an even better one, Andre Dawson, fell to the eleventh round in 1975 before the Montreal Expos made the Florida A&M product the 250th player chosen. Dawson made his debut toward the end of the next season, then won the NL Rookie of the Year Award in 1977, launching a twenty-one-year career in which he amassed 2,774 hits, 438 home runs, and 314 stolen bases. The quintessential five-tool player, he was also a stellar outfielder who won eight Gold Gloves and made eight All-Star teams.

In 1978 future Hall of Famer Ryne Sandberg slipped into the twentieth round (511th overall) before the Phillies took a chance on him. In 1979 Don Mattingly fell to the nineteenth round (493rd overall) before the Yankees took him. Both players would have been drafted sooner if not for concerns about their signability. Sandberg appeared headed for Washington State on a football scholarship, while Mattingly appeared headed for Indiana State to play baseball, but both ultimately chose to forgo college to play minor league baseball.

Joining Mattingly as a steal in the 1979 draft, Bowling Green University junior Orel Hershiser lasted until the seventeenth round when the Dodgers made him the 440th player chosen. After deciding not to return to college for his senior year, Hershiser won 204 big league games, a Cy Young Award, and a World Series MVP trophy.

When it came time for the 1982 draft, two other stellar pitchers waited until the later rounds before hearing their names called. The Royals took Reseda, California, schoolboy Bret Saberhagen in the nineteenth round (479th overall), figuring he might play shortstop. And the Rangers took Plant City, Florida, schoolboy Kenny Rogers in the thirty-ninth round (815th overall) with the thought that he might be a decent big league outfielder some day. Two and a half seasons later Saberhagen was pitching in the big leagues and winning the first of his two Cy Young Awards at age twenty in 1985. He won 167 big league games in all, or, to put it another way, 124 more than the first pitcher selected in his draft class—Jim Jones, whom the Padres took third overall. As for Rogers, his conversion to the mound took a bit longer to pay dividends. He made his major league debut in 1989, and went on to win 219 games and make more than $80 million in the big leagues before retiring after the 2008 season.

The first round of the 1985 draft is often cited as one of the most productive opening salvos in draft history. Indeed, the first four picks were B. J. Surhoff, Will Clark, Bobby Witt, and Barry Larkin, respectively, while Barry Bonds went sixth, Pete Incaviglia eighth, Walt Weiss eleventh, and Rafael Palmeiro twenty-second. In total, twenty of the twenty-eight first-round picks reached the majors. But it wasn't until the last pick of the twenty-second round that the best pitcher of the lot was nabbed. The Tigers took John Smoltz 574th overall, and even they didn't know how wise a pick they'd made. They traded the big righty to the Braves in 1987 for the aging Doyle Alexander, and then watched as Smoltz won 213 games and saved 154, picking up a Cy Young Award and eight All-Star nods along the way (through 2009).

Thirty-ninth-round draft-pick Kenny Rogers—pictured here making a rehab start for the West Michigan Whitecaps in 2007—earned more than 200 wins. COURTESY OF WIKIMEDIA COMMONS

In 1988 the Dodgers stumbled upon what rates in our opinion as the very best late-round draft pick ever. In the sixty-second round, Los Angeles took an unheralded twenty-year-old first baseman from Miami-Dade College. Mike Piazza, the 1,390th player selected that year, was selected just five picks from the very end of the draft. The Dodgers only drafted him, in fact, as a favor to Dodgers manager Tommy Lasorda, who was a friend of Piazza's father, Vince, the two men having forged a relationship in their mutual hometown of Norristown, Pennsylvania. With a conversion to catcher and scrupulous hard work in the batting cage, Piazza eventually blossomed into a surefire first-ballot Hall of Famer. The Dodgers needed to be patient, though. In Piazza's first minor league season, he batted .268 with 8 home runs in 198 at-bats in the Low-A Northwest League. The next year, he advanced to the High-A Florida State League, where he batted .250 with 6 homers in 272 at-bats. Then, playing a third year at Class-A, for Bakersfield in 1991, he began bashing balls out of California League parks with regularity and the Dodgers took notice. Piazza batted .277 with 29 homers in 448 at-bats that year, and by the end of the next season, he'd landed in Los Angeles. Over a sixteen-year career, he batted .308 and collected 2,127 hits. He hit 427 home runs, including a record 396 while playing the catcher's position. He made twelve All-Star teams, and though his defensive skills never put him in the running for a Gold Glove, he won ten Silver Slugger Awards.

For enjoying such remarkable success despite being drafted on a whim, Piazza is the clear choice as the best draft steal of all-time. But for the sake of covering this interesting baseball topic as thoroughly as possible, let's also acknowledge some other recent stars who were plucked from the scrap heaps of the later rounds too. The Blue Jays made Jeff Kent their twentieth-round pick (521st overall) in 1989, and Kent went on to rack up 2,461 hits and 377 home runs in a career that lasted from 1992 until 2008. Along the way, he made five All-Star teams, won four Silver Slugger Awards, and set the record for most long balls by a second sacker with 351 dingers during the games he played at second base.

The Yankees, meanwhile, unearthed a diamond in the rough in 1995 when they used a twentieth rounder to nab Mike Lowell. After selecting the Florida International University second baseman with the 562nd pick and cultivating his skills in the minors for five years, the Yankees gave up on him too soon. In the years since New York traded Lowell to Florida in 1999, he has made four All-Star teams, won four Gold Gloves at third base, and won a World Series MVP Award for the Red Sox.

Pitcher Roy Oswalt slipped to the twenty-third round of the 1996 draft before Houston made him a draft-and-follow pick as the 684th player chosen. Oswalt played the 1997 season at Holmes Community College before signing with the Astros just before their exclusive rights to his services would have expired with the start of the next year's draft. In 1998, meanwhile, lefty Mark Buehrle lasted until the thirty-eighth round when the White Sox took him 1,139th overall. In 1999 Jake Peavy went unclaimed until the fifteenth round when the Padres took him 472nd. All three have since established themselves as staff aces and have appeared in multiple All-Star Games.

The Cardinals uncovered a gem when they drafted Albert Pujols with their thirteenth-round pick in 1999, 402nd overall. After one year of minor league seasoning, the former Maple Woods Community College standout won the NL Rookie of the Year Award in 2001 after enjoying one of the most prolific offensive seasons ever by a first-year player. He's been a perennial All-Star and MVP contender ever since.

The best sleeper pick since Pujols didn't pay off for his original organization, or his second, or even his third. The Expos took Gonzaga University outfielder Jason Bay in the twenty-second round (645th overall) in 2000. Over the next three years, Bay was traded to the Mets, then to the Padres, then to the Pirates. Given the chance to play at the big league level in Pittsburgh, he became the 2004 NL Rookie of the Year, then made the All-Star team in 2005 and 2006. In 2008 Bay was traded to the Red Sox in a three-way deal that sent prospects to the Pirates and Manny Ramirez to the Dodgers. In 2009 Bay led Boston in home runs and RBI.

As for the hundreds of other late-round picks still toiling in the minors today, the jury is still out on them. Surely many will reach the big leagues and thus become the "next" Jason Bay or Roy Oswalt. But it seems unlikely that any one among them will emerge from such depths of obscurity to ever become the next Mike Piazza. Of course, we'll have to stay tuned, though. As long as there are amateurs waiting for their phones to ring on the draft's second day, anything is possible.

23

THE WORST ROOKIE OF THE YEAR

He Was a One-Hit Wonder

Remember Shane Spencer? How about Wally Bunker? Dave Fleming? We didn't think so. Despite enjoying red-hot starts to what were otherwise tepid careers, these shooting stars didn't claim Rookie of the Year (ROY) honors. Thus, once their luster wore off, they stuck around for several years in the bigs, but eventually faded, rightfully, into the furthest reaches of most fans' memory banks. Today, their names—unlike those of similarly fleeting stars who *did* win top rookie honors—get hardly a mention in the annals of baseball lore.

As for those rookies who did take home their freshman class's hardware, well, they do get their just due in the *Baseball Encyclopedia,* even if the fraternity to which they belong isn't quite all it's cracked up to be. To wit, consider the roster of entirely pedestrian recent rookie award winners: Pat Listach (1992), Bob Hamelin (1994), Marty Cordova (1995), Ben Grieve (1998), Eric Hinske (2002), and Angel Berroa (2003). Mind you, these are merely the least impressive Rookies of the Year in the past two decades. And they've been giving out the trophy since 1947. Our task in this chapter is to crown the worst ROY winner ever. But first, we'll review the history of the award and tip our caps to some of the future stars and Hall of Famers who won it.

Since the inception of the ROY, the National League has

Jackie Robinson—whose exploits are depicted on this poster that hangs at Tucson Electric Park in Arizona—set a high bar for subsequent Rookies of the Year to pursue.

had far more luck than the American League in honoring players bound for long-term success. During the first two years of the award's existence, when only one winner was picked from both leagues, the NL claimed the first two honorees: Jackie Robinson and Alvin Dark. After the format changed to honor a player from each league each year, Don Newcombe carried the torch for the NL in 1949, while Roy Sievers became the first AL winner. In the years since, the NL has used the award to herald the arrival of such stars as Willie Mays (1951), Frank Robinson (1956), Orlando Cepeda (1958), Willie McCovey (1959), Frank Howard (1960), Billy Williams (1961), Pete Rose (1963), Dick Allen (1964), Tom Seaver (1967), Johnny Bench (1968), Andre Dawson (1977), Bob Horner (1978), Rick Sutcliffe (1979), Fernando Valenzuela (1981), Darryl Strawberry (1983), Dwight Gooden (1984), Vince Coleman (1985), David Justice (1990), Jeff Bagwell (1991), Mike Piazza (1993), Albert Pujols (2001), Ryan Howard (2005), Hanley Ramirez (2006), and Ryan Braun (2007). Meanwhile, the AL has acknowledged its share of future All-Stars with the award, too, but it has also crowned far more duds. Some years have simply offered a dearth of exceptional candidates, giving the baseball writers who do the balloting little choice but to tap a middling player like Ozzie Guillen (1985), Walt Weiss (1988), Listach (1992), or Bobby Crosby (2004)—four shortstops who had mediocre first seasons at the outset of predictably mediocre careers. Other years have offered well-qualified winners like Mark Fidrych (1976) or Joe Charboneau (1980)—who followed their solid debuts with brief and undistinguished careers. The AL winners who maintained their initial excellence over the long haul include Gil McDougald (1951), Luis Aparicio (1956), Tony Oliva (1962), Rod Carew (1967), Lou Piniella (1969), Thurman Munson (1970), Carlton Fisk (1972), Fred Lynn (1975), Eddie Murray (1977), Lou Whitaker (1978), Cal Ripken Jr. (1982), Jose Canseco (1986), Mark McGwire (1987), Tim Salmon (1993), Derek Jeter (1996), Nomar Garciaparra (1997), Ichiro Suzuki (2001), and Dustin Pedroia (2007).

Now then, let's begin our review of the Rookies of the Year who didn't enjoy enduring big league success. We'll start by stipulating that the "worst" ROY ever should satisfy two criteria. First, his rookie season should have been nothing all that spectacular. Perhaps he only won due to a dearth of other viable candidates in his rookie class. And second, his career as a whole should be worse than mediocre. If we weigh both criteria equally, we should eliminate from consideration such big-time flameouts as Fidrych (19-9 with a 2.34 ERA as a rookie, but just 10-10 with a 4.28 ERA over the remainder of his injury-riddled career) and

Charboneau (.289, 23 home runs, 87 RBIs as a rookie, but just .211, 6 home runs, 27 RBIs over his remaining two seasons). At least these players and others like them enjoyed one very good season in the bigs. Similarly, the second criterion will extend a reprieve to candidates like Weiss (.250, 44 runs, 39 RBIs as a rookie, and .258, 623 runs, 386 RBIs over a fourteen-year career) who were average from the start, but at least stuck around in the major leagues for a long time. Instead, we hope to find the ROY who comes up shortest in both categories, the one who had neither a stellar first season nor a prolonged career to follow.

The NL offers Ken Hubbs (1962) who might well have been our eventual winner, if not for a terrible accident. The second baseman excelled in the field for the Cubs and to his credit became the first rookie ever to win a Gold Glove Award, but he also struck out a league-high 129 times and grounded into a league-leading 20 double plays while batting only .260 with a .299 on-base percentage and .346 slugging percentage. The next season, he batted .235/.285/.322, placing him in jeopardy of being farmed out. But then Hubbs, who'd taken up piloting in hopes of overcoming a lifelong fear of flying, crashed his plane in Utah and died shortly before the start of the 1964 season. His premature death leaves too small a body of work for us to judge him.

Other particularly unimpressive NL winners have included Chris Sabo (1988), Jerome Walton (1989), and Todd Hollandsworth (1996), all of whom had unexceptional first seasons and then failed to remain big league starters in the seasons ahead. Walton was the worst of this lot, collecting just 423 hits over parts of ten big league campaigns, or, to put it another way, just 284 hits after his 139-hit debut for the Cubs, when he batted .293 with 5 home runs and 46 RBIs. While Walton makes a strong case for the weakest ROY, he did spend parts of ten seasons in the majors, which counts for something. Sabo and Hollandsworth also stuck around for nine and twelve seasons, respectively, even if they were bench players, so we'll cut them some similar slack too.

As for the AL winners who were nothing special, the best early example is Philadelphia A's pitcher Harry Byrd (1952), who had a 15-15 record and a 3.31 ERA in his debut. He lasted another six years in the bigs before hanging up his spikes with a 46-54 record and 4.35 ERA. Those are pretty underwhelming career numbers, but here's betting we can find worse. After all, stats like that get Scott Boras clients four-year $40 million contracts these days.

Washington Senators outfielder Albie Pearson (1958) batted .275 with 3 home runs and 33 RBIs to win the Rookie of the Year Award in the finest of his nine utterly unremarkable seasons, putting him in the same class as Walton, Sabo, and Hollandsworth. Twins third baseman John Castino (1979) won the award, hitting .285 with 5 home runs and 52 RBIs, then posted similar stats over the next five years, before leaving the game at age twenty-nine. Again, pretty mediocre, but we can find worse.

The 1990s and 2000s offer a wealth of candidates to consider. Listach (1992) actually had a decent rookie season for the Brewers, batting .290 with 54 stolen bases, but he finished his six-year career with just a .251 average, 444 hits, and 116 steals. Fellow shortstop Berroa (2003) similarly had a fine first season, batting .287 with 17 home runs and 73 RBIs for the Royals but he hasn't approached those numbers since, even though he was still bouncing back and forth between the big leagues and minors as recently as 2009.

Perhaps the strongest case of all may be made for another former Royal: Bob Hamelin (1994). The burly slugger batted .282 with 24 home runs and 65 RBIs in 101 games during his work-stoppage-abbreviated debut season. Now, at first glance those numbers look quite respectable. Further scrutiny reveals, however, that Hamelin collected just 88 hits in his ROY campaign. Then, after a longer than usual off-season while the players and owners haggled over the labor agreement, Hamelin never regained his form. He began so slowly in 1995 that he was playing Triple-A ball in Omaha by June. He carried a .175 batting average back to the minors. And by the time he was recalled to Kansas City later that season, the holes in his swing had only grown larger. His sophomore stats are easily the worst by an ROY winner: In seventy-two games he batted .168/.278/.313 with just 35 hits, 7 home runs and 25 RBIs. He struck out 56 times in 208 at-bats.

Over the next four seasons, Hamelin shuttled between the big leagues and minors for the Royals, Tigers, and Brewers. His best "comeback" season was 1997 when he hit .270 with 18 home runs and 52 RBIs. Still, he collected just 86 hits that year, marking the second-best total in a career that would end after the next season. He retired after parts of six big league seasons with a .246 average, 313 hits, 67 home runs, and 293 strikeouts in 497 games.

For being considerably worse than mediocre after a not-so-dazzling debut, Bob Hamelin is our choice for worst Rookie of the Year. But let's not be too hard on him. Unlike most current and retired players, and certainly unlike most readers of this book, The Hammer can still boast to his friends back home that he is a former Rookie of the Year Award winner.

[24]

THE WORST CY YOUNG AWARD WINNER

His Career Was Otherwise Unremarkable

Shortly after the great Cy Young ascended to that big baseball field in the sky in 1955, Commissioner Ford Frick championed the creation of a new annual award to be named in Young's honor that would recognize each season's best pitcher. By then, baseball already had the Most Valuable Player and Rookie of the Year awards, so a trophy for top hurlers was a logical next step. Between 1956, when

Don Newcombe became the first Cy Young Award winner after going 27-7 with a 3.06 ERA for the pennant-winning Brooklyn Dodgers, and 1966, when Sandy Koufax won it after going 27-9 with a 1.73 ERA for the pennant-winning Los Angeles Dodgers, only one recipient was named to represent both leagues. Then, in 1967, baseball began picking a winner from each league.

Through the years, the award has come to embody pitching excellence. Upstarts have added it to their résumés upon arriving with a splash in the big leagues—à la Fernando Valenzuela, who also claimed the Rookie of the Year trophy in 1981, or Dwight Gooden

Cy Young has been a tough act to follow for future hurlers.
COURTESY OF THE LIBRARY OF CONGRESS

and Bret Saberhagen who were the winners in the National League and American League, respectively, in 1985, when they were just twenty and twenty-one years old.

Eventual 300-game winners who've won the award include Warren Spahn, Early Wynn, Gaylord Perry, Tom Seaver, Steve Carlton, Roger Clemens, Greg Maddux, and Tom Glavine. Meanwhile, other 300-W clubbers like Don Sutton and Nolan Ryan surprisingly never took home the Cy.

Clemens, who never managed to throw a no-hitter—something his Texas idol Ryan did seven times—won a record seven Cys. Fellow flame-thrower Randy Johnson ranks second with a quintet of best-pitcher trophies to his credit, and shares with Maddux the record for winning the Cy in four consecutive seasons. In total, fifteen pitchers have won the award more than once.

All of the pitchers who have won the Cy have at least one thing in common: For one season they were deemed the best in their league. But that doesn't mean they all had exceptional careers. And in some cases even their Cy seasons were not as special as one might expect. The goal of this chapter is to weigh both of these criteria—quality of career and quality of Cy season—and to decide which Cy Young Award winner was the least remarkable of all, and thus appears as something of an anomaly when listed among the many truly great pitchers who have won the award.

Our first candidate, 1980 winner Steve Stone, was 78-79 over the first nine years of his big league career before he went 25-7 with a 3.23 ERA for the Orioles to claim the Cy. The next season, Stone went 4-7, before an arm injury abruptly ended his playing days, and opened the door to his broadcasting career. Before stepping behind the mike, he compiled a 107-93 record with a 3.97 ERA over eleven seasons. Stone was certainly an unlikely winner, but there's no doubting that his Cy season was worthy. We might say the same about Pete Vuckovich, who went 18-6 with a 3.34 ERA for the Brewers in 1982, but just 93-69 with a 3.66 ERA overall in his career, as well as Mike McCormick, who went 22-10 with a 2.85 ERA for the Giants in 1967, but just 134-128 with a 3.73 ERA in sixteen seasons.

As for the least statistically eye-popping Cy seasons, it's hard to find fault with the starting pitcher who won the fewest games on the way to the award, Valenzuela, seeing as the Mexican phenom was 13-7 in the strike-shortened 1981 campaign. The mark for second-least wins in a Cy season, 16 W's, is shared by Maddux and David Cone, who both did so in the similarly shortened 1994 campaign, 2006 NL winner Brandon Webb, 2009 winner Zack Greinke, and 1984 NL winner Rick Sutcliffe. Sutcliffe's inclusion here is misleading, though. The righty was 16-1 with a 2.69 ERA for the Cubs that season, but only after he had gone 4-5 with a 5.15 ERA in fifteen first-half starts in Cleveland. Thus, if we consider only Sutcliffe's twenty NL starts, he had a spectacular Cy season. If we look at his cumulative stats, his 20-6 record is worthy, but his 3.64 ERA is high. Indeed, crunching the numbers this way means Sutcliffe's 3.64 mark was the second-highest ERA ever for a Cy winner. Only 1983 winner LaMarr Hoyt, who was 24-10 with a 3.66 ERA for the White Sox, allowed more earned runs per game. Hoyt's lifetime record of 98-68 with a 3.99 ERA over eight seasons includes fewer wins than usual for a Cy-caliber hurler too, but his .590 winning percentage is solid.

The next highest ERAs submitted by Cy's in their winning seasons belong to Clemens, who was 20-3 with a 3.51 ERA for the Yankees in 2001, and Bartolo Colon, who was 21-8 with a 3.48 ERA for the Angels in 2005. Although the still-active Colon has a career ERA a hair over 4.00, he has won more than 60 percent of his decisions and claimed 153 wins, so we can hardly call him the worst Cy Young Award winner to date.

As for pitchers who have won the Cy with double-figure totals in the loss column, Pat Hentgen, who was 20-10 with a 3.22 ERA for the Blue Jays in 1996, is the most recent example. That's still a solid season. And while Hentgen's 131-112 career mark includes a Cy-high 4.32 ERA, he was nonetheless a winning pitcher in a hitter's era. Meanwhile, two-time winner Gaylord Perry had a far better career, winning 314 games, but holds the record for the most losses in a Cy season. In 1972 Perry went 24-16 with a 1.92 ERA for an Indians club that finished tenth in the twelve-team AL in scoring.

Four years later, a National Leaguer came within shouting distance of Perry's loss total and still won the Cy. And this is where we get our first break in pursuit of Cy mediocrity. In fairness, Randy Jones's 1976 season was pretty darned good. That year the Padres lefty went 22-14 with a 2.74 ERA to beat out a quartet of other 20-game winners on the NL ballot. A finesse pitcher who induced ground-outs aplenty, Jones struck out just 93 batters in 315 innings for a Padres team that scored the second-fewest runs in the NL. No doubt, Jones was a worthy selection. But the six straight losing seasons that followed cemented his legacy as an average pitcher at best. Jones followed up his Cy season by going 6-12 with a 4.58 ERA in 1977. Then he submitted another losing season, and another, and another, and well, you get the picture. He never again enjoyed a winning campaign and finally ended his ten-year career with a 100-123 record and 3.42 ERA. While a strong case can be made for Jones as the most mediocre Cy Young Award winner ever, another Padres southpaw who came along a decade later makes for an even less impressive candidate.

Mark Davis enjoyed two really good seasons over a fifteen-year career and won the Cy Young in one of them. During his first six years in the bigs, Davis bounced between the starting rotation and bullpen for the Phillies and Giants, compiling a 22-44 record and 4.37 ERA. Then, midway through the 1987 season, the Giants traded him to the Padres, who converted him to a full-time reliever. He responded well and, pitching out of the bullpen the next season, went 5-10 with 28 saves and a 2.01 ERA. In 1989, he excelled to an even greater degree, going 4-3 with 44 saves in 48 opportunities while maintaining a 1.85 ERA. The only 20-game winner in the NL that year was Mike Scott, who went 20-10 with a 3.10 ERA for the Astros to finish a distant second to Davis in the Cy balloting. For the converted reliever, the future looked bright. Davis was still only twenty-nine when he signed a lucrative free-agent deal with the Royals shortly after being named the NL's top pitcher. In Kansas City, he joined a staff that already boasted Saberhagen, the reigning AL Cy. But things did not go as planned for either pitcher in 1990. Saberhagen struggled with injuries, going 5-9 in twenty starts, while Davis turned in a successful first week in the AL before his season turned into a nightmare. After being unscored upon and notching three saves in his first four appearances, he surrendered four runs in the ninth inning of a loss to the Rangers on April 27. And he never regained his form. By mid-May Davis had lost the closer's job. By the end of the year the reigning NL Cy Young was a situational lefty with a 2-7 record, 6 saves, and a bloated 5.11 ERA. He played parts of five more seasons—bouncing between the big leagues and minors until 1997—but earned only five more saves, en route to a 51-84 lifetime record with 96 saves and a 4.17 ERA. For his spectacularly unsuccessful post-Cy career, losing lifetime record, and for his high ERA, Mark Davis is our choice for the Worst Cy Young Award winner.

THE WORST WORLD SERIES WINNER

It Stood Tall When the Stakes Were Highest

Since the first modern World Series occurred in 1903, teams have often risen from the ashes of tepid springtimes to seize baseball's championship in autumn. This phenomenon has grown only more common since the onset of divisional play in 1969, and the realignment to six divisions and three playoff tiers in 1994. Today eight teams advance to baseball's postseason tournament, as opposed to the two who did so during the first seven decades of big league play, when just one team from each league participated in the "second season." Not surprisingly then, three of the six teams who have won World Series after seasons in which they won fewer than 90 games have accomplished the feat in the past two decades. These recent overachievers include the 2006 St. Louis Cardinals (83-78, .516 winning percentage), 2000 Yankees (87-74, .540), and the 1987 Twins (85-77, .524). Remarkably, since 1986 only two teams that reached 100 wins in the regular season (the 1998 and 2009 Yankees) have won the World Series, despite the fact that historically thirty-four World Series champions have done so.

In this chapter, we will scrutinize the six teams that won fewer than 90 games on the way to claiming the World Championship, with the goal of determining which one deserves to be called the least talented team to ever win a World Series.

Let's begin by looking at the three teams in this group who competed prior to the elongation of the regular season from 154 to 162 games, which occurred in 1961 in the AL, and 1962 in the NL. The 1926 Cardinals were the first team to win a World Series with fewer than 90 wins (discounting the Red Sox who won just 75 games in 1918 when the season was cut short due to World War I). The Cardinals went 89-65 (.578) to finish two games ahead of the Reds that year, despite weathering a slow start to their season. After dropping their fourth straight game to the Reds on May 29, their record stood at 21-23, eight games out of first place. But they rallied over the second half and moved into first place to stay on September 17. They were playing their best ball as the World Series dawned and prevailed in

Grover Cleveland Alexander was a member of the 1926 St. Louis Cardinals, the first team to win the World Series with fewer than ninety wins. COURTESY OF THE LIBRARY OF CONGRESS

seven games over a Yankees squad that had gone just 91-63 itself. Just how good were the 1926 Cardinals? Well, they had five future Hall of Famers on their roster, including second baseman Rogers Hornsby (.317, 11 home runs, 93 RBIs), first baseman Jim Bottomley (.299, 19 home runs, 120 RBIs), outfielder Billy Southworth (.317, 11 home runs, 69 RBIs), and pitchers Jesse Haines (13-4, 3.25 ERA) and Grover Cleveland Alexander (9-7, 2.91 ERA). And their top-scoring offense was complemented not only by their pair of Cooperstown-bound hurlers but also by Flint Rhem (20-7, 3.21 ERA) and Bill Sherdel (16-12, 3.49 ERA). The Cards led the NL in runs, home runs, and slugging percentage, and their 3.67 ERA ranked third. They outscored opponents 817–678 to account for a league-best runs differential of 139. Despite their low win total, they were a very talented team.

In 1945 it was the AL's turn to send an 80-something-game winner into October play. The Tigers finished 88-65 (.575) to narrowly edge the 87-67 (.565) Washington Senators in the wartime season. The race was tight all summer, but Detroit never relinquished its grasp on the top spot after wresting control of it on June 12. The Tigers batted just .256 as a team to rank fifth in the eight-team AL, and their .322 on-base percentage ranked sixth. But their lineup received a shot in the arm in June when Hank Greenberg returned from the military and proceeded to homer in his first game back. Over the final 78 games, he batted .311 with 13 home runs and 60 RBIs, and set a new record with 11 multihomer games in a season. First baseman Rudy York (.264, 18 home runs, 84 RBIs) and outfielder Roy Cullenbine (.277, 18 home runs, 93 RBIs) were the team's other offensive cogs. Still, no Tiger scored more than 80 runs or drove in more than 93. On the mound, the Tigers were anchored by future Hall of Famer Hal Newhouser, who went 25-9 with a career-best 1.81 ERA. Dizzy Trout (18-15, 3.14 ERA) and Al Benton (13-8, 2.02 ERA) also chipped in admirably. The Tigers outscored their opponents by 68 runs, which was a better differential than any other team posted, except, surprisingly, for the fourth-place Yankees, who scored 70 runs more than their opponents during an 81-71 season.

The Tigers entered the World Series as underdogs against the 98-56 Cubs. In the first game, Chicago battered Newhouser for seven runs in 2⅔ innings en route to a 9–0 romp. But the Tigers bounced back, and Newhouser did too. The hard-throwing lefty stood tall in Games Five and Seven, submitting complete-game efforts to deliver Detroit's first championship in ten years and leave the Cubs and their fans muttering something about a billy goat's curse.

In 1959 the Dodgers advanced to meet the White Sox in the World Series despite having just 88 wins under their belt. They were actually 86-68 (.558) during the regular slate of games, finishing in a first-place tie with the Milwaukee Braves. They then padded their regular season win total and clinched the pennant by winning the first two games of a best-of-three playoff series. The first West Coast team to reach the October Classic was powered by aging holdovers from the franchise's Brooklyn days like Gil Hodges (.276, 25 home runs, 80 RBIs) and Duke Snider (.308, 23 home runs, 88 RBIs). Newcomer Wally Moon (.302, 19 home runs, 74 RBIs), who'd been acquired in an off-season trade with the Cardinals, also excelled. Meanwhile, shortstop Don Zimmer batted just .165 in 97 games, before losing his job to speedy rookie Maury Wills. The league's third-highest-scoring offense supported a quintet of young pitchers who led the Dodgers to the league's third-best ERA. At the head of the rotation was twenty-two-year-old Don Drysdale (17-13, 3.46 ERA), followed by twenty-six-year-old Johnny Podres (14-9, 4.11 ERA), twenty-three-year-old Sandy Koufax (8-6, 4.05 ERA), twenty-six-year-old Danny McDevitt (10-8, 3.97 ERA), and twenty-nine-year-old Roger Craig (11-5, 2.06 ERA). The Dodgers outscored their opponents by just 35 runs, however, a margin that both second-place Milwaukee and third-place San Francisco bested, but thanks to a 33-22 record in one-run games (including both playoff wins against the Braves) they advanced to face a White Sox team that had posted 94 W's and held the top spot in the AL since July.

Because Dodger manager Walter Alston had used Drysdale, Podres, and Koufax in the final playoff game, the Dodgers sent Craig to the mound in Game One and suffered an embarrassing 11–0 defeat. They won the next three games though, all tightly-played affairs behind Podres, Drysdale, and reliever Larry Sherry. Then they lost Game Five 1–0, before bouncing back to end the Series with a 9–3 laugher in Game Six, as Sherry picked up another win and claimed MVP honors.

With the arrival of the 162-game schedule shortly thereafter, more than four decades passed before another sub-90-game winner claimed the October prize in a nonstrike-shortened season, although the 1973 Mets (82-79, .509) came frighteningly close, before falling to the A's in a seven-game World Series. Instead, it was an AL team, the 1987 Twins, who lowered the bar for World Champions to 85 wins. Minnesota was a remarkable 56-25 in games played on its bright green Metrodome turf that year, but a woeful 29-52 on the road. Nonetheless, the Twins' 85-77 (.525) record placed them two games ahead of the Royals in the AL West. The unusual October opportunity was the by-product of an imbalance in power between the two AL divisions. If the Twins had been playing in the AL East, their record would have been good for just fifth place, behind a quartet of teams that won 89 games or more, but in their division they and the Royals were the only teams to finish with winning records. Remarkably, the Twins were outscored by their opponents 806–786, and their 4.63 ERA ranked just tenth in the fourteen-team circuit. Just one Twin reached 100 RBIs—Gary Gaetti (.257, 31 home runs, 109 RBIs)—and not a single Twin reached 100 runs scored. Only two Minnesota pitchers reached double figures in wins, Frank Viola (17-10, 2.90 ERA) and Bert Blyleven (15-12, 4.01 ERA), who were, in fact, the team's only starters with winning records. Manager Tom Kelly juggled ten different pitchers in the third, fourth, and fifth slots in their rotation, including Les Straker (8-10, 4.37 ERA), Mike Smithson (4-7, 5.94 ERA), forty-two-year-old Joe Niekro (4-9, 6.26 ERA), and forty-two-year-old Steve Carlton (1-5, 6.70 ERA). In fairness, Gaetti wasn't the only spark in the lineup. Kent Hrbek (.285, 34 home runs, 90 RBIs), Kirby Puckett (.332, 28 home runs, 99 RBIs), and Tom Brunansky (.259, 32 home runs, 85 RBIs) were also solid sluggers.

In the ALCS the Twins won all four games started by Viola and Blyleven to vanquish the Tigers in five games. In the World Series, they relied on their only two passable starters again—and on their home-field advantage—to beat the Cardinals in seven games. Fifty-five thousand Homer Hanky–waving Minnesotans cheered them to victory in all four home dates, while they dropped all three middle games on the road. The series MVP was Viola, who went 2-1 in three starts.

More than a decade later, the Yankees became the first team in the three-tier playoff era to win the World Series with fewer than 90 wins. The two-time-defending World Champs made it three titles in a row in 2000, despite going

87-74 (.540). Unlike the 1998 and 1999 pinstripe editions that finished first and second, respectively, in the AL in ERA, the 2000 club finished sixth at 4.76. The staff consisted of Roger Clemens (13-8, 3.70), Andy Pettitte (19-9, 4.35 ERA), David Cone (4-14, 6.91 ERA), and Orlando Hernandez (12-13, 4.51 ERA) before mid-season acquisition Denny Neagle (7-7, 5.81 ERA) joined the fray. New York held onto at least a share of first place from July 7 on, though, as Bernie Williams (.307, 30 home runs, 121 RBIs), Paul O'Neill (.283, 18 home runs, 100 RBIs), and Derek Jeter (.339, 119 runs, 15 home runs, 73 RBIs) paced an offense that scored 871 runs, sixth most in the league. The team outscored its opponents by 57 runs, which looks pretty good compared to those outscored 1987 Twins, but, like the Twins, the Yankees finished the season with just the fifth-best record in the league. They would have placed third in either of the other two AL divisions in 2000.

Nonetheless, the Yankees had confidence and playoff experience on their side. First, they knocked off the A's in a five-game Division Series, then they bounced the Mariners in a six-game ALCS, before finally rolling over the crosstown Mets in a five-game World Series. O'Neill and Jeter batted .474 and .409, respectively, in the Subway Series.

Finally, we arrive at baseball's losingest champion yet, the 2006 Cardinals, who won the NL Central with an 83-78 (.516) record. If St. Louis had played in either of the other two NL divisions or in the AL West, their record would have ranked them third. If they had played in the AL East or AL Central, they would have placed fourth. The Cardinals had just the thirteenth-best regular-season record in baseball. To their credit, they managed to outscore their opponents 781–762. To their discredit, they won just 52 of the season's final 114 games. Their strength was their offense, which scored the sixth-most runs in the NL, thanks to thumpers Albert Pujols (.331, 49 home runs, 137 RBIs) and Scott Rolen (.296, 22 home runs, 95 RBIs), and to the unexpected contribution from rookie Chris Duncan (.293, 22 home runs, 43 RBIs). Like the lackluster Yankees and Twins before them, the Cardinals didn't have a dominant pitching staff. In fact, only two St. Louis starters had decent seasons—Chris Carpenter (15-8, 3.09 ERA) and Jeff Suppan (12-7, 4.12 ERA). Jason Marquis (14-16, 6.02 ERA) was the only other hurler to reach double figures in wins. Expected ace Mark Mulder went 6-7 with a 7.14 ERA before shutting down his season in August due to an injury. Jeff Weaver was 5-4 with a 5.18 ERA in fifteen second-half starts, after being acquired in a trade with the Angels. The Cardinals' 4.54 ERA ranked ninth in the NL.

The Cardinal starters came through in the first round of the playoffs against the Padres, though. Carpenter won the opener, as well as the fourth and final game, allowing just three runs in 13⅓ innings. And Weaver pitched five shutout innings to earn a victory in Game Two. In the NLCS against the Mets, Suppan rose to the occasion, going 1-0 with a 0.60 ERA in two starts—including seven innings of one-run ball in Game Seven. In the World Series against the favored Tigers, St. Louis pitchers combined for a 2.05 ERA in a five-game romp.

The debate over which of these six champions should be considered the worst team to take home baseball's highest prize comes down to the 1987 Twins and 2006 Cardinals, both of whom possessed only two legitimate big league starting pitchers. The Twins won 85 games; the Cardinals won 83. But at least the Cardinals scored more runs than their opponents during the regular season, something the Twins didn't come close to doing. The Cardinals also claimed their World Championship rather handily in 5 games, whereas the Twins needed 7 games to win theirs and almost certainly would have fallen short if they hadn't had the good fortune of home-field advantage. For these two reasons especially, and for being mediocre or worse in every other way, the 1987 Twins earn our grudging respect as the worst World Series winner yet crowned.

THE WORST OF THE WORST

[26]

THE WORST BIG LEAGUE HITTER

He Couldn't Hit His Way Out of a Wet Paper Bag

While debates over which legendary batsman should be regaled as baseball's best hitter are sure to invoke surnames like Williams, Ruth, Cobb, Gehrig, and Aaron, our present pursuit is a bit different. Okay, it's a lot different. We seek not the most capable big league hitter ever, but the one who deserves to forever wear the crown of shame—made, no doubt, of splintered bats, pine tar, and tattered batting gloves—that belongs rightfully to the worst hitter ever.

Now, surely you're thinking that the worst hitter ever would have never made it to the bigs or that he would have been immediately farmed out if by some miracle or misunderstanding he did. And you're right. So let's clarify our objective. What we're looking for is the worst hitter who stuck around for an appreciable amount of time in the Major Leagues. So, to eliminate the role players, September call-ups, and other short-lived big leaguers who really didn't belong in the Show in the first place, let's say that just as a hitter must accrue 3,000 career plate appearances to be taken seriously on baseball's all-time leader boards in ratio categories like batting average, on-base percentage, and slugging percentage, so too will a hitter need at least 3,000 plate appearances to be considered for our worst hitter ever designation. This translates to roughly five full seasons hitting (or *trying* to hit) at the bottom of some team's order as a regular or ten seasons as a platoon player. This provision will also give a free pass to all of the weak swingers who have made it to the big leagues through the decades thanks to their pitching prowess. Only the great Cy Young, who batted .210 over his twenty-two-season career, has reached 3,000 plate appearances among pitchers.

At the outset, then, we might conjecture that our eventual winner will have possessed—not unlike a pitcher—other virtues that kept him in the game for a prolonged period of time. Perhaps his defensive acumen was so great as to compensate for his offensive deficiencies. Or perhaps his untapped potential as a hitter outweighed the reality of his meager output. Or perhaps he happened to have compromising photos of some team's general manager. We'll see.

But before we begin our review of the likeliest candidates, let's tip our caps to two swingers who were weak-hitting enough to gain mythic stature in the game and to become parts of our American pop culture lexicon, even if they didn't reach the 3,000 plate appearances we require presently. When the topic of horrid hitters rears its head, Bob Uecker comes immediately to mind. And for good reason. He has reminded us of his ineptitude repeatedly, as part of his shtick, ever since he retired in 1968 with a career batting average of exactly .200, after 843 plate appearances and six seasons. The self-effacing back-up catcher then parlayed his mediocrity and good humor into a "personality" that led to an announcing career, and to starring roles in beer commercials, in the 1980s sitcom *Mr. Belvedere*, and in the movie *Major League*. There have been plenty of backup catchers who were worse with the stick than Uecker, however; they just weren't as proud of their ineptitude.

The second famously foundering flailer was the inspiration for the term *Mendoza Line*, which, as most fans know, refers derogatorily to a .200 batting average. This unofficial divider between bad and *really* bad owes its existence to Mario Mendoza, whose ears begin ringing, no doubt, in April or May each season when players and pundits lament the struggles of hapless hitters. Mendoza played parts of nine years in the big leagues, batting above .200 four times, including a high of .245 in 1980. The worst of his five years below .200 was his final season, 1982, when he batted .118 in just 17 at-bats. According to baseball lore, Mendoza Line was coined by George Brett, who was competing for batting titles for the Royals while Mendoza was trying to keep his head above water with the Mariners and Rangers. While no one would relish having their name linked to futility in their profession, at least Mendoza can take solace in the fact that he batted .215—.015 above the Mendoza Line—over his 1,337 career at-bats. Furthermore, he was only the successor to a generation of shortstops like him who had struggled with the bat a decade before. And with a review of some of their weak offensive performances, we will now begin our review in earnest.

By the 1960s, the balance between hitting and pitching had tilted significantly toward moundsmen, resulting in low-scoring games and a mind-set throughout baseball that putting a good defensive squad on the field was paramount. The most active and important defensive position, shortstop, came to be increasingly viewed as a defense-first proposition. Among the players of the era who epitomized this trend, Orioles shortstop Mark Belanger was, and still is, most prominently known. Like his peers Ray Oyler, who batted .175 in 1,265 at-bats for the Tigers, Seattle Pilots, and California Angels between 1965 and 1970, Ed Brinkman, who batted .224 in 6,045 at-bats accrued mostly with the Tigers and Washington Senators between 1961 and 1975, and Bobby Wine, who batted .215 in 3,172 at-bats for the Phillies and Montreal Expos between 1960 and 1972, Belanger couldn't hit a lick but sure could flash the leather. He won eight Gold Gloves and nearly won seven in a row at one point, if only Brinkman hadn't wrested away the shiny Rawlings trophy in 1972. In 5,784 career at-bats, spread over eighteen seasons, Belanger batted .228 with a .300 on-base percentage and meager .280 slugging percentage.

Brinkman, who retired with a slightly lower batting average than Belanger and a lower on-base percentage of .280, had a slightly higher .300 slugging percentage. Wine finished behind Belanger in all three ratio categories. Yet Belanger is remembered as the weakest hitter of his generation and as the personification of the good-field, no-hit middle infielder, due primarily to the memories fans have of him as a really good fielder. Neither Brinkman, Wine, nor Belanger rank as the weakest-hitting middle infielder ever, though. That distinction belongs to Davy Force—a 5-foot 4-inch tall utility man whose pre-1900 career included such consistent failure at the plate that his presence on big league diamonds must have been something of a farce. Initially, Force enjoyed success in the National Association, baseball's first professional league, then, once the National League was founded, he struggled mightily. During a nomadic five-year stint in the big league precursor, he batted above .300 four times, playing for teams in Washington, Troy, Baltimore, Philadelphia, and Chicago. After joining the National League in its inaugural 1876 season, Force batted .211 in 3,081 trips to the plate over ten seasons. He finally concluded his career with a .182 performance over 242 at-bats for the Washington Nationals in 1886. He had one career home run and 209 RBIs. His .211 batting average is the second lowest ever submitted by a player with 3,000 plate appearances.

Now, before we get to the only player with a worse success rate than Force's over the requisite number of trips to the batter's box, we'll offer the hint that he was a catcher and say a few words about this defense-first position that still features plenty of battered warriors who manage today to chisel out big league careers while hitting in the low-.200s. The current game's best representative of this creature is career backup Kevin Cash, who, through 2009, had hit just .186 in 527 at-bats for four different AL East teams over seven big league seasons. Previous backstops who struggled at the plate, while donning the "tools of ignorance" behind it, include Choo Choo Coleman, who batted .195 in 462 at-bats for the Phillies and Mets over four seasons in the 1960s, Mike Ryan, who batted .193 in 1,920 at-bats for the Red Sox and Phillies over eleven seasons mostly during the 1960s, and future big league pitching coach Dave Duncan, who batted .214 in 2,885 at-bats (and 3,151 plate appearances) for several teams in the 1960s and 1970s. When it comes to the worst of this putrid bunch, however, no player stunk it up quite so fabulously as Bill Bergen, who spent three seasons with the Cincinnati Red Legs and eight with the Brooklyn Superbas between 1901 and 1911, and managed to bat an all-time-worst .170 over 3,028 at-bats.

In ten of his eleven seasons Bergen failed to finish above .200. His career on-base percentage was .194, and his slugging percentage was .201. He never walked more than 14 times in a season, despite routinely making 300 trips to the plate. And, not surprisingly, his teams finished with a record above .500 only once, when the Reds went 74-65 in 1903 when Bergen enjoyed a career year, batting .227. Immediately after that campaign, the catcher was traded to Brooklyn, where his offensive production dwindled to the tune of a .182 average in 329 at-bats in 1904. It was in Brooklyn, however, that Bergen also distinguished himself as the finest-fielding backstop

Bill Bergen, depicted on this baseball card issued by the American Tobacco Company, batted just .170 over his eleven-season career. COURTESY OF THE LIBRARY OF CONGRESS

of his generation. Although he played long before the advent of the Gold Glove, Bergen was widely considered the best catcher in the game. He once famously threw out six would-be base stealers in a game against the Cardinals in 1909, and his 202 assists in 1909 and 1,444 lifetime assists still rank in the top-ten all-time among catchers. Despite his strong arm, Bergen is also remembered for suffering through the worst offensive season ever submitted by a player with enough at-bats to qualify for a batting title in 1909, when he hit just .139 in 346 at-bats. And he is remembered for enduring the longest batting slump ever among nonpitchers—a 0 for 46 stretch the same year. For struggling through miseries such as these, he is our choice as the worst hitter ever.

[27]

THE WORST TEAM EVER

It Blighted the Diamond Like No Team Before or Since

Every few years a big league team starts the season in truly horrendous fashion, prompting the talking heads on ESPN to begin comparing its struggles to those of the pitiful 1962 New York Mets. And fairly so. After all, those expansion Metropolitans set the twentieth-century low-water mark for baseball futility, suffering through an abysmal 40-win, 120-loss season to finish 60½ games behind the first-place San Francisco Giants, whose old Polo Grounds the Mets were then inhabiting. In the years since, would-be challengers to this dreadful record have occasionally arisen. But usually by Memorial Day or the Fourth of July, they've managed to paste together a modest win streak and to silence the "worst-team-ever" chatter. And so, with their regrettable record for the worst winning percentage in the modern era secure for another season, the woeful Mets of Casey Stengel, Gil Hodges, Frank Thomas, and Richie Ashburn fade once more into the pages of baseball history.

At least that's the way it usually goes. Even the 1988 Baltimore Orioles, for example, who started the season with 21 straight losses before winning their first game on April 29, had improved to 24-57—good for a .296 winning percentage—by July 4. Some teams have kept the worst-ever chatter alive deeper into the season though. The 2003 Detroit Tigers, for instance, kept it alive until the season's final week. Those not-so-roaring Bengals lost their first nine games and sixteen of their first seventeen, then suffered through losing streaks of eleven, ten, nine, eight (twice), and seven games as the season progressed. They remained on pace to break the Mets' modern record for ineptitude as late as September 22, when they stood at 38-118 (.248) before they rallied to win five of their final six games to finish 43-119 (.265). The Tigers were outscored by 337 runs over 162 games, and starting pitchers Jeremy Bonderman (6-19), Mike Maroth (9-21), Adam Bernero (1-12), and Nate Cornejo (6-17) bore the bruises to prove it.

While acknowledging that the 1962 Mets' 40-120 record speaks for itself, we wonder if those Mets really were the worst team to ever pose as a big league outfit.

For the sake of enlivening a discussion about which most baseball historians seem to have already made up their minds, let's change the question a little bit though, so that it asks instead: Which was the worst team without a darned good excuse for being so terrible?

What qualifies as a darned good excuse? Well, this obviously brings a bit of subjectivity into the query, but it seems reasonable to offer an expansion team like the Mets at least one season's grace. After all, expansion teams are supposed to stink. And we might say the same of war-era teams, like the Philadelphia Phillies of the early and mid-1940s, for example, who were especially terrible while many of the regulars were overseas. So, leaving aside expansion teams and wartime-replacement teams, what other clubs deserve derision, along with the 2003 Tigers, among baseball's worst clubs ever? To begin, let's travel back in time to the dying days of the pre–modern era.

The year was 1899 and baseball's modern era was still a year away from dawning. Prior to the start of the next season, the shape of home plate would change from a 12-inch square to a pentagon that measured 17 inches wide. And a year after that, the first two foul balls would count as strikes instead of do-overs, the catcher would be required to catch third strikes before they touched the ground, and the infield-fly rule would be instituted. As you can see, the game still had many evolutionary steps to take in 1899. And that's why the 1962 Mets are generally considered the worst baseball team ever, instead of the pre-modern Cleveland Spiders of 1899, who went a ghastly 20-134 (.130) and finished 84 games behind the Brooklyn Superbas in the National League standings. The Spiders were outscored by a whopping 723 runs, as they surrendered 1,252 tallies while crossing the plate just 529 times themselves. But, like the Miserable Mets who would one day follow in their eight-legged footsteps, the Spiders had a reasonable excuse for being terrible: They were a glorified farm team. The story goes something like this. As the 1890s played out, Cleveland appeared to be displaying the makings of a proud baseball city. On three separate occasions the Spiders finished second in the NL and advanced to the Temple Cup, a World Series precursor. In 1898 they finished fifth in the twelve-team NL with a respectable 81-68 mark, but fan apathy had begun to set in, so the Spiders played eighty-three of their final eighty-seven games on the road in the face of dwindling attendance at their League Park. This occurred at a time when attendance was falling throughout the game, it should be noted, as a national recession dampened fan interest. Compounding Cleveland's problems, though, was a local law that prevented the Spiders from playing games on Sundays, when crowds were usually the largest. Still, the Spiders were a decent team and their fans had reason to expect they would be contenders again in 1899. But during the ensuing off-season, Spiders owner Frank Robinson purchased the St. Louis Browns. Then he transferred ownership of the Spiders to his brother Stanley. Then he proceeded to not-so-covertly transfer all the best Spiders players to St. Louis through a series of lopsided trades and sales. Among the players Robinson and Robinson relocated were future Hall of Famers like Cy Young and Jesse Burkett, along with every other Cleveland starter. Rather than reacting with outrage, the other NL teams responded by mimicking this underhanded approach to team building, so that before long Brooklyn's owner had purchased Baltimore,

Chief Zimmer batted .342 in twenty games for the hapless 1899 Cleveland Spiders before being sold to the National League team in Louisville.

and four different teams claimed ownership shares of the New York Giants. In effect, the NL soon consisted of a subset of powerhouses who were using other league members as their feeder teams. The situation would be rectified in the winter of 1900 when the NL Reduction Committee eliminated Baltimore, Cleveland, Louisville, and Washington and established an eight-team league. But by then, the Spiders made history. Fielding a team of semipro and minor league players, the Spiders won neither baseball games nor fans. They began the season losing thirty of their first thirty-eight games, during what, unbelievably, was their best stretch of the season. After drawing fewer than two hundred fans per home date during the first three months, they announced on July 1 that most of their remaining "home" games would be played on the road. The Spiders played just seven more games in Cleveland, finishing 9-25 at home, and 11-109 in other NL cities. Their longest winning streak was two games, which they accomplished once, in mid-May. They lost forty of their final forty-one games. Their best pitchers were Jim Hughey (4-30) and Charlie Knepper (4-22). Their home attendance for the season was 6,088. As for the Browns, who benefited from the influx of Spiders, they finished fifth, exactly where the Spiders had stood the year before.

While it is hard to argue there has ever been a worse major league team than the 1899 Cleveland Spiders, they did have a pretty good excuse for being so terrible. Their owner wasn't trying to win. So, let's consider the Spiders the worst team in the pre–modern era, and let's call the Mets the worst expansion team ever, while continuing to look for a team worse than the 2003 Tigers to bear the worst modern-era-team-without-an-excuse mantle.

A case can surely be made for the 1916 Philadelphia A's, who had the misfortune of taking the field during one of Connie Mack's infamous down cycles, as their 36-117 (.235) record attests. The mercurial Mack made a regular practice, of course, of building championship teams and then selling his players off to the highest bidders and starting all over from scratch. That year, the A's worst offense in the AL featured Hall of Fame second baseman Nap Lajoie, who hit an uncharacteristic .246 in his final big league season. Meanwhile, the league's worst pitching staff was led by Joe Bush (15-24) and Elmer Myers (14-23), who were the only A's pitchers to win more than two games. Fellow starter Jack Nabors finished 1-20 and swingman Tom Sheehan finished 1-16. Philadelphia also had the league's lowest fielding percentage. And all of these factors combined to create a team that was outscored 776–447 on the way to finishing 54½ games behind the first-place Red Sox. Perhaps more tellingly, the A's finished 40 games behind the next-to-last-place Washington Senators, who finished 76-77.

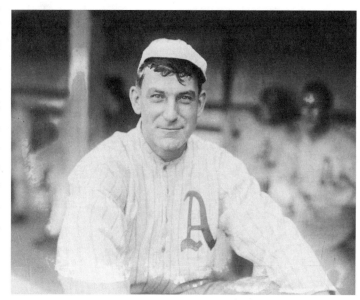

Hall of Famer Nap Lajoie batted just .246 for the 36-117 Philadelphia A's of 1916. COURTESY OF THE LIBRARY OF CONGRESS

Even the sickly Spiders finished "only" 35 games behind eleventh-place Washington in their losing season, and the miserable Mets finished "only" 18 games behind ninth-place Chicago in theirs. And perhaps this is the best barometer of a team's futility: How much worse was it than the next worst team in the league? As for the 2003 Tigers, they stack up relatively well compared to the other AL also-rans in their seasons of discontent, having finished just 20 games behind the Tampa Bay Devil Rays and 25 behind the Cleveland Indians in the AL standings.

Even if we include the expansion teams and war-replacement teams, no team has ever finished as far from next-to-last as the 1916 A's. And that's the main reason why this club, which started the season with fifteen wins in its first fifty contests, lost twenty straight between July 21 and August 8, and finished with just eighteen wins over its final eighty-one games, earns our disdain as the worst team ever without a darned good excuse for being so awful.

[28]

THE WORST TRADE IN THE PAST FIFTY YEARS

It Was as Lopsided as a Corked Bat

Whenever a general manager pulls the proverbial trigger on a deal with one of his fellow team builders, he accepts a certain degree of risk. In short, for any baseball trade to take place, both architects of the deal have to think their club is getting the better end of the bargain. Sometimes the gambles that GMs take are small ones, as in the case of swaps made strictly on the basis of short-term needs of both teams, when, for example, one club trades a spare utility infielder for another team's situational lefty. Likewise, trades at the other end of the talent spectrum, those rare blockbusters that involve established veterans on both sides of the transaction, also carry limited risk, seeing as the players changing hands are known entities, who, barring injury, should continue to perform in line with how they have in the past. Trades involving young players—be they at the major league or minor league level—carry the most risk, on the other hand, owing to the difficulty even the most skilled baseball talent evaluators have in assessing how a prospect's raw tools will translate into eventual success at the big league level. Our goal in this chapter is to identify the worst—or best, depending on your point of view—baseball trade of the past half century. We chose to limit our review to the past fifty years to remove from consideration the scores of players swapped and/or sold in the sordid players-for-cash deals of the first half of the last century, which have since been made illegal.

Despite the emphasis teams have placed recently on developing and keeping their own talent—as they've realized the benefits of holding onto pre-free-agent eligible stars—there have been plenty of recent deals that teams and their fans continue to lament. The July 30, 2004, deadline deal that sent Victor Zambrano and a minor leaguer from the Devil Rays to the Mets for former first-round draft pick Scott Kazmir and another minor leaguer is one such example. Zambrano, a twenty-eight-year-old with a 35-27 career record at the time, won two of his first three starts for the Mets, then went on the disabled list in mid-August and was a nonfactor on a team that finished twenty-five games out of first place in the NL East. Zambrano went 8-14 for the Mets over the next two seasons before being released. On the other side of the trade, Kazmir nearly immediately emerged as one of the most exciting young pitchers in the game. The hard-throwing lefty posted double-figure win totals in each of his first four full seasons in Tampa Bay, maintaining an ERA in the 3.00s every season. Even after a lackluster 2009 season, during which he was traded from Tampa Bay to the Los Angeles Angels of Anaheim, Kazmir was only twenty-six years old with a bright future ahead of him. The fact that the Mets traded one of their most highly regarded pitching prospects—a lefty, no less—for a middling pitcher during a season in which they clearly weren't headed for the playoffs still has New Yorkers fuming.

Another bad 2000s trade occurred in November of 2003 when the Giants sent a trio of young pitchers—Joe Nathan, Francisco Liriano, and Boof Bonser—to the Twins for catcher A. J. Pierzynski. The bristly backstop spent just one season in San Fran before earning his release. The Twins, meanwhile, watched Nathan blossom into one of the game's premier closers, Liriano into one of the most dominant young left-handers, and Bonser into a serviceable back-of-the-rotation starter.

The July 2000 trade that sent infield prospect Michael Young and another minor leaguer from the Blue Jays to the Rangers for Esteban Loaiza rates as another recent bamboozle. The Blue Jays missed the playoffs as Loaiza went 5-7 over the season's second half, while Young quickly established himself as an everyday player—first at second base, then at shortstop, and then at third—and became a perennial All-Star and .300 hitter.

But the worst trade of the past decade was the six-player swap in which the Montreal Expos sent a trio of future standouts to the Indians for a pitcher that helped them finish 19 games out of first place and 12½ games behind the Wild Card winner in 2002. Bartolo Colon held up his end of the deal, going 10-4 for the Expos. But it didn't make much of a difference in the standings. And after the season, the foundering Montreal franchise decided it couldn't afford to keep him, so it dealt him to the White Sox. The Indians, meanwhile, are still reaping the benefits. Grady Sizemore has proven to be the rare player who possesses both exceptional speed and power. And Cliff Lee won in double figures four times in five full seasons in Cleveland—including 2008 when he went 22-3 and won the Cy Young Award—before being traded to Philadelphia midway through the 2009 campaign. The third player the Indians received for Colon, second baseman Brandon Phillips, didn't make good in Cleveland, but has since become a solid everyday player in Cincinnati. A trio like this would surely have boosted the profile of those Expos heirs, the Washington Nationals, as they moved to their new city and opened their new ballpark.

The 1990s too saw several stars-in-waiting change hands, including Bobby Abreu, Curt Schilling, and Jeff Bagwell, all of whom seem likely to receive Hall of Fame consideration when they become eligible. Abreu broke into the bigs with fifteen games for the Astros in 1996 and fifty-nine more in 1997. Then he was selected by the Devil Rays in the November 1997 expansion draft. But the Devil

Cliff Lee was one of three future stars acquired by the Indians for Bartolo Colon. COURTESY OF WIKIMEDIA COMMONS

Rays immediately shipped him to the Phillies for shortstop Kevin Stocker. It was a trade the expansion team soon regretted. Stocker batted a meager .208 in 112 games during Tampa Bay's inaugural season, while Abreu has averaged more than 100 runs and 100 RBIs per year since 1999 with a .300 batting average.

Schilling was actually traded three times before he became a frontline starter and recurring postseason hero. First, the Red Sox traded the burly righty, along with Brady Anderson, for Baltimore's Mike Boddicker, midway through the 1988 season. Then the Orioles traded him along with Steve Finley and Pete Harnisch for Houston's Glenn Davis in 1991. The Astros then spun him to the Phillies for Jason Grimsley in 1992. In this case, three teams could commiserate that they had given up too soon on a pitcher who would win 216 games over twenty big league seasons, as well as World Series games in 1993, 2001, 2004, and 2007. For their part, it should be noted, the Red Sox were able to get Schilling back, via a 2003 trade with the Diamondbacks, and put him to good use during their championship runs in 2004 and 2007.

In 1990, the Red Sox were on the losing end of another trade that haunted them throughout the ensuing decade. As the Red Sox zeroed in on an AL East title, they moved to bolster their bullpen by sending Double-A third baseman Jeff Bagwell to the Astros for middle reliever Larry Andersen. The veteran pitched well for the Red Sox down the stretch, but was a nonfactor as they were dismantled in the opening round of the playoffs by the World Series–bound Oakland A's. Then Andersen departed via free agency after the season. The Astros, meanwhile, moved Bagwell across the diamond to first base, where he suddenly found his power stroke. After hitting just 6 homers in two minor league seasons, Bagwell went on to hit 449 big league taters, and the rest, as they say, is history.

During the 1980s two youngsters were traded at the outset of careers that have since earned them induction into the Hall of Fame. Additionally, two other young players traded during the decade are likely to receive their due in Cooperstown when they become eligible. The Cubs pulled off a steal when they traded shortstop Ivan DeJesus to the Phillies for shortstop Larry Bowa and second base prospect Ryne Sandberg in January 1982. DeJesus struggled to hit .250 in three seasons in Philadelphia, while Bowa himself struggled in Chicago. But Sandberg became the face of the Cubs over the next decade and raised the bar for power-hitting second basemen. Similarly, in December 1981 the Cardinals pulled off a swindle, heisting fourth-year shortstop Ozzie Smith from the Padres for shortstop Garry Templeton. Templeton lasted nine seasons in San Diego, but his career paled in comparison to the wizardly Smith's.

Surely, the trajectories of the Philadelphia and San Diego franchises would have been different had they held onto these Cooperstown-bound infielders. The same could be said of the Tigers, concerning a pitcher they dealt in 1987. Detroit sent unknown minor leaguer John Smoltz to the Braves at midseason that year to acquire veteran right-hander Doyle Alexander. Smoltz, whom the Tigers had drafted in the twenty-second round two years before and who had struggled to an 11-19 record in two minor league seasons, must not have seemed like much to sacrifice at the time, especially to the Tigers who were battling for the AL East crown and needed to shore up their rotation. The deal looked even better for Detroit after Alexander went 9-0 with a 1.53 ERA in eleven starts for the Tigers, who won the AL East by two games over the Blue Jays. The team lost to the Twins in the playoffs, though, and Alexander was just 20-29 over the next two seasons before retiring. Smoltz, for his part, won 210 games and saved 154 more for the Braves over the next two decades. He helped Atlanta to thirteen postseason berths and was 15-4 in 27 postseason starts. He was still pitching in 2009, first with Boston, and then with St. Louis.

In a similar swap of raw youth for veteran savvy, the Expos dealt Randy Johnson and two other young pitchers to the Mariners in May 1989 for Mark Langston and a minor leaguer. Langston won 12 games in Montreal before becoming a free agent and signing with the Angels after the season. Johnson notched his 300th win in 2009.

The two worst trades of the 1970s included two future Hall of Famers who were once teammates in New York. First, the Mets traded Nolan Ryan and three other players to the Angels for shortstop Jim Fregosi in December of 1971. Then, six years later, in June 1977, they traded Tom Seaver to the Reds for Pat Zachry, Doug Flynn, Steve Henderson, and minor leaguer Dan Norman. Both were terrible deals, but while Seaver "only" had ten solid seasons and 122 wins remaining in his right arm, Ryan had his entire career ahead of him. It's easy to understand what the Mets were thinking at the time: The twenty-five-year-old Texan could throw the ball faster than anyone they'd ever seen, but he'd never been able to harness his great stuff. He'd gone just 29-38 over his first four seasons, walking nearly as many batters as he struck out. Everything clicked for him as soon as he landed in Anaheim though. Ryan went 19-16 with a 2.28 ERA and 329 strikeouts in 1972 and was on his way to becoming a legend. As for Fregosi, the player the Mets acquired for Ryan, he played just 1½ seasons in New York, batting .232. Then he was sold to Texas midway through 1973.

Because Ryan went on to win a total of 324 games, struck out more batters than any other pitcher in history, and authored a record 7 no-hitters, and because Fregosi returned so little value to the Mets, this trade is our choice as the most lopsided—or worst—one in the past fifty years.

For the sake of tying up loose ends before closing, we should also acknowledge the poor judgment, lack of foresight, and plain bad luck that went into trades involving two other future Hall of Famers during the 1960s. Midway through the 1964 season, the Cubs and Cardinals pulled off a six-player swap that resulted in sophomore second-sacker Lou Brock landing in St. Louis where he became a star. The three players the Cubs received in return—Ernie Broglio, Bobby Shantz, and Doug Clemens—all had brief and forgettable careers in Chicago. Another bad deal was consummated in April 1966 when future Hall of Famer Ferguson Jenkins and two other youngsters were traded from the Phillies to the Cubs for veteran pitchers Larry Jackson and Bob Buhl. Jenkins won at least 20 games in each of his first six full seasons in Chicago and claimed 282 of his 284 lifetime wins after the trade. Meanwhile, Jackson and Buhl combined to win 47 games over the remainder of their careers.

29

THE WORST BASEBALL BLUNDER

It Begot the Game's First "Goat"

When things go bad for a baseball team, there's usually plenty of blame for fans and pundits to spread around. Sometimes the criticism is fair, while other times the recipients of onlookers' derision don't entirely deserve the harsh treatment they receive. But just the same, baseball's most devout rooters frequently see fit to tar and feather those players whom they hold responsible for their team's failure. And as the years pass, these favorite sons–turned–scapegoats seem only to grow more and more prominent within the mythology surrounding the team's history. Thus, Boston grandfathers have passed down to their sons, who have passed down to *their* sons, the lamentation that "Pesky held the ball," in 1946, allowing the Cardinals' Enos Slaughter to race home from first base on a single to centerfield and deprive the Red Sox of a Game Seven World Series victory. Whether shortstop Johnny Pesky really double-clutched before he relayed the throw from outfielder Leon Culberson is today irrelevant. In the minds of Red Sox fans—most of whom never saw the play—he did. Although Pesky—like some, but not all the other legendary goats—has since been forgiven by most Boston fans, he'd surely like to shake the now six-decade-old rap that he cost his team a World Series . . . but he carries it still.

As fans, our inability to simply accept our team's shortcomings creates in us the need to boil things down to a simpler, more visceral, rationalization. Rather than simply admitting that the other team was better than ours, we point the finger of blame at one player, and he becomes the lightning rod into which all of our frustration and anger is directed. He is the reason, the only reason, our guys lost. Otherwise they were just as good as—actually, better than—their opponents.

As the decades have flown past, this basic human tendency to scapegoat has manifested itself time and again within the sport. Every contending team in every near-miss season has at least one player who becomes symbolic for its failure to put together that winning streak, reach first place, stand tall down the stretch, or win the big game in the playoffs. It is in the playoffs, of course, where players truly have the chance to forever etch their names into the annals of baseball infamy with one untimely error, mental mistake, base-running gaffe, or other blunder.

In this chapter, we will examine the most famous baseball blunders of all time in the hope of identifying the most costly, devastating, worst one of all. Ultimately, the boneheaded play that came when the stakes were highest—and that perhaps really did decide the fate of a team all on its own—will be our winner.

To begin, we'd like to reiterate that every major league team carries its own litany of insidious offenses that imperiled its fortunes at one time or another. And no doubt each and every blunder has scarred the souls of the disappointed fans who witnessed and then mythologized it. But we believe five blunders stand above, or below, the rest as the most boneheaded ever. To start, the infamous Merkle Boner, as it's been remembered, is one gaffe that presented the classic case of an athlete snatching defeat from the jaws of victory by way of a moronic mental mistake. Though as notorious as this base-running snafu has remained through the years, it actually didn't occur in the World Series but during the regular season; however, it did have World Series implications. The 1908 season was winding down when the Cubs visited New York for a crucial September affair against the Giants. With a week to play, the two teams were tied atop the National League standings. No one imagined they'd still be tied at the end of the day. The skies proffered no threat of rain, so the game would certainly be played to its conclusion, enabling the winner to assume sole possession of first. As the afternoon progressed, the game entered the latter innings as a classic pitcher's duel.

After 8½ frames the score stood at 1–1. Finally, with two outs in the bottom of the ninth, the Giants advanced Moose McCormick to third base on a long single to rightfield by nineteen-year-old first baseman Fred Merkle, who was starting his very first game of the season that fateful day in place of an injured teammate. The Polo Grounds crowd rose to its feet, the roused grandstand fans joining the many onlookers who had been standing all game long behind roped off areas in the deepest recesses of the outfield. The Giants crowd anticipated a victory that would propel their team into first place. And the next batter, Al Bridwell, delivered. He lined a clean single into right-centerfield. Bridwell sprinted triumphantly toward first base. McCormick trotted home from third. And the game was over. Or so it appeared. There was only one problem: Merkle, who had been on first, never ran to second base. He took several steps toward the keystone sack, but then, as the jubilant crowd spilled onto the field, he got spooked and took a right turn toward the Giants clubhouse, which was located out beyond the centerfield fence. The rest of Merkle's teammates began to make the harrowing trek too, but their point of origin was the dugout, not first base. However understandable Merkle's panicked flight may have been, the play was still technically live as long as there was a potential force out for the Cubs to make at second base, and Merkle was still a live runner. And so, savvy Chicago second baseman Johnny Evers braved the stampeding masses to retrieve a ball—whether it was the actual one Bridwell hit was later debated—and then stepped on second base to end the inning and negate the apparent winning run that McCormick had scored. The umpires conferred and then ruled Merkle out. The game was still tied. But with the crowd on the field it was impossible to resume play, so the umps ruled the game a tie. The two teams played out the remainder of the schedule and finished the season a week later with identical 98-55-1 records.

To determine the NL champion, the two teams made up the controversial tie by starting a new game on October 8. The Cubs prevailed 4–2. Simply because Merkle had failed to run from first to second on a single—well, actually a fielder's choice—his team was denied a trip to the World Series. He would be derided as a Bonehead for the rest of his career, but would fortunately have five future chances to play in the October Classic over fourteen big league seasons. Unfortunately, though, his teams lost all five series and he committed another big-time blunder in one of them that combined with another Giants' mistake to sabotage his team yet again. But before we get to that second boneheaded Merkle play, there are some other more recent postseason miscues we should review.

In Game Two of the 2005 American League Championship Series, Angels catcher Josh Paul channeled the ghost of Merkle when he committed a similarly mindless mistake. Ironically, the game situation was the same as it had been at the time of the Merkle debacle, tied 1–1 in the bottom of the ninth. With two out and no one on base, the White Sox sent A. J. Pierzynski to the plate to face Kelvim Escobar. Escobar delivered two strikes, then threw a pitch in the dirt that Pierzynski swung at and missed. Strike three. Escobar pumped his fist and headed for the dugout, assuming the game would head to extra innings. There was only one problem. Paul had trapped the pitch against the ground after a short hop. But he never tagged out Pierzynski. He merely rolled the ball back to the mound before heading for the dugout himself. Pierzynski took a step or two in the direction of his own dugout, then made a beeline for first base before the Angels could retrieve the ball. The disheartened Angels returned to their positions in the field in order that the bottom of the ninth could continue with two outs and a man on first. Then they quickly unraveled.

After White Sox manager Ozzie Guillen sent Pablo Ozuna into the game to pinch run for Pierzynski, Ozuna promptly stole second. Then Joe Crede hit a game-winning double. Instead of entering extra innings and a chance to take a two-games–to–none lead in the series, the Angels found themselves tied in games at 1-1, and worse, utterly deflated by a silly mistake that cost them a game. Not surprisingly, they lost the next three games, and just like that their season was over.

A World Series mistake is even worse than a Championship Series one, of course. And the most infamous World Series whiff of the past few decades was committed by Red Sox first baseman Bill Buckner, who failed to come up with Mookie Wilson's groundball in Game Six of the 1986 Series. The through-the-wickets grounder allowed the Mets to score their third run in the bottom of the tenth inning and to claim a series-tying victory. Through the years Buckner has been widely lambasted, and not entirely fairly. His goof was, after all, a fielding error, not a mental mistake like the previous two we've discussed. And today, few fans remember that there was actually a Game Seven still to play afterward in which the Red Sox enjoyed a 3-run lead in the sixth inning before blowing that lead too. Many Buckner critics also fail to remember that at the time of Buck-ner's blunder the Mets had already erased Boston's 2-run lead to tie the game. In fact, before the ball rolled through the gimpy first baseman's legs the Red Sox had committed a pair of equally disastrous mistakes that had already diminished their chances of winning. First, with Boston just one strike from victory, pitcher Bob Stanley uncorked a wild pitch—that just as easily could have been ruled a passed ball on catcher Rich Gedman—to allow the tying run to score and the eventual winning run to advance to second base. Then, moments later, Stanley had an opportunity to pick off Ray Knight from second base when second sacker Marty Barrett sneaked over the bag unobserved by Knight and called for the ball. But Stanley never looked back, and delivered a pitch home to Wilson instead. And we all know how that turned out. Is Buckner the most famous World Series goat of our time? Certainly. But his wasn't the most egregious blunder, and his rap as a player who cost his team a World Championship is unwarranted.

Much longer ago, a worse World Series meltdown that didn't come to define its principal offender's career in the way Buckner's bungle did was committed by no less a star than the mighty Babe Ruth. The Bambino played in ten October

Babe Ruth was caught stealing to end the 1926 World Series.
COURTESY OF THE LIBRARY OF CONGRESS

Classics and performed exceptionally well in them (see Chapter 10). In 1926, though, Ruth's Yankees were playing the Cardinals and as the seventh game entered the bottom of the ninth inning, the Pinstripes trailed 3–2. As the Yankees readied for their final at-bat, surely no one would have guessed that a Ruth miscue would seal the home team's sorry fate. Ruth had already hit a home run in the game when he stepped to the plate with two outs and no one on base, with fans dreaming that he'd do something heroic. Instead, he worked the count full and then walked, bringing up Bob Meusel, a solid swinger who had batted .315 with 12 home runs and 81 RBIs in 108 games that season. With a gap hit the Yankees could tie the game.

With a homer, they could win it. But on pitcher Grover Cleveland Alexander's first pitch—which Meusel took for a strike—Ruth broke for second base. Cardinals catcher Bob O'Farrell threw to Rogers Hornsby, who tagged Ruth out and the series was over. Afterward it came to light that the Bambino was running on his own impetus, without prompting from the dugout. It was a low-percentage gamble, as Ruth had stolen 11 bases that season, and had been caught trying to steal 9 times. In his career, Ruth was successful on just 123 of 240 stolen-base attempts. To this day, no other World Series has ended on a caught stealing.

Seeing as Ruth's team was trailing when he committed his boneheaded play, it's impossible to say whether the Yankees would have tied or won the game had Meusel been allowed to take his hacks. We can say for sure, however, that had Merkle and one of his Giants teammates made one of two routine plays they botched in the final inning of the 1912 World Series, the Giants would have won the World Championship. Instead, they fell to the Red Sox. With the Series knotted at three

Fred Merkle (top row, fourth from left) and Fred Snodgrass (top row, second from right) pose with their Giants teammates at the Polo Grounds in 1912. COURTESY OF THE LIBRARY OF CONGRESS

Fred Snodgrass made a key error in the final innings of the 1912 World Series. COURTESY OF THE LIBRARY OF CONGRESS

games apiece, the Giants carried a 2–1 lead into the bottom of the tenth inning of the finale. The first batter against Christy Mathewson, pinch-hitter Clyde Engle, lifted a high fly ball that Giants centerfielder Fred Snodgrass settled under. But Snodgrass muffed it. The ball hit his glove and popped out, allowing Engle to reach second base. Mathewson then induced a sacrifice fly that advanced Engle—the potential tying run—to third. After a walk to Steve Yerkes, Tris Speaker came to the plate and hit a routine foul pop on the first-base side. Both Mathewson and catcher Chief Meyers looked to Merkle, the first baseman, as the logical candidate to make the play, but Merkle never budged. The ball fell a few feet from him in the first-base coach's box. After being given a second life, Speaker hit Mathewson's next offering into rightfield to tie the game and advance Yerkes—the potential winning run—to third. Mathewson issued an intentional walk to load the bases, then Boston's Larry Gardner lifted a sacrifice fly to right to plate Yerkes with the winner. Had either Snodgrass or Merkle converted just one of the two bungled plays, the Giants would have won the game and the Series. For their meltdowns at the worst possible time, we dub theirs the worst baseball blunders ever.

30

THE WORST BALLPARK TRAGEDY

Winning and Losing Suddenly Didn't Seem So Important

In this chapter our grim pursuit involves revisiting those dark moments when the realities of life—fleeting and fragile as it is—have crept into the baseball world and shattered the illusion of the ballpark as a sanctuary immune to the everyday worries and vexations we all face. During the course of our investigation into the worst ballpark tragedies, we may observe that many of baseball's most distressing moments have resulted in corresponding rule and/or equipment changes that have safeguarded future generations of fans, players, coaches, and umpires from particular kinds of harm.

While the crux of this chapter involves tragedies that have struck the game's on-field personnel at the major and minor league levels, let's first devote a few paragraphs to the risks of rooting. Some readers may be surprised to learn that untimely ballpark deaths are not so uncommon, especially ones involving fans. According to a study published in 2003 by the baseball journal *Nine,* there were thirty-five fan fatalities between 1900 and 2000 at professional baseball stadiums. Most of these were the result of accidents unrelated to the game, occurring on rickety grandstands, slippery concourses, or on flights of stairs.

Back in 1903, the support joists holding up the balcony of Philadelphia's Base Ball Grounds gave out when a crowd rushed to the top of the bleachers to see why a little girl was screaming on the street outside. When the balcony came crashing down, more than 200 people fell into the bleachers below, and twelve unfortunate souls met their maker. It wouldn't be long before concrete and steel became the ballpark building materials of choice. But even so, later fans remained vulnerable to rapid spectator exoduses. In 1929, a lightning storm sparked a similar ballpark panic at Yankee Stadium and set off a stampede that left more than sixty people injured and two dead.

In perhaps the most mysterious ballpark fatality of all, fifty-six–year-old Bernard Boyle was shot to death while sitting in the Polo Grounds watching a Fourth of July doubleheader in 1950. Police never found the marksman, but suspected the shot had come from outside the stadium. That death came three years after a fan had been similarly shot at Sportsman's Park in St. Louis; though, in that case, the mysterious wound was not fatal.

Recent news stories suggest that today's fans need still be vigilant, if not for flying bullets, then at least for potentially hazardous ballpark infrastructure. In 2008, a twenty-five-year-old man fell 150 feet down a stairwell and died at Turner Field in Atlanta. That same year, a thirty-six-year-old man slipped on an escalator and died at Shea Stadium. The latter fatality was the third death of its kind in New York City alone in recent memory, following similar stairwell falls that led to the 1985 death of a man at Shea and to the 1999 death of a man at Yankee Stadium. Likewise, a sudden escalator failure at Coors Field in 2003 injured more than thirty fans, including one who had to have part of her leg amputated.

These ballpark infrastructure-related tragedies enter our public consciousness, usually as Page Three news stories, and then fade away just as quickly. Meanwhile, deaths involving the game's participants get far more attention. A still painful memory for fans involves Mike Coolbaugh, whose tragic end in August 2007 garnered massive media attention and an outcry of sympathy from fans around the country. A first-base coach for the Texas League's Tulsa Drillers, Coolbaugh suffered a life-ending injury when a foul ball struck him in the temple as he stood in the first-base coach's box. The thirty-five-year-old baseball lifer left a pregnant wife and two young children behind. As a small silver lining to this awful tragedy, we can only hope that the rule changes it prompted may save some future base coach from harm. In 2008 baseball instituted two new rules. The first stipulated that base coaches could no longer leave their designated boxes in order to stand closer to home plate. The second mandated that all coaches must wear helmets while on the field.

A similar near-tragedy that could have been a whole lot worse than it turned out occurred nearly a decade before Coolbaugh's death, when Yankees bench coach Don Zimmer was struck in the head by a foul ball while sitting in the dugout of a 1999 American League Division Series game. Zimmer was minding his own business on the bench when Chuck Knoblauch didn't quite get around on a fastball and sent a low screamer careening off the aged coach's skull. Zimmer's jaw and left ear were badly cut, but the next day he returned to the bench wearing an army helmet bearing a Yankees logo. The next year the Yankees added protective screens in front of both dugouts in the Bronx, an innovation that soon became standard issue throughout the big leagues.

While umpires frequently suffer minor injuries—especially those home-plate umps who sometimes seem like foul-ball magnets behind the plate—usually their protective gear keeps them from harm. In fact, the most memorable tragedy involving an umpire had nothing to do with his padding or headgear. It occurred on Opening Day of 1996 when home plate arbiter John McSherry collapsed and died of a massive heart attack at Riverfront Stadium. To be clear, McSherry's death was not the result of an on-field injury but it did prompt baseball to ensure umpires keep themselves in better physical condition. McSherry died just seven pitches into the first game of the year in Cincinnati. After signaling for the second base umpire to replace him behind the plate, he started to walk toward the Reds dugout but didn't make it. The fifty-one-year-old was pronounced dead less than an hour later and the game between the Reds and Expos was suspended. In her inimitable fashion, Reds owner Marge Schott was reported to say, "Snow this morning and now this. I don't believe it. I feel cheated. This isn't supposed to happen to us, not in Cincinnati." The rest of the baseball world mourned though. Deaths occurring as the direct result of events taking place within the course of the game and afflicting the game's players would seem most resonant, and by that measure most tragic, if there is such a thing as deeming one death more horrific than another.

There have been several close calls in the major leagues through the years but only one big league player has actually died. The minor leagues, however, have presented a much different story. According to a 2003 study written by Bob Gorman and published by the University of Nebraska Press under the title "I Guess I Forgot to Duck," since 1883 no less than twenty-six bush leaguers have passed away due to injuries incurred on the field. The study subdivided fatalities by cause, noting thirteen deaths due to pitched balls, one due to a thrown ball, three as the result of collisions, one due to a batted ball striking a player, four due to on-field heart attacks, one due to physical exertion, one due to a poisonous snake bite, one due to a lightning strike, and one to mysterious causes. On the brighter side, only two of the deaths cited in the study occurred since 1961, thanks, presumably, to improvements in minor league ballpark lighting, improvements in player equipment, improvements in medicine, and an improving skill level throughout the minor leagues.

The two more recent player tragedies struck a twenty-year-old Class A pitcher for the Gastonia Rangers named Ronaldo Romero, who suffered a heart attack on the mound in 1990, and an eighteen-year-old Class A outfielder for the Salem Pirates named Alfredo Edmead, who suffered a brain hemorrhage when he collided with a teammate in pursuit of a pop-up in 1974. The last player to die after being struck by a pitched ball was the Dothan Browns' leading hitter, Ottis Johnson, who suffered a fractured skull when he was hit in the head by a Jack Clifton pitch in an Alabama-Florida League game in 1951. Ironically enough, Clifton pitched for a team named the Headland Dixie Runners in the Class D circuit.

The only case Gorman's study cites of a pitcher expiring after being struck by a batted ball dates back to 1902, and, surprisingly does not involve a blow to the head. Midlothian pitcher Charles Harrington was struck in the chest by a liner off the bat of a Texas League opponent, and then picked up the ball and threw the batter out at first base. Harrington got back up on the hill, began his windup, and dropped dead.

The only death-by-reptile incident the game has known claimed the life of James Phelps, an outfielder for an independent league team in Rayville, Louisiana. Phelps was snake-bitten while playing the field in 1909, but didn't tell anyone until after the game, a short time before he passed away. The lightning death occurred in 1951 when Crawley Millers centerfielder Andy Strong was struck by a wayward thunderbolt and died in the sixth inning of an Evangeline League game.

While there have been several scary moments in recent major league memory, none has involved snakes, lightning, or even pitched balls. Incidents involving line drives and broken bats flying toward pitchers tend most commonly to cause fans and players to hold their collective breath and hope for the best. Recent liners that cracked into the noggins of pitchers like Bryce Florie and Matt Clement come immediately to mind as near-

Yankees pitcher Carl Mays threw a pitch in 1920 that killed the Indians' Ray Chapman.
COURTESY OF THE LIBRARY OF CONGRESS

tragedies that thankfully didn't result in fatalities. In the more distant past, old-timers still talk about the sorry turn Herb Score's career took after he was struck in the right eye by a liner off the bat of Gil McDougald in 1957.

Likewise, batters have suffered some serious injuries as the result of pitched balls—the 1987 incident in which Andre Dawson was struck in the face by an Eric Show pitch stands out as a memorably close call—but thanks to the batting helmets now in use, none of these incidents has resulted in death. Interestingly, even after Tony Conigliaro was struck and seriously injured by a Jack Hamilton pitch in 1967, major league players were still not required to wear batting helmets for another four years. The

Ray Chapman is the only Major League player to die as the result of injuries suffered in an official game.
COURTESY OF THE LIBRARY OF CONGRESS

hard hats were finally made mandatory for rookies in 1971, but established big leaguers had the choice to don them or not, until they became fully mandatory in 1980. This, despite the fact that the hard-headed antihelmet holdouts of the 1970s must have known that the only big leaguer ever to suffer a fatal injury in an official game was a batter struck by a pitch.

And that brings us to the worst baseball tragedy ever. Ray Chapman was a twenty-nine-year-old Cleveland Indians shortstop in the prime of his career when he stepped into the right-handed batter's box at the Polo Grounds to face Yankees pitcher Carl Mays on August 16, 1920. Chapman was leading off the fifth inning, no doubt hoping to get on base and help his team expand upon its 3–0 lead. Little did he know that the plate appearance would be his last and that his final seconds were already ticking away. Mays was a submarine-style right-hander whose ball ran back inside on right-handed batters. And he was known throughout the league as a headhunter. But he had no reason to be throwing at Chapman at the time, given the game situation: The score was tight and Chapman was leading off an inning. Whether he intended to or not, however, Mays unleashed a delivery that headed up and in on Chapman. Squinting into the glare of the late afternoon sun, the doomed batter never moved. The ball crashed into his skull, making a thud so loud that Mays thought it had hit the bat. The pitcher picked up the ball, which had rolled nearly all the way back to the mound, and threw it to first base. Chapman, meanwhile, lay writhing on the ground. He was eventually able to stand up and walk halfway to the Indians clubhouse with the support of teammates on either side, but then his legs gave out and he collapsed. Doctors knew right away that the situation was critical. According to the game story that ran the next day in the *New York Times,* "The blow had caused a depressed fracture in Chapman's head 3½ inches long." His limp body was rushed to St. Lawrence Hospital where an operation removed part of his skull in hopes of relieving the pressure on his brain. But the surgeons noticed several blood clots that had already formed and by the next morning Chapman had slipped away.

The death brought two important changes to the game. First, baseball outlawed the widely accepted practice of pitchers dirtying up new balls with tobacco juice, black licorice spit, and mud. And second, the spitball, which was known for its late-darting movement, was outlawed (although enforcement of this edict would prove difficult at times through the years). Hopefully these, and other later changes to the way the game is played will go a long way toward ensuring that Chapman's death will remain Major League Baseball's only on-field player fatality, but given the game's history of tragic and near-tragic events, it seems likely the Grim Reaper may someday infiltrate the American ballpark again, especially if today's batters continue swinging the thin-handled maple bats that have been shattering with increasing frequency in recent years.

THE BEST BASEBALL TASTES AND PLACES

31

THE BEST BALLPARK TREAT IN THE MAJORS

Buy Me Some Peanuts and . . . Garlic Fries

Once upon a time, back when teams still scheduled doubleheaders on the Fourth of July and players still worked part-time jobs in the off-season, hungry ballpark fans were content with fistfuls of flaccid ballpark franks and cups of lukewarm beer. Today, however, ballpark voyagers expect a little bit more—okay, a lot more—when it comes to chowing down at the ballpark. And fortunately, the teams we root for have responded by offering more diverse game-day menus than our forefathers could have ever imagined. Insert your family's resident octogenarian here, asking in his most flummoxed voice, "Sushi at the ballpark? Are you sure?" Yes, Uncle Vit, I'm sure. They serve it at Safeco Field in Seattle, partly as a nod to the many Japanese fans that Ichiro Suzuki has attracted to the Mariners and partly as a nod to, well, the many people of all backgrounds who just happen to like sushi.

Of course teams aren't just trying to be all-inclusive for exclusivity's sake with their spiffy new menus. The fact is, as the game has evolved into a bigger business its teams have figured out that concession sales put nearly as much money in their coffers as ticket transactions. That's why, while ticket prices have risen as a whole, some small market teams have recently taken the innovative approach of making thousands of seats available for just a few dollars each. We're talking about the remote Rockpile Seats that sell for $4 in Colorado, or the altitudinous Uecker Seats that sell for a dollar—as in one hundred pennies—in Milwaukee. Get fans through the turnstiles, so this line of thinking goes, and they'll fork over wads of dollars for pricey munchies. And when it comes to this type of revenue, unlike the money from ticket sales, home teams don't have to share their revenue with visiting teams. So, if teams are counting on their fans to eat big at the park, it makes sense not only for them to provide something for every taste, but also for them to each offer a signature culinary item or two, unique to their local community, that fans may embrace as a special part of the ballpark experience in their city. Thus, it has become a Padres tradition to eat fish tacos at Petco Park, and an Orioles tradition to enjoy crab cakes at Oriole Park at Camden Yards.

In some cases these ballpark flavors become such important aspects of the home team's identity that they even find marketing traction outside the ballpark. Visit any supermarket in New England and you can purchase a package of Fenway Franks to boil in the comfort of your own kitchen. Visit any convenience store in Cleveland and you'll find a jar of Stadium Mustard just waiting for you to take home.

Now, it may be true that no food will ever surpass the hot dog as the ballpark delicacy of choice—after all, baseball and the frank have been linked ever since the turn of the last century when legendary vendor Harry Stevens started dishing out dogs from a wicker basket at the Polo Grounds. The hot dog will always be the first course of the nation's first sport. But for major league fans looking to indulge their pallets still further, there are some real treats out there in baseball land to devour these days, and in a book like this the better ones seem to deserve a few pages of mouth-watering attention. So, without further ado, here are our picks for the best ballpark foods that fans are sampling at today's big league parks.

The aforementioned fish tacos at Petco Park represent the best fish dish among baseball's rapidly expanding seafood options. They pay homage to San Diego's proud Mexican heritage and to Southern California's eclectic taste. This fish taco is the brainchild of an entrepreneur named Rubio, who owns restaurants throughout Greater San Diego. It consists of beer-battered Alaskan Pollock, smothered in salsa and a tangy white sauce, topped with shredded cabbage, and wrapped in a soft tortilla. It's not only delicious but also light enough to leave room in your stomach for another one three or four innings later.

The stout rooters in Pittsburgh, meanwhile, enjoy an appropriately richer ballpark treat at PNC Park. The ballpark pirogue is the comfort food fans turn to as they try to stay cheerful while their Pirates endure one losing season after another. The buttery dumplings, which come stuffed with potato, onion, or garlic, also serve as a tribute to Pittsburgh's robust Polish population.

Another ballpark culinary phenomenon certain to ward off vampires or overly affectionate significant others who threaten to divert the hard-core fan's focus from the game are the Garlic Fries at AT&T Park in San Francisco. These deep-fried potatoes come topped with minced garlic and grated Parmesan cheese. They not only taste great going down but even better the next morning as they remind fans of good times had at the ballpark while lingering on the palate.

Making the list on the basis of comedic value are the Rocky Mountain Oysters at Coors Field. When Rockies fans take out-of-towners to the ballpark, they often find themselves subjected to playful jabs about how the thin air in Denver makes a mockery of the game. And they don't take this indignity sitting down. Rather, they get up and head to the concession stand to buy these deep fried mystery balls. Then they return to their seat and offer some to their wayfaring friend, being careful to hold back their laughter until the critic pops a few. Finally, they bust out laughing and disclose that the unsuspecting sucker has just eaten a fried bull testicle. Rocky Mountain Oysters have long been a treat at country fairs and festivals out west, but sometimes it takes a while for easterners to wrap their mind around the idea of them, even if locals swear they're delicious.

A less controversial treat, the Toasted Raviolis at Busch Stadium in St. Louis consist of crispy pockets of deep-fried cheese or ground beef, served with warm marinara sauce for dipping. They're a tribute to the Gateway City's proud Italian community, which spawned future big leaguers like Yogi Berra and Joe Garagiola.

Boog's Barbecue in Baltimore is another local favorite, and in fact, serves up an array of sandwiches that are even more scrumptious than Oriole Park's originally intended trademark food, the aforementioned crab cakes. And more than just filling the air with smoky billows and filling bellies with juicy goodness, Boog's started a trend that has infused new flavor throughout the game. For all the barbecue pits across the big leagues today, we fans owe Mr. Boog Powell a tremendous debt of gratitude for serving as their inspiration. The heavy-hitting former Oriole star first opened his joint in 1993, and since then former players like Manny Sanguillen (Pittsburgh), Gorman Thomas (Milwaukee),

The brats and sausage in Milwaukee are so popular that they've inspired a quintet of mascots (pictured here at the Brewers' spring training park in Arizona).

Randy Jones (San Diego), and Greg Luzinski (Philadelphia) have begun smoking meat at their favorite ballparks. None has matched Boog's melt-in-your-mouth pork and beef yet, or his special barbecue sauce, but their efforts are nonetheless appreciated and well worth a taste.

The bratwurst at Miller Park in Milwaukee is one of those local delicacies that taste even better when served with a side of big league game action. Topped with the stadium's secret sauce and chased by a spicy Italian sausage or Polish sausage, this miracle in a bun causes even the fiercest critic of Bud Selig to reconsider his disdain. We shouldn't give too much credit to the commish for this ballpark innovation, though; proper thanks go out instead to Wisconsin's large German population.

And what could be better than the best ballpark sausages in the Midwest? Well, how about a nearly-as-good sausage topped with dripping Italian beef? The Italian beef and sausage combo at Wrigley Field fits the bill. But consider yourself warned. Fans usually have puddles of greasy jus on their Carlos Zambrano jerseys by the time they're finished.

Finally, we arrive at the mouthwatering concoction that narrowly edges all the other delicious treats we've discussed so far to earn this chapter's most effusive praise. Not surprisingly, perhaps, the pick reflects what you may have already perceived to be your author's cased-meat bias. While out-of-towners may more readily associate a trip to Boston's Fenway Park with such specialties as the Fenway Franks and cups of hot New England clam chowder, which are served at the grand old

Sausage vendors line the street behind Fenway's fabled Green Monster.

Author Josh Pahigian displays a Fenway Sausage.
PHOTO BY HEATHER PAHIGIAN

stadium, Fenway is also home to the best sausage in baseball . . . well, sort of. In fact, the better Fenway sausages are sold not at the concession stands inside the park, but rather outside the turnstiles where fans find a contingent of private vendors hawking their meat on Lansdowne Street, right behind the Green Monster. Fans can smell these beauties sizzling on their vendors' griddles from as far away as Kenmore Square as they approach the ballpark. Loaded with a heaping helping of grilled peppers and onions, they're as much a part of the Boston tradition as Pesky's Pole and that big green wall. Well, that's the list—just one heavy eater's menu of favorite flavors currently defining the game. If you disagree with one or two of the selections, please feel free to add a bottle of Maalox and a Tide-to-Go stick to your overnight bag and hit the road for a taste test of your own.

32

THE BEST PLAYER-NAMED WATERING HOLE

Sating Our Appetite for All Things Hardball

While some retired players are content to man barbeque pits bearing their names at their favorite ballpark, others are even more ambitious in the forays they make into the food and beverage market. These former big leaguers attach their names to sports bars or restaurants that parlay their good name and hopefully their good menu sensibility into profitable businesses. They succeed by plastering the walls with memorabilia from their playing days, hanging HDTVs above, behind, and around the bar, and by offering menus that reflect their own personal taste. They also make regular appearances at their joint, becoming part of the attraction themselves. Sometimes a retired player—or in some rare cases, a still active player—owns "his" establishment outright, while other times, his stake in the venture is shared with friends, investors, or other people who know more about running a restaurant than he does. In some cases, such a restaurant outlives the player around whose legend it was created, and thus continues bearing his name and images as a sort of shrine after he's no longer available to chat with dinner guests among its tables.

Player-affiliated baseball hangouts are popular because they fuse the passion fans have for their beloved stars with the enjoyment they derive from watching the game on a nice TV in a cozy place with fellow fans, good food, and a few frosty beverages. The goal of this chapter is to review the better player-named eateries and to ultimately pick the one that best epitomizes this special type of baseball haven.

To start, we should tip our caps to St. Louis, a city that really steps up to the (dinner) plate and delivers when it comes to player-affiliated restaurants. The Gateway City boasts not one, not two, but three hangouts built upon the local celebrity of former Cardinals. Less than two blocks from the new Busch Stadium, Al Hrabosky's Ballpark Saloon offers a high-energy environment for fun-loving party animals seeking a place to let their hair down and enjoy life a little bit on game days. Originally, Hrabosky (aka the Mad Hungarian) earned a place in baseball lore with his spitting, sputtering, stomping mound presence, Fu Manchu mustache, and blazing fastball. He spent eight seasons with the Cardinals during the 1970s, during which time he was one of the most dominant relievers of his time. Then he spent two years in Kansas City and three in Atlanta before taking a place behind the microphone to do color commentary on Cardinals telecasts in the 1980s. Now his saloon provides a rollicking good time to fans.

Former Red Bird Mike Shannon, meanwhile, has his own restaurant in St. Louis. Mike Shannon's Steaks and Seafood is pricier and more refined than Hrabosky's, but Shannon, who is also a Cardinals broadcaster, is a regular guy who likes to mingle with patrons. Inside, Shannon's décor features burnished mahogany, as opposed to the airport hangar motif familiar to fans of Mad Al's. Diners at Shannon's enjoy a finer collection of memorabilia too, including a photo tile that depicts Shannon in his prime during the 1960s, floor-to-ceiling columns of autographed baseballs, cases of autographed bats, photographs of favorite Cardinals, and more. As for Shannon, he visits after every home game to broadcast a postgame show from his favorite table.

The third and most welcoming Cardinals nest of all is the one named after Hall of Famer Ozzie Smith. Ozzie's Restaurant and Sports Bar fits right between Hrabosky's and Shannon's in the middle of the low- to high-culture scale. It boasts more than fifty TVs and a pub menu that serves St. Louis favorites like toasted raviolis. The walls are absolutely swathed in Cardinals gear and keepsakes. The most impressive display is the one that showcases all thirteen of Smith's Gold Glove Awards. And even on nights when the resident namesake isn't on hand to rub elbows with fans, patrons can still leave with an autograph if they visit the gift shop and shell out a few bucks for a ball signed by the Wizard.

Of course, there are other Hall of Famers besides Smith who have their own haunts "where everyone knows their name"—to borrow a phrase from the TV show *Cheers*, which was set, as you may recall, at a bar owned by fictitious former Red Sox pitcher Sam Malone. Their ranks include the late Mickey Mantle and Joe DiMaggio as well as the still-living Willie McCovey and Nolan Ryan.

Mantle was once a regular patron at upscale Mickey Mantle's Restaurant and Sports Bar in Manhattan. Today, the Central Park South establishment regularly hosts Yankees players, retirees, coaches, and front-office types among its dinner guests, as well as other celebrities and everyday fans who come to enjoy the good company, juicy steaks, and vast array of baseball relics on display courtesy of the in-house memorabilia store. Interestingly, at Mantle's most of the baseball keepsakes adorning the walls are for sale; hence, the turnover of merchandise guarantees that each visit will offer a unique viewing experience. One item that stays on the premises, though, is the original plaque that hung at Monument Park in honor of Mantle from 1969 until 1996, when a new monument was installed. A scaled down replica of Yankee Stadium is another favorite attrac-

Prior to his death in 1995, Mickey Mantle was a frequent dinner guest at the restaurant that still bears his name. PHOTO COURTESY OF MICKEY MANTLE'S

tion, as is the life-size cutout of Babe Ruth, autographed by more than 150 big leaguers. Another unaffiliated Mantle-inspired joint is located in Oklahoma City, where fans find in Mickey Mantle's Steakhouse a place to honor the Sooner State's favorite native son.

Joe DiMaggio's Italian Chophouse, which features classy black-and-white images of the Yankee Clipper, is located in San Francisco, near his boyhood home. It offers fine dining served with a side of Golden Age decadence. A more family-friendly option that is actually owned by the same company as the one that operates DiMaggio's is McCovey's Restaurant, found in the San Francisco suburb of Walnut Creek. McCovey's was designed to reflect the regal brick exterior of the Giants' home ballpark. Inside, the tables are cleverly arranged into infield and outfield sections within the boundaries of a miniature baseball diamond. The trophy that McCovey was presented in 1963 for winning the National League home run crown is prominently displayed, along with the trophy he snagged in 1969 for winning NL MVP. Other items of interest for fans to peruse include old jerseys, photographs, bats, balls, and autographed memorabilia paying tribute to other giants of the game such as Ted Williams, Hank Aaron, Cal Ripken Jr., Johnny

Bench, Tony Gwynn, Willie Stargell, Jackie Robinson, and Willie Mays. As for Mr. McCovey, he usually dines in the private McCovey Room, but finds time to chat with fans on his way in and out.

Nolan Ryan's Waterfront Steakhouse is located in Three Rivers, Texas, near Ryan's favorite fishing hole. Meanwhile, non-Hall-of-Famer Pete Rose can be frequently spotted sipping a drink and chatting about his playing days at the Pete Rose Ballpark Café in Boynton Beach, Florida. Rose's place caters to families, offering lots of TVs for the hard-core fans, arcade games for the kids, and the requisite memorabilia.

Although he is better remembered as a big league skipper, Bobby Valentine played ten seasons in the major leagues with the Dodgers, Angels, Padres, Mets, and Mariners. Since his playing career ended in 1980, he has owned a popular sports bar in his hometown of Stamford, Connecticut, and has even occasionally opened satellite locations in the big league cities where he's managed. Today, Valentine is overseas guiding a team in Japan's Nippon Professional Baseball League, so he doesn't play quite as large a role at Bobby Valentine's Sports Gallery Café as he once did, but he's still actively involved in business decisions. In Stamford, fans find uniquely named menu items like the Rollie (Chicken) Fingers and Gold Glove Quesadillas, as well as six specially topped hamburgers—one to represent the local flavors popular in each of the six big league towns where Valentine played or managed. Fans enjoy this fare amid plenty of baseball cards, autographed photos, and old uniforms.

Joints owned by a couple of current big leaguers deserve praise as well. Jeff Suppan and his wife opened Soup's Sports Grill in Woodland Hills, California, in 2008. The restaurant features authentic seats from the recently demolished Busch Stadium II; seating sections inside dugouts featuring railings, steps, and roofs; and chairs shaped like giant baseball mitts. The restaurant also has six different listening zones so that fans can listen to the audio broadcast of the baseball game that fits their rooting preference. Don't worry. The menu includes plenty more beside the popular Soup of the Day.

Yankees reliever Mariano Rivera is another pitcher who has recently ventured into the restaurant business. Mo's New York Grill opened in New Rochelle, New York, in 2006. Its main hallway and dining room are decorated with stunning photos of Rivera and his pinstriped teammates. The menu, meanwhile, offers nods to the house namesake, including Mo's No. 42—a whopping 42-ounce porterhouse steak. As for Rivera's personal favorite, it's the Panama Special—a marinated skirt steak served with mashed yucca and sweet plantains.

So which of these fan-pleasing places offers the most to fans? Well, that probably depends on which team you root for and which of these players you've most enjoyed watching through the years. The pick here, though, and this is coming from an unabashed Yankees Hater, is for the Mickey Mantle's in New York City. Perhaps more than any other player, Mantle personified a special time in the life of the game, a time before baseball became a big business, when we still looked at our diamond kings—rightly or wrongly—as true heroes. With its wealth of memorabilia and its A-list crowd, Mantle's does well to recapture and re-create this lost innocence and glory.

33

THE BEST BALLPARK SEAT IN THE MINORS

It Offers a One-of-a-Kind Baseball Experience

Within intimate settings where winning takes a backseat to the intrinsic pleasures of the game, the ballparks of baseball's bush leagues offer dozens of one-of-a-kind seating options that fans may today enjoy. This chapter is dedicated to exploring the quirkiest minor league vantage points of all, the ones that go above and beyond traditional notions of what a ballpark seat should be to present fans with uniquely delightful viewing experiences. We'll touch upon several seating jewels along the way to picking the one seat that stands, or perhaps we should say "sits," above the rest.

To start, let's offer three cheers for three minor league parks that house vast sections of special seats by virtue of crafty architects who were forward-thinking enough to look back in time for inspiration in their design. First, there's the home of the Southern League's Montgomery Biscuits—Montgomery Riverwalk Stadium—which utilizes a pre-existing railroad storage facility, or "train shed," as locals call it, as part of its seating bowl. The long thin building, which has stood in the city since 1898, today runs along the first base line of a ballpark the rest of which opened in 2004. The Train Shed's second level houses six seating boxes, from which fans may hover over the infield, while downstairs the structure's first level provides space for concessions and restrooms. The train shed succeeds in adding character to the ballpark while also providing a viewing locale that goes above—literally and figuratively—the normal concept of stadium seating.

Fifth Third Field in Toledo is another bush league park that made use of the pre-existing cityscape to create a special area for fans. Thanks to a wedge of seats suspended between two old warehouse buildings high above rightfield, the home of the International League's Mud Hens boasts 282 highly coveted Roost Seats. Appropriately, this third-story deck is reminiscent of the overhanging upper deck that once existed at Tiger Stadium in Detroit, a flourish surely appreciated by fans of this Tigers farm club. The first three rows of the Roost extend over the rightfield warning track, with half of them sitting in fair territory and half in foul territory. Thus, the Roost is the place to be for glove-toting youngsters hoping to get their mitts on a home-run ball . . . or a long foul.

In Visalia, California, the hometown Oaks took the opposite approach to enhancing the fan viewing experience. Instead of embracing an old building at an otherwise new facility, they added a modern facility to a California League park that dates back to 1946. And instead of placing their special seats high above the field, they placed them underground. Well, mostly underground. In 2007, while renovating Recreation Park, the Oaks added a "fan dugout" down the third base line. The dugout situates spectators in a recessed, enclosed seating area just like the dugouts the players use. This unusual stadium nuance offers the best chance fans will find of enjoying a player's-eye view of the game.

Fans find another California League yard with its own special way of cherishing the game, at Banner Island Ballpark in Stockton. There, a protrusion, or bubble, in the rightfield fence creates a peninsula of seats jutting into right-centerfield. These aren't just any seats either. The Back Porch, as it's known, houses fifty decadent wooden rocking chairs that sit in the shade of an unobtrusive roof. On rainy spring nights or hot summer days, this is the sweetest—and most comfortable—spot in the ballpark.

Clear across the continent, another sun-soaked minor league venue presents an equally alluring oasis in its own home-run territory. Bright House Field offers fans of the Florida State League's Clearwater Threshers a place to sip fruity frozen drinks and watch the game in style from its five rows of steeply rising Tiki Seats atop the leftfield fence. A straw-thatched roof, like the kind adorning the watering holes at

The Tiki Seats are set above the left field fence in Clearwater, Fla.

nearby Clearwater Beach, shades fans to complete the quintessentially Floridian picture. Like the much more altitudinous Green Monster Seats at Fenway Park in Boston, these pavilion seats consist of barstools along spacious counters where fans can set down their refreshments and scorecards. And unlike the impossibly hard-to-come-by seats in Boston, the Tiki Seats aren't just for high-rollers. They're available on a first-come, first-served basis as soon as the ballpark gates open.

A similar but less dramatic signature seating structure may be found in western Pennsylvania. At Blair County Ballpark, fans of the Eastern League's Altoona Curve enjoy a single row of Rail King Seats tucked in the leftfield corner. These special chairs on the party deck are as scarce as they are delightful: Only forty spectators per night have the privilege of plopping their fannies down onto their comfortable padding some 325 feet from home plate and 16 feet above the warning track.

Even more exclusive are the select few grandstand seats in Tacoma, Washington, that position fans side by side with a local baseball legend. At Cheney Stadium, home of the Pacific Coast League's Rainiers, those lucky individuals in Section K get to watch the game in the company of a life-size bronze statue of stadium namesake Ben Cheney. Cheney sits frozen in his seat with a bag of peanuts in his hand, peanut shells and a scorecard at his feet, and a joyous smile lighting his face. Mr. Cheney was a local lumber tycoon who contributed $100,000 to the stadium's construction back in 1960. Today, in this section just to the right of home plate, his likeness occupies the first seat of the first row. Further adding to the nostalgic effect, fans seated in this part of the stadium get to sit in the actual seats that once resided within the grandstands of legendary Seals Stadium, a Pacific Coast League ballpark that stood in San Francisco from 1931 until 1959.

As you can see, all of these seats certainly do their best to contribute to an utterly pleasant trip to the local field that's different from the adventures we fans enjoy anywhere else. And indeed, nearly every minor league park has one or two seating areas that are special in some way. Doing them all one better, though, and earning our praise as the very best seat in the minor leagues, is a special chair at Midway Stadium in St. Paul, Minnesota.

The home of the American Association's St. Paul Saints embodies the "fun is good" mantra espoused by Mike Veeck and fellow executives at the Goldklang Group, which owns several bush league teams. In St. Paul, bizarre promotional nights and hilarious giveaways are the norm, not the exception. But the most wonderful seat in the house exists in a quiet tranquil place where a fan, who may have previously thought he'd seen it all, may enjoy an introspective moment and connect with the game on a deeply personal level. In exchange for a small donation, patrons may enjoy half an inning of special handling in Midway Stadium's massage chair, which is located down the third-base line. Here, Sister Rosalind Gefre, an octogenarian nun who's been a fixture at Midway for years, works her magic. And as her healing hands deliver each patient into a dreamy trance, the sounds and smells of ballpark nirvana come into greater relief, fostering a new perspective from which fans may appreciate the game. The crack of the bat never sounded quite so profound as it does when relaxing with one's eyes closed in Sister Rosalind's chair, and the aroma of those simmering ballpark franks never smelled so mouthwateringly divine. And if you're sore from too much road-trip travel, well, the massage sure puts your achy muscles in a better place too. For putting our bodies at ease while opening our senses to the possibility of a world beyond what is most immediately before us, the massage chair at Midway Stadium is our pick for the best seat in the minor leagues.

[34]

THE BEST OLD-TIME BALLPARK IN THE MINORS

It Continues to Stand and to Stand the Test of Time

Today's minor league parks may be refreshingly affordable and intimate when viewed in light of their major league counterparts, but they also tend to homogenize the ballpark experience in certain ways. Despite offering some very inspired seating options—as detailed in the previous chapter—many of today's minor league stadiums were built over the past two decades and were designed by the same few architectural firms. They're comfortable. They're modern. Their seats provide cup holders for our massive souvenir sodas. Their concourses offer ample room to roam between innings. Their foul territory provides plenty of space for goofy promotions and between-inning festivities. They are fun, family-friendly places to spend a summer's night. But the game-day experience at most of today's bush league yards is rather uniform. There are exceptions though—holdovers from an earlier era in time when ballparks truly were places to experience a game, not just to watch one and have a few laughs. Although their numbers continue to dwindle, there are still several old-time ballparks opening their gates regularly today, and this chapter is dedicated to exploring the best of them. They are quaint and charming places. They are magical. But they also require that we look past some imperfections in the creature-comfort department. Their grandstands often house wooden seats that may be deemed too narrow by larger-bottomed fans or too hard by those without sufficient rear padding. Their roofs are often supported by steel pillars that block the sightlines of those fans sitting nearby. But they succeed in connecting us to the game and its historic roots in ways that later-generation parks simply do not. And for that, we should be grateful, even if we find ourselves rubbing a sore butt the next morning.

Before we review the most likely candidates for the distinction of best old-time park still in use in the minors today, let's establish some parameters. First, let's stipulate that our best golden oldie should date back to an original construction prior to 1950, and second, let's say that it should host at least one minor league game per season—to eliminate from consideration still-standing relics that have either fallen into disrepair or been converted to serve lower levels of competition (like Durham Athletic Park which has stood in Durham, North Carolina, since 1939 but which hosts only college and youth games today). And let's also remove from consideration venerable parks that have been so substantially renovated through the years that they've shed much, if not all, of their original appearance and charm (like John O'Donnell Stadium in Davenport, Iowa, which is now called Modern Woodmen Park and bears little interior resemblance to the facility that first opened in 1931).

Now then, let's begin our review of the best old-time parks. The first of three New York–Penn League facilities worthy of mention has thankfully been "restored" through the years, rather than more aggressively "renovated." Accordingly, it has retained much of its original essence, even if it has yielded some ground to the forces of modernity and innovation. Bowman Field originally opened its gates in Williamsport, Pennsylvania, in 1926. Today, more than eight decades later, it serves as the home of the short-season Crosscutters and looks much the same structurally as it did way back in the days of Prohibition. Outside, it projects the illusion of an ancient two-story castle, with a series of triangular arches and a conical ticket office that rises like a tower to greet visitors. Inside, a low-hanging roof creates a cozy atmosphere for those in the grandstand below. The demands of the current state of minor league affairs did, however, necessitate the replacement of the park's original light towers, which happened to have been the ones that had once upon a time lit up the sky at Polo Grounds. Those lights, in case you're wondering, had been contributed by Williamsport's big league affiliate at the time, the Mets, who donated them in 1964. Furthermore, plastic stadium seats have replaced the wooden ones that filled the stands for generations. But such is the price of progress. Want history? Bowman Field is the place where the Williamsport Grays—one of the New York–Penn League's charter members and later an Eastern League affiliate—played for four decades. It's where Oscar Charleston, who would later become a star of the Negro Leagues, hit the ballpark's very first home run during an exhibition game. It's where up-and-comers like Schoolboy Rowe and Jim Bunning proved their mettle while dreaming of the big leagues.

Today, when the Williamsport team sets its compass for the northeast and travels to play the rivals in Oneonta, New York, its players enter a ballpark that also captures the essence of a long-past time in the game's history. Damaschke Field has been renovated several times since opening in 1939, but it continues to provide a no-frills atmosphere that puts the focus squarely on baseball while leaving hardly any room for such distractions as mascots, flashing scoreboards, and blaring sound bites. This antique yard, which is fittingly situated just twenty-five miles from the National Baseball Hall of Fame, can barely be called a stadium. There is little in the way of a ballpark structure, just some freestanding shacks that provide concession and restroom spaces behind the seating banks. A picket fence separates the concourse behind the seats from the parking lot. The old-fashioned main seating area consists of a tiny covered grandstand behind home plate with just five rows of seats and then several rows of benches. Atop this structure protrudes a roof, topped itself by a minuscule press box. Modern seating has been added down the baselines. Visiting Damaschke Field, it's easy to pretend you're watching a New York–Penn League game in the 1960s or even a Can-Am League contest in the 1940s.

The third stadium from this short-season league that earns a place in our discussion can be found in Burlington, Vermont. There, Centennial Field serves as home to the University of Vermont Catamounts, as well as to the Vermont Lake Monsters. It opened as a college field in 1906, saw the construction of the concrete-and-steel grandstand that still stands today in 1922, and hosted its first minor league game in 1955. Today, from the parking lot outside or from the seats inside, it looks much the same as it did back in those earliest days of Green Mountain State baseball. The green wooden seats pack fannies close together in four sec-

Centennial Field is home to the Vermont Lake Monsters and UVM Catamounts.

tions around the infield, while steel pillars rise to support the wooden roof. Many seats are partially obstructed by the supports, but on a rainy night the roof, which covers the entire grandstand, comes in handy. On either side of the grandstand, highly unusual concrete bleachers provide excellent views to savvy cushion-toting fans. Meanwhile, beyond the fence in leftfield, a small scoreboard runs along the back of the adjacent football field's press box. Aside from the sound bites that play over the PA and the antics of Champ, the lake monster mascot, the environment is as pristine as it must have been back in the early part of the last century when out-of-town big leaguers like Smokey Joe Wood, Harry Hooper, Tris Speaker, Larry Gardner, and Ray Collins were trekking to Burlington to play exhibition games.

A ballpark that barely meets one of our initial requirements—the one that says parks must still see use as minor league facilities today—Birmingham's Rickwood Field hosts exactly one game per season. But it makes such a dramatic impression and carries such a rich history that it shouldn't be overlooked. Dating back to an initial construction in 1910, the stadium was designed to look like Forbes Field, which had just opened the year before in Pittsburgh. Today, Rickwood's main entry plaza showcases a pale green– and cream-colored ballpark face. Several square openings beckon fans inside to where they find a large grandstand covered by a long, low-hanging roof that extends all the way from rightfield home-run-territory to home plate and then back out past third base. The manually operated scoreboard in leftfield looks like it could be an original but is in fact a replica, added in the 1990s, during filming of the movie *Cobb*. A gazebo sits high atop the roof above home plate, providing a place for the public address announcer to watch

the game. The light banks thrust out off the roof on metal staging so that the bulbs hang over the field, creating an effect similar to the lights that once shined at old Tiger Stadium in Detroit. After serving as the home park of Birmingham's minor league teams for nearly eight decades—and also serving the Black Barons of the Negro Leagues— Rickwood Field passed the local baseball torch to a new park in 1988, when the Southern League's

Rickwood Field still hosts one Birmingham Barons game per season.
PHOTO BY CHRIS FREY, COURTESY OF THE FRIENDS OF RICKWOOD

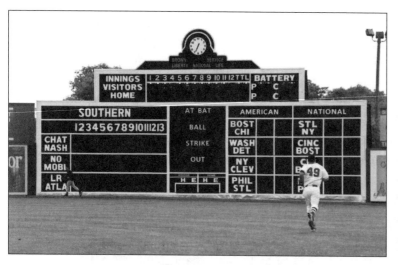

The replica scoreboard at Rickwood Field was added during the filming of the movie *Cobb*. PHOTO BY CHRIS FREY, COURTESY OF THE FRIENDS OF RICKWOOD

Barons moved to nearby Hoover. But a dedicated group of local citizens has seen to it that this National Historic Landmark not only be preserved but also remain active. Thus, Rickwood Field welcomes amateur players to its grounds all summer long, and once a year hosts the Rickwood Classic, which pits the Barons against one of their Southern League opponents on a night when both teams take the field in throwback jerseys.

If it hosted more than one minor league game per season, we would crown Rickwood Field the best old-time minor league park in the United States. Truly, it fosters a more thoroughly old-time atmosphere than any other facility in the minors, right down to such intricate details as the advertising signs that hang on the outfield fences replicating the ones that hung in the park in the 1920s. But as far as every-day venues go, we must tab McCoy Stadium in Pawtucket, Rhode Island, the best throwback park.

The home of the Pawtucket Red Sox, or PawSox, McCoy Stadium opened in 1942 after being built as part of President Franklin Delano Roosevelt's Works Projects Administration. Several renovations later there are new seating areas along the baselines and across the outfield, but the spacious original grandstand is still essentially intact. After passing through the turnstiles at ground level, fans climb a spiraling ramp that leads to a concourse halfway up the grandstand. All along this ramp are colorful murals of those members of the home team who went on to achieve big league success. Among the notables are Jim Rice, Mo Vaughn, and Marty Barrett, as well as dozens of others. On the concourse behind the seats, meanwhile, fans find a veritable museum's worth of artifacts detailing the stadium's rich history. The most prominent display tells the story of the longest game in American professional baseball history—a thirty-three-inning affair between the PawSox and Rochester Red Wings in 1981. The epic match took eight hours and twenty-five minutes to complete, spread over two different days. It featured twenty-five future big leaguers, including Cal Ripken Jr. and Wade Boggs, and encompassed 219 at-bats, 882 pitches, and 60 strikeouts. After fans learn more about this and other historic events in the park's life, they enter a grandstand that rises steeply around the infield. A wooden roof provides shelter, its wide steel supports obstructing views for many seat holders but adding oodles of character. And, interestingly, the first row of seats is more than ten feet above field level, which leaves room for the dugouts, which are not, in fact, dug out, but reside at field level. In addition to providing a delightfully quaint setting for a game, McCoy Stadium benefits from a PawSox stadium operations approach that keeps the distractions to a minimum so that fans may become entranced by the game. McCoy Stadium is our choice as the best old-time park in the minor leagues.

McCoy Stadium was built as part of FDR's Works Projects Administration.

[35]

THE BEST HISTORIC BALLPARK SITE IN THE MAJORS

Where the Ghosts of Yesteryear Play On

More than any other American sport, baseball tends to attract as fans sentimental types, prone to waxing poetic about the heroes of our youth, those idealized players whose daily triumphs and foibles taught us so much about life, even when we didn't realize we were learning anything more than how to keep score or trick our mothers into thinking we were asleep when we were actually listening to the West Coast game with a radio beneath our pillow. As we grow into adulthood, as much as we still enjoy the game, it is never quite so pure and pristine as it remains in our childhood memories. And for this reason we hold a special place in our collective baseball heart for the ballyards across the country where our oldest memories related to the Grand Old Game were formed.

In a few cities, of course, it is still possible to return to the very seats where we ate our first ballpark hot dog or scampered after batting-practice balls for the first time. But more often, the wrecking ball has spoken with stark finality and our childhood rooting grounds have been paved over. The hallowed field where Jackie Robinson broke baseball's accursed color barrier, Ebbets Field, is today the site of a dilapidated apartment complex. The field where Harmon Killebrew began bashing his path to Cooperstown is now the site of a shopping mall, as only a lone stadium chair, mounted high above the Mall of America, marks the spot where a monstrous Killebrew home run touched down at Metropolitan Stadium one day. Most shoppers go about their business without ever noticing the seat, and many would be shocked to learn there had once been a big league park where they buy their BVDs and bed linens.

But in some cities the game's hallowed grounds have left more permanent and visible impressions on the local landscape. At these places, where it's possible to reach out and touch history, we may step back in time, if only for a few moments, to reclaim our childhood awe. History remains alive at these places and speaks to us in ways that a museum exhibit simply cannot. It's pretty mind-blowing, for example, to visit the spot where more than a century ago Cy Young delivered the first pitch of the first World Series game ever played. A life-size statue of Young stands where the mound once rose at Boston's Huntington Avenue Grounds. And if you can look past the Northeastern University students shuttling back and forth from classes on the campus quad, you can dig in beside home plate, stare right back at Young, and almost believe you're Honus Wagner gearing up for your first at-bat of the 1903 "World Series of Baseball." It's impossible not to feel goose bumps as you confront baseball history at places like these. And in the end, that's what baseball's historic ballpark sites accomplish: They give us goose bumps. They make us feel like little kids again, even if we weren't born when the most memorable moments related to their history played out.

This chapter is dedicated to the handful of special cases where significant portions of classic major league parks still stand, and thus offer the chance to reconnect with the game and its history on just such goose-bump-invoking levels. For the purposes of this discussion, we'll set aside the two old-time parks—Fenway Park and Wrigley Field—that still see professional use today, and focus

on the best remnants of now extinct parks. Three historic yards in particular stand above the rest, easily trumping other would-be contenders like Tiger Stadium, of which only the dugout-to-dugout portion still stands as Detroit mulls whether to finish the job and demolish it completely or to convert the remainder into a museum, and Olympic Stadium, which still stands in Montreal, though it hardly qualifies as historic or, for that matter, as a ballpark.

A statue of Cy Young stands on the campus of Northeastern University, marking the spot where the first World Series game was played.

A treasured baseball relic may be found in the parking lot across the street from Turner Field in Atlanta. Here, fans can visit the spot where Hank Aaron staked his claim to what was then the most prestigious record in American sports. On a rainy night in April 1974, Aaron supplanted Babe Ruth atop baseball's all-time home run list, and in so doing consecrated Atlanta–Fulton County Stadium as sacred ground. Very little of the old ballpark remains, but there is just enough to send a shiver of truth down any fan's spine as he steps into a batter's box laid in brick, peers out at the portion of the leftfield fence that still rises 385 feet away—the fence over which Aaron's 715th long ball sailed. After taking a phantom swing, sojourners may trace Aaron's triumphant, if frenzied, steps around the bases. Remember those racist threats Aaron endured? Remember how he persevered? Imagine the relief he felt as he connected with that Al Downing fastball. Imagine the fear he must have initially felt when those two loonies ran onto the field to follow him around the sacks. It was a glorious moment for the game, but also one that brought to light how divided our nation still was. Today, baseball pilgrims seek this place in the Deep South, where a black man broke a record once deemed unbreakable, and where the tides of social change ebbed dramatically in the direction of progress.

When it comes to preserving a magical moment, this tiny piece of Atlanta–Fulton County Stadium—the Hank Aaron Wall—belongs at the top of the list, but the ballpark itself was a generic cookie-cutter that didn't host too many other games of historic significance. And little of the park remains. Ideally, we'd like to find a more intact old stadium as this chapter's most worthy nominee.

League Park is one such old-time stadium that still stands in greater proportion in Cleveland. In addition to the old diamond, which today serves as a youth field, the original brick ticket office and a sizable portion of the brick facade remain. The ballpark certainly welcomed plenty of legendary players to its grounds and hosted some important games, but it is not as revered as some of the storybook cathedrals of its era. Perhaps it should be. The first big league game at this site took place all the way back in 1891, when Cy Young pitched the Cleveland Spiders past the Cincinnati Reds. The concrete-and-steel retaining wall that stands today was erected in 1910 to create a setting where fans would witness Ruth's 500th long ball, Nap Lajoie's and Tris Speaker's 3,000th hits, and the end of Joe DiMaggio's 56-game hit streak. The knock on League Park for our purposes would be that the Indians were hardly an iconic franchise during the years it was in use. And the Tribe only used it sporadically during much of the team's history, as the construction of Municipal Stadium in 1934 began a stretch of thirteen years when the team bounced back and forth between the two sites, depending upon how large a crowd was expected. In short, if the Indians possessed the list of canonized games and names associated with franchises like the Yankees or Cardinals, League Park would be widely known and recognized as the best historic ballpark site and baseball pilgrims would be flocking to its brick facade. Despite coming up short in the historical significance department, it still belongs in the top three for offering fans a glimpse of what a classical era park was like.

An old field that does much more in terms of satisfying our historical significance criterion while making a similarly profound physical impression is Forbes Field in Pittsburgh. Before Forbes opened in 1909, ballparks were made of wood and tended to burn down with regularity. But Forbes was made of concrete and steel, and its success prompted builders across the country to make these materials staples of ballpark construction. As for magical moments, the Pirates capped their very first season at Forbes with a World Series victory party. Then, in 1921, the first big league radio broadcast emanated from Forbes. In 1935, Babe Ruth slugged the final three home runs of his career at Forbes as a member of the Boston Braves. In 1951, the classic movie *Angels in the Outfield* was shot at Forbes. And most memorably of all, the final game of the 1960 World Series took place on the Forbes lawn. On that October day, the Pirates bested the heavily favored Yankees—who wound up outscoring them 55 runs to 27 in the seven-game series—to win the championship. Pittsburgh prevailed in dramatic fashion when Bill Mazeroski broke a 9–9 tie in the bottom of the ninth inning with a home run off Ralph Terry. The ball sailed over the head of helpless Yankees leftfielder Yogi Berra— who was splitting catching duties by that point in his career with Elston Howard and Johnny Blanchard—and landed in the tree branches outside the park. The Pirates had won their first title in thirty-five years.

Today, Pirates fans still gather on October 13 each year at the appreciable portion of the Forbes Field outfield fence that still remains to listen to the radio broadcast of the famous homer. The remnants of the park are located on the campus of the University of Pittsburgh, and while the actual field and grandstand have long since been folded into eternity, most of the brick outfield wall still stands. The 12-foot-high edifice sprouts a healthy crop of ivy in the summer months, while still displaying the same distance-from-home plate markers—457 to the deepest part of right-center and 436 to center—as when the Pirates played their final game at Forbes in 1970. The flagpole, which stood in fair territory—as was often the case at old-time parks—is also still in place. And after the wall ends, a line of brick laid in the sidewalk traces the footprint of the old wall to a plaque in leftfield where Mazeroski's famous homer landed. Not far away, beneath glass in its original location, home plate lies in the lobby to the university's business school.

On any day of the year, a walk along the Forbes Field outfield fence is a special treat for anyone who appreciates the game's old parks, legends, and lore. And on the anniversary of the most dramatic home run in baseball history, such a stroll is magical, especially for today's Pirates fans yearning to remember better times in their team's history. Forbes Field is our pick for best historic ballpark site.

THE BEST BASEBALL
WORDPLAY

THE BEST PLAYER NICKNAME

His Was a Play on Words

Long before ESPN funnyman Chris Berman began rechristening practically every player in the baseball universe with a clever new name—who can forget such classics as Frank Tanana "Daiquiri," Todd "Mercedes" Benzinger, and Jack "the Whiffer" Clark?—nicknames were already ingrained in baseball culture. Back before the dawn of the twentieth century, in fact, the game spawned a number of creative player tags that remain recognizable today. Denton True Young, known as Cy, short for Cyclone, was renamed for the ferocity of his windup. Johannes Peter Wagner went by a couple of pseudonyms that conspired to wipe his given name clean out of the record books. When he was a child his mother called him Hans, but by the time he reached the big leagues he was Honus. Later, his fans called him the Flying Dutchman in tribute to his German heritage and acrobatic playing style. Likewise, the name Adrian Constantine Anson probably doesn't ring a bell to many fans, but Cap Anson sure does. Cap was short for captain, the role Anson proudly filled for his Chicago Nationals teams.

Throughout the generations since, the game has included a legion of players identifiable by names other than the ones their moms and dads scribbled on their birth certificates. Sometimes these nicknames refer to their style of play—as in Charlie Hustle (Pete Rose)—and other times to their personality or physical appearance—as in Spaceman (Bill Lee) or the Big Unit (Randy Johnson). Still other baseball nicknames refer to players' prowess afield—as in "Hammering Hank" Aaron. Sometimes, though, a nickname celebrates a player's nonbaseball-related abilities—as in "Oil Can" Boyd, who once drank so many cans of beer, or oil as his buddies in Mississippi called their brew, that he would never again be known as Dennis.

There have been hundreds of colorful baseball pseudonyms through the years, and needless to say, narrowing down such a lengthy roster into a short list of the cleverest will involve a fair amount of subjectivity. But let's at least set the parameter that our winner should have a name that refers in some way to his experiences within the game, and let's also say that the best baseball nickname of all-time should be easily recognizable to even the most casual of fans.

At the outset, let's pay tribute to some of the better nicknames in the style-of-play classification. Like Charlie Hustle, Lenny Dykstra was known as a gritty warrior, a player who was tough as nails; hence his nickname Nails. Al Hrabosky, on the other hand, was known for stomping histrionically around the mound, which led to his rap as the Mad Hungarian. Harry Walker had a typical demeanor but took forever to get into the darned batter's box due to an obsessive-compulsive habit of tugging on his cap between pitches, a routine that eventually earned him the title Harry the Hat. It took even longer for Mike Hargrove to finish his between-pitch adjustments, which included checking his helmet, batting gloves, and sleeves, and earned him the not-so-flattering reputation as the Human Rain Delay.

Don Mattingly played the game the right way, earning his stripes as Donnie Baseball. Ernie Banks was the face of Chicago's North Siders for so long that he came to be known as Mr. Cub. Leo Durocher was always yapping, hence his nickname Leo the Lip. Orioles third baseman Brooks Robinson devoured nearly every ball hit his way to earn the title the Human Vacuum Cleaner. On the other hand, Dick Stuart couldn't field a lick at first base for the Red Sox—he amazingly made 29 errors in 1963 and 24 more the next year—on the way to becoming Dr. Strange-glove, which played off the title character of the popular movie *Dr Strangelove*. The slick-fielding Ozzie Smith took his nickname from cinema too, becoming the Wizard of Oz, or simply the Wizard for his brilliance at shortstop. Proving that managers can get dramatic nicknames too, Sparky Anderson was known as Captain Hook, as a nod to the *Peter Pan* villain, because he yanked pitchers off the mound so frequently. As for the most complimentary nickname in this grouping, it has to be Mr. October, bequeathed on Reggie Jackson after he hit three home runs on successive swings in Game Six of the 1977 World Series.

As for the better nicknames that described players' personalities, these would include goofy brothers Dizzy and Daffy Dean, the jovial Albert "Happy" Chandler, the classy "Gentleman Jim" Lonborg, the popular and superfriendly "Mayor" Sean Casey, and the "Georgia Peach" Ty Cobb, whose name may have been intended as ironic, as he was anything but cordial to fellow players, even if he came from the Peachtree State.

Players labeled according to how they filled out a uniform include hefty Boomers George Scott and David Wells, diminutive stars "Pee Wee" Reese and "Wee Willie" Keeler, and larger than life behemoths like Frank "the Big Hurt" Thomas, "Big

Ty Cobb was known as "The Georgia Peach," even though his demeanor was far from peachy.
COURTESY OF THE LIBRARY OF CONGRESS

Dan" Brouthers, Don "Big D" Drysdale, David "Big Papi" Ortiz, and Japanese giant Hideki "Godzilla" Matsui. Then there are the Hall of Fame brothers known as Big Poison and Little Poison, Paul and Lloyd Waner. Paul was in fact shorter than his "little" brother, but three years older.

Mordecai "Three Finger" Brown lost two digits off his pitching hand in a farming accident when he was a child. Antonio "El Pulpo" Alfonseca was born with six fingers on both hands, which still doesn't explain why his nickname translates to "the Octopus," an animal with eight appendages. Perhaps the person who gave El Pulpo his nickname couldn't count? Tris "the Gray Eagle" Speaker, meanwhile, saw his brown hair turn prematurely gray when he was still in his early thirties, but

The Seventh Inning Stretch

remained a speedy ball hawk in centerfield. These characteristics-based names are all interesting, but the best of the class in our opinion is Godzilla, which Matsui earned with exceptionally long home runs in Japan and brought with him to New York. For its epic nature, appropriate tie to Japanese culture, and international appeal, it stands alone.

Nicknames that pay tribute to baseball prowess are common, particularly ones that acknowledge speedy throwers and long hitters. Some of the best fastballs in history were thrown by Bob "Rapid Robert" Feller, the "Nolan Ryan Express," Roger "the Rocket" Clemens, Walter "the Big Train" Johnson, and "Pud" Galvin, whose heater was so fast it turned hitters' knees into pudding, or so the legend went. Frank "Home Run" Baker, has the best name a hitter could ask for, even if he "only" hit 96 dingers during baseball's dead-ball era. "Hammering Hank" Aaron, who hit 755 long balls, joins Baker, along with Harmon "Killer" Killebrew, "Joltin' Joe" DiMaggio, and Jimmie "The Beast" Foxx, in the homering-hero-handle gang.

Sometimes a player is so dominant that he sheds his given name entirely, as Steve Carlton became known simply as Lefty and Mickey Mantle as the Mick. Alliterative names like Ted "the Splendid Splinter" Williams and Ron "Louisiana Lightning" Guidry, which roll off the tongue while also saying something profound about a player's ability, are our favorites in this baseball prowess category.

As for the nicknames that emanated from baseball anecdotes or myths, George Herman Ruth's nickname, the Babe, and the shoeless part of "Shoeless Joe" Jackson's name are classic examples. Ruth became the Babe when he arrived at his first minor league camp with the Baltimore Orioles in 1914 as the prodigy of team owner Jack Dunn who had signed him out of a Baltimore reform school. The Orioles veterans called him Dunn's Baby and the name stuck. Jackson was playing semipro ball at a dusty field in Greenville, South Carolina, when he decided his cleats were causing his feet to blister, so he took them off, and stepped back into the batter's box in his stockings. He promptly banged out a hit, or so the story goes, and the legend of a country kid named Shoeless Joe came to life. Jackson carried the name like a bad case of foot fungus for the rest of his life with the name coming to carry particular resonance—because it recalls the image of a down-on-his-luck hero—after Jackson's banishment from baseball.

The story of how Jim "Catfish" Hunter came by his colorful nickname isn't all that colorful after all. Oakland A's owner Charlie Finley simply decided that "Jim" was too boring and told Hunter he planned to list him as Catfish in the team's forthcoming media guide. Harry "Suitcase" Simpson had a name that made more sense, since he was always packing up and leaving town. Simpson played for seventeen different teams in eleven years in the Negro Leagues and major leagues.

So what's the best baseball nickname ever? This writer's pick is Mr. October, because it so aptly conveys a player's dominance on the game's grandest stage and because it is so universally known. There are dozens of cleverly and creatively named candidates in this realm of baseball culture though, so feel free to disagree with the player-turned-writer once known as Stats (owing to a starring role spent beside the coach on the bench, keeping the scorebook in Senior Babe Ruth League "play").

[37]

THE BEST MAJOR LEAGUE TEAM NAME

Is a Royal a Royal by Any Other Name?

Have you ever found yourself wondering, "So, what exactly is a Dodger, anyway?" Or have you noticed, perhaps, that Billy Beane's moneyballing Oakland Athletics are, in fact, anything but athletic, seeing as Beane perennially fills out his roster with slugging DH types? Or how about those Pittsburgh Pirates: Ever wished you had stayed awake that day back in eighth-grade history class when your teacher talked about those savage pillaging pirates who wrought havoc up and down the Allegheny? Or was the campaign waged along the banks of the Monongahela? You'll never know. Even two bastions of the game like the Red Sox and White Sox have names to make fans scratch their heads, or at least their athlete's foot. So their players wore red and white socks back in the early days of the American League . . . and they chose to build their franchise identities around that?

If you have wrestled with conundrums such as these, rest assured you're not alone. In every fan's coming of baseball age there is that one sleepless night when we lie awake, running all the AL and NL team monikers through our heads and asking why, why, why? By dawn we accept that we're a bit obtuse, that our grasp of geography and U.S. history is lacking, or that, golly gee, there really are forces at work in the universe too complicated for us to understand. After all, tigers in Detroit, ha! And yet something seems just right about the Detroit Tigers, doesn't it? So we must accept that the baseball gods had their reasons and that the names our teams go by made perfect sense once upon a time. Some tigers escaped from a circus, maybe, and staggered into Navin Field, or maybe there really were tigers prowling the shores of Lake Michigan when Ty Cobb was sliding spikes up into first base . . . you know, before all the wild cats were herded off to Africa and India.

Along the way to deciding which big league team has the most fitting, and therefore best, nickname, in this chapter we will at long last answer some of your burning baseball naming questions. Because, in fact, you see, there never were actual tigers in Detroit or Pirates in Pittsburgh. At least not literally. As for the Dodgers nickname, however vexing it may be today, it did make some sense back in the time when it was first introduced. It was bequeathed upon the Brooklyn nine by local fans to supplant such lackluster monikers as the Bridegrooms, after several players who were married in the 1880s; the Robins, after popular manager Wilbert Robinson; and the Superbas, after a superb bunch of players. The name that stuck began as the Trolley Dodgers, before being shortened to Dodgers. It first appeared around the turn of the century when Brooklyn fans began referring to themselves as "trolley dodgers," owing to the difficulty they had in traversing the busy city streets around their downtown ballpark. Think of the old Atari game Frogger, where the frog is trying to cross five lanes of racecars and Mack trucks to hop on a mate and eat a fly, only the Brooklyn fans were trying to dodge trolleys

Before becoming the "Dodgers," the Brooklyn team was named the "Robins," after affable manager Wilbert Robinson. COURTESY OF THE LIBRARY OF CONGRESS

to hop in and sit on a stadium bench, watch nine innings, and eat a few hot dogs. Eventually, the franchise adopted the identity of its fans. And so, because the city of Brooklyn's early trolley system was one of the most sophisticated in the nation, while its sidewalks and crosswalks were too narrow, the NL club that has played in Los Angeles for the past half century is known as the Dodgers.

The Athletics name dates back even earlier, to an 1860s semipro team that went by the Athletic Club of Philadelphia. Although the since-abbreviated handle has stood the test of time and endured two franchise relocations, to contemporary fans it may ring a bit self-congratulatory, as if the team is trying to compliment itself on being so swift and agile. Maybe that's why the Oakland club more commonly refers to itself as the A's. Two other names that come off as boastful are the Royals—anyone who's been to Kansas City knows there are no castles there, and the Giants—insert your own Barry Bonds rapidly expanding hat size joke here.

The White Sox and Red Sox may be two of the AL's founding franchises, but neither club socked the ball out of the park when it came to picking a name. According to most historic reference books, hosiery was no more admired and celebrated by sports junkies in the early 1900s than it is today. To name a team after stylish stockings is just silly. This is baseball we're talking about, after all, not kickball or ballet.

The Tigers too were also named at the turn of the last century, deriving their handle from a local militia, formally known as the Detroit Light Guard, informally as the Tigers. The unit, which was regaled for its ferocity, served with distinction in the Civil War and Spanish-American War. This isn't a bad nickname. Tigers are ferocious, which is to be desired in a ball club, and there is a local connection that reflects the city's heritage. But the Tigers are just one of several teams who borrow their names from animals, and the rest are somewhat trite. Birds are especially popular, with brightly colored ones like orioles, blue jays, and cardinals appealing to the inner-birdwatcher within every beer-bellied baseball fan, while diamondback snakes, devil rays, marlins, and bear cubs also make their presences felt in the baseball kingdom. At least there is a type of bird specifically called the *Baltimore* Oriole, whereas blue jays and cardinals aren't especially unique to the cities that claim them, so it's hard to see the point in them. As for the Cubs, maybe Yogi gave them a bad rap, but bears seem like lazy beasts to which to hitch a team's proverbial wagon, and these aren't even adult bears we're talking about, these are cute, little, helpless cuddling cubs like the ones on that baby animals calendar you get your Aunt Eloise for Christmas every year. As for diamondbacks, most people find snakes repulsive and creepy, so why name a team after them, unless you're trying to increase your fan representation among biker gangs? And for the two Sunshine State teams named after fish, they have good names for swim teams, not baseball.

Names that make geographic sense work the best, which explains why the Pittsburgh Pirates name seems discordant, even if it possesses one of the more interesting backstories. It arose out of a dispute between the Athletics and Pittsburgh Nationals in the early 1890s. Following the dissolution of the Players

League, the players who had abandoned their NL and American Association teams to play for the start-up circuit were returned to their original teams, provided those teams had previously placed them on a reserved list; otherwise they became free agents. Because the Philadelphia club had neglected to reserve the rights to second baseman Lou Bierbauer, Pittsburgh inked him to a contract, which incensed Athletics fans to the point where they labeled their state rivals—you guessed it—Pirates.

Other names that play off geographic or regional identity include the Los Angeles Angels of Anaheim and Philadelphia Phillies—neither of which does much more than reiterate the home team's locale. Also belonging to this category are the slightly more creative Minnesota Twins, for the Twin Cities of St. Paul and Minneapolis, and the New York Mets, for the booming Metropolis that is Queens. The Rockies do well to celebrate a national treasure in their midst. The Washington Nationals at least ensure that the Senators won't strike out for a third time. The Braves and Indians honor or debase, depending upon your viewpoint, their cities' local Native American populations. The Padres name is less controversial, paying tribute to the fathers of the city's Spanish missions. The Yankees would have a pretty good nickname if only 90 percent of New Englanders didn't consider themselves old-fashioned Yankees (defined by one *Webster's* entry as "a native or inhabitant of New England") while still hating the team that goes by the name in New York.

Teams that offer a nod to the local fans who support them score points in our book. They include the salty seafaring Mariners of Seattle, the innovative Astros, whose rooters blazed a trail to the cosmos, and the gunslinging Rangers, whose fanatics will certainly shoot first and ask questions later if Tom Hicks ever tries to bring back Chan Ho Park for a second tour of duty. However clever these entries are, the facts remain that knowing one's way around a captain's galley, designing a spaceship, and firing a six-shooter have little to do with hardball. And that's why the Milwaukee Brewers are our choice as the most aptly named big league squad.

Milwaukee is known for its many breweries, and its citizens are known for their love of beer, so the name makes sense in a geographic sense. But more than that, baseball and beer go together. Whether you're a blue-collared bratwurst-loving fan from the Midwest, or a suave Manhattanite who prefers the ballpark knish of the Big Apple to any other ballpark treat, chances are you wash down your game-day munchies with a cold cup of suds. Having a frosty plastic cup of brew at the ball game is as much a tradition as singing "Take Me Out to the Ball Game" during the seventh-inning stretch or booing the opposing team's cleanup hitter. It just comes naturally to us.

Although Bud Selig deserves some credit for naming his prospective team the Milwaukee Brewers back in the late 1960s, he doesn't deserve all the credit. In fact, the very same name belonged to one of the AL's charter members, the 1901 Milwaukee Brewers, who finished in eighth place out of eight teams that inaugural year with a 48-89 record and then promptly moved to St. Louis to become the Browns. The name outlived the major league's desertion, though, as it continued to belong to Milwaukee's professional team, the American Association Brewers, from 1902 through 1952. Since being reborn at the big league level, the Brewers have embodied the nickname well, often starring big-bellied sluggers like the ones who powered the 1982 AL Championship team known as Harvey's Wallbangers, and more recently fun-loving heavy-hitter Prince Fielder. For making regional sense, baseball sense, and historic sense, the Brewers are the pick.

[38]

THE BEST MINOR LEAGUE TEAM NAME

Manatees, T-Bones, and Biscuits, Oh My!

Unlike their prim and proper cousins in the bigs, the more than 240 teams comprising baseball's affiliated and unaffiliated minor leagues may be as goofy and gimmicky as they desire when it comes to marketing their product. After all, the successful minor league business model doesn't revolve so much around winning and losing but rather on engaging and entertaining fans of all age and interest levels. To keep the turnstiles turning and concession coffers coughing, the first and arguably most important order of business each team faces when it comes to chiseling out its place in the hearts and minds of local fans concerns choosing just the right name for itself.

A few decades ago, the typical minor league franchise was still sporting the moniker of whichever big league club was currently providing its players. This was less than ideal for the bushers, though, seeing as player-development relationships changed frequently—as they still do—which resulted in minor leagues full of teams with regularly changing names. From a marketing standpoint, this dynamic positioned minor league teams as outposts of faraway cities rather than stalwarts of their local communities. The frequent changes also created merchandizing headaches, since teams found themselves often discarding boxes of unsold T-shirts and caps whenever their name and logo changed.

Fortunately, recent decades have ushered in minor league owners eager to fashion their own team names and to build their own franchise identities, without the help of their parent organizations. Often newly created teams, as well as old ones looking to spiff up their image, have turned to area fans for inspiration in this regard, picking a winning nickname from entries submitted in fan balloting. Other teams have turned to professional marketing companies to identify the one- or two-word handle that might best stick with consumers, generate hat sales, and translate into a colorful mascot.

In this chapter, we seek to laud the minor league team with the most apropos, creative, and expressive nickname of all. As we review the better candidates, we'll award points for teams with a sense of humor, tip our caps to those whose names succeed on a local level, and compliment especially those teams whose names allow for a baseball-specific level of interpretation.

First, let's run down some of the goofier minor league team names, starting with a quartet of entries that might be subcategorized into the Edible Division. Biscuits are a staple of southern cuisine, and by embracing them the Montgomery Biscuits certainly cooked up a name that smells good in the local market. Like the biscuit itself, the name is light and a bit flaky. Other than the biscuits they sell at the concession stands of Montgomery Riverwalk Stadium, however, the connection between biscuits and baseball is marginal.

The Modesto Nuts' name embraces their region's agricultural tradition. COURTESY OF THE MODESTO NUTS

Likewise, the Kansas City T-Bones score points for good humor and regional marketing sizzle, but come up short in the makes-good-baseball-sense department. The same can be said of the Cedar Rapids Kernels who play in the heart of corn country, and wisely make the corncob that appears in their logo into a sort of cob/baseball bat hybrid. Another team, the Modesto Nuts, deserves praise for satisfying all three better-team-name criteria, since fresh roasted nuts are a traditional ballpark favorite, Modesto is a leading producer of almonds and walnuts, and the name itself is slightly nutty.

Outside the realm of edibility, other funny and local, but not quite baseball-related names include the Albuquerque Isotopes, who pay tribute to New Mexico's

The Cedar Rapids Kernels offer a corny logo that's a big hit with locals. COURTESY OF THE CEDAR RAPIDS KERNELS

history of nuclear innovation; the Las Vegas 51s, whose alien mascot offers a tip of his cap to the mysterious Area 51, to which so many UFO conspiracy theories have been traced; the Augusta Green Jackets, whose name references the famous green blazer awarded to the winner of golf's first major tournament each season, which takes place a couple of miles from Lake Olmstead Stadium; and the Lansing Lugnuts, whose name honors an Oldsmobile factory that stood in the Michigan city for generations.

Funny or miscast animals constitute another wacky subclassification of bush league taxonomy. This group includes the Brevard County Manatees, Greensboro Grasshoppers, and Savannah Sand Gnats.

Interesting names that reference points or citizens of local pride include the Kannapolis Intimidators, whose moniker matches the one that once belonged to NASCAR star Dale Earnhardt, who hailed from Kannapolis and held an ownership stake in his hometown team at the time of his death; the Round Rock Express, who are owned in part by Nolan Ryan, who once baffled hitters with a fastball nicknamed the "Nolan Ryan Express"; the Frederick Keys, whose ballpark sits across the street from the cemetery where Francis Scott Key—the man who wrote the "Star Spangled Banner"—is buried; the Inland Empire 66ers, who play just a few blocks from where famous Route 66 passes through San Bernardino; and the Chattanooga Lookouts, whose fans yell "Heads-up!" when foul balls enter the stands at a ballpark that sits in the shadow of Lookout Mountain.

While the above entries all speak volumes for the creativity and vivid imagination of minor league team owners, the finalists in this baseball argument do them one better by offering clearer connections to not just their communities but to baseball itself. The Louisville Bats pay tribute to the Hillerich and Bradsby Company, which has been lathing planks of ash and maple into Louisville Sluggers in their city since the 1880s. You won't find a team name with a more overt baseball connotation than this one, but the Louisville club loses points in the originality department, seeing as other cities have used Bats as a team nickname before—the Greensboro Bats of the 1990s come immediately to mind. Louisville Sluggers might have been an even better name for this team, since it would have provided the same local tie while also projecting the Louisville club as a hard-hitting bunch, but perhaps the local bat manufacturer would have objected.

The Clinton LumberKings succeed in announcing to the baseball world that their boys can flat-out hit. Their name also pays tribute to Clinton, Iowa's, proud lumbering history, and, indeed, local mascot Louie the LumberKing can swing an armful of two-by-fours as swiftly as some minor leaguers swing a baseball bat. Succeeding for similar reasons, the Tulsa Drillers simultaneously offer a wink to their city's oiling history, and a nod to terrified Texas League pitchers whom they drill into submission at hitter-friendly Drillers Stadium.

Another cleverly named team to consider is the Altoona Curve. On a level apparent even to those fans who have never visited Altoona, Pennsylvania, the Curve name honors one of baseball's most common pitch types. To ballpark visitors, the name makes even more sense, since an amusement park lies immediately beyond the rightfield fence at Blaire County Ballpark, and its famous wooden roller coaster shows off plenty of dips and curves. What's more, locals who take pride in Altoona's cultural and commercial history are well aware of the set of famously U-shaped railroad tracks just east of downtown—a stretch known as the Horseshoe Curve.

Finally, our pick for the best minor league team name goes to a club that hitches its wagon most ambitiously to a seminal moment in baseball mythology, if not baseball history: the Auburn Doubledays. For

The Auburn Doubledays are named after Abner Doubleday, who was once considered "the father of baseball." COURTESY OF THE LIBRARY OF CONGRESS

years, upstate New York was said to be the game's birthplace, owing to the widely held belief that Civil War general Abner Doubleday invented the sport. Doubleday was credited with devising baseball's rules and designing its diamond and spreading its joy wherever he traveled in the 1830s. One hundred years later, in 1939, baseball gave further credence to the myth by building the National Baseball Hall of Fame in Cooperstown, just a few blocks from the pasture where Doubleday was said to have overseen the very first game.

Later historians, however, pointed to a man named Alexander Cartwright as the game's true father, and then, later still, others concluded that the sport had no single father but evolved instead thanks to the many men and women who contributed to its development throughout the 1800s. Even if the Doubleday Myth is just that, a myth, the Auburn Doubledays deserve credit for the witty tribute they pay to their region's reputation as baseball's Mecca. The substitution of Auburn for Abner is a clever bit of wordplay. And while it's true that Auburn is 120 miles from Cooperstown, it's also true that Mr. Doubleday spent part of his childhood living in the town, so the name does make geographic and historic sense.

[39]

THE BEST BASEBALL SLANG

A Language of Its Own

As any seamhead can attest, baseball culture has a vernacular that is as charming to diehards as it is mystifying to the pink hats and luxury box Larrys who wouldn't sit in a Uecker Seat if you paid them and couldn't distinguish between a big fly and big league fly ball off the bat. Since the days of the dead ball, back before radio's rookie season when beat writers would spin a yarn to re-create games in the green fields of each fan's mind, colorful terms and witticisms have defined the national pastime. And like the *Oxford English Dictionary*, the lexicon we use to describe the players and plays that fill our dog days with delight is not a static compendium, but one that continues to develop, like a prospect with lots of upside.

This chapter is meant as a short ode to baseball slang. Hopefully it will tickle your funny bone or at least your rotator cuff, whether you're a stat head, purist, or lifer. Along the way, we'll try to demystify some of the more familiar baseball terms, so that the newbies and baseball widows out there in reader land will no longer feel like hardball half-wits. We'll stop short of picking one single baseball saying as the best, but offer instead an entire essay full of them. So here goes . . .

After the five-o'clock hitters take their best cuts in BP and the skippers post their starting nines, the home team's starter—be he a crafty portsider or flame-throwing horse, climbs the hill and toes the rubber. If he's got some good cheese, then the hitters had better choke up and remind themselves not to climb the ladder. On the other hand, if his out-pitch is a hammer—also known as the deuce or Old Uncle Charlie—then hitters had best remember not to step in the bucket. Either way, they'll be waiting for a meatball in the wheelhouse or some salad over the dish, so they can swing from the heels and tattoo it. As for the pitcher, he'll be hoping to paint the corners like a Picasso—you know, a control artist—and if he's a head-hunter, he'll mix in some chin music to make sure the batter doesn't dig in.

Most top of the order hitters are speedsters, of course, guys with good wheels who know how to pick 'em up and put 'em down. More often than not these guys are banjo hitters though, whose bats make more of a twang than a crack. These Punch and Judy hitters can be tough outs though, even if they can barely hit their way out of a wet paper bag. They set the table with dying quails and Texas Leaguers—like the bloopers Texas League players once hit when ball hawks had to play deep to prevent frozen ropes from shooting up the gaps of sunburned Lone Star State lawns.

If the pitcher is blowing gas and putting mustard on his heater, there will be plenty of bleeders that leave hitters picking splinters from their hands. The outfielders will still see their share of rainmakers and probably a few cans of corn—balls that drop straight down from the heavens like the cans grocers used to knock off high shelves with poles for shoppers. If a pitcher is throwing lollipops, on the other hand, instead of aspirin tablets, then hitters in the Show will tee off on him and hit everything on the screws, according to a term that originally referred to solid contact between a golf ball and one of those old-fashioned wooden drivers that had a contact plate screwed onto its face. When the pitcher surrenders a screamer, he can only hope an outfielder will come up with a snow cone or make a circus catch. Or maybe one of his infielders will flash some leather and say, "Look what I found." Sometimes an outfielder will track down a blooper too, by getting a good bead on it, hopping on his horse, and making a shoestring catch. After the inning, the hot dog will brag to teammates that he had it all the way.

A filthy pitcher with stuff that falls off the table will induce hitters to go fishing. They'll hit worm burners and daisy cutters, and only once in a while will a seeing-eye single sneak through the box or through the hole. There may be a Baltimore Chop—like the kind John McGraw's Orioles used to pound into the hard clay around home plate at their ballpark in the 1890s—mixed in too. These balls will bounce so high that infielders have to eat them or put them in their back pocket. But rest assured if there's a pitcher on the mound, not a chucker, and his stuff truly is nasty, he'll induce a nubber, squibber, or comebacker so his team can turn two. That is, as long as an infielder doesn't have a tin glove, or stone fingers, in which case he'll boot the twin killing, unless he gets a room-service hop.

Because you never know when a fielder is going to throw a parachute to first base that allows a hitter to beat one out, it's always best to have a flamethrower on the mound, a guy who gets punch-outs and racks up K's whether he's facing a contact hitter or mistake hitter. He'll be more apt to put goose eggs on the board and whitewash the opponent than one of his noodle-armed stablemates who always lets the opposition put crooked numbers on the board. Nonetheless, by the middle innings the man on the slab will probably find himself in a jam, and then, after a powwow with his pitching coach and batterymate, he'll give a dead-red hitter the four-fingered salute, especially if there's a base open. This strategy will almost certainly pay off if the on-deck hitter is on the interstate, or hitting just a buck and change, or below the Mendoza Line, as they say, but once the bases are juiced there won't be any room at the inn, so he'll have to come in with it. With all those ducks on the pond, the hitter will be thinking ribbies, but he'll know better than to press, because that's the most certain way to get stuck in the yard. If the pitcher hits his spots, he may dodge a bullet. If he throws a fat one, he may wake up the next morning with whiplash.

Whether the game's a nail-biter or a slugfest, unless the pitcher's a workhorse with a rubber arm, chances are by the eighth inning his skipper will dial 911 and send him to the showers. If the game's a blowout, a mop-up man will be first out of the chute. If it's a pitcher's duel, a lefty specialist or shortman will precede the fireman. Unless it goes extras, the long men in the pen will know their services aren't needed and start surveying the crowd for Baseball Annies.

A few minutes after the closer shuts the door, the players will tell the scribes that they just have to take it one day at a time, and that the season's a marathon, not a sprint. They'll say they have to stay within themselves. In the winning locker room, the star hitter will shrug his shoulders and say he's just in the zone. The winning pitcher will credit his catcher for calling a good game. In the losing clubhouse, a pitcher who got lit up will lament that he didn't have his good stuff. And a hitter will chastise himself for not working the count. Hitters who took the collar will say they need to spend time in the cage. And hitters who are really slumping, like the one who earned a Golden Sombrero by whiffing four times, will know their struggles are beyond that kind of help. Instead, they'll head off in search of a slump buster, a Baseball Annie who may not be easy on the eyes but practically guarantees the player will get lucky sometime soon.

[40]

THE BEST BASEBALL QUIPS AND QUOTATIONS

They Speak Volumes about the Grand Old Game

Through the years baseball has inspired hundreds upon hundreds of people to offer their own two cents of wisdom concerning the sport's capacity to mesmerize us, why it occupies such an important place in our national psyche, and why it truly is the greatest game ever invented. From pundits to fans, players to team owners, and even diehard Red Sox fans to diehard Yankee fans, we Americans have never been hesitant to offer our thoughts about what makes baseball wonderful. Often, these quips might well be interpreted as commentaries on more than just the game, but on a wider sphere of human interactions as well. The list of quotations to follow includes some of the most insightful, humorous, and philosophical baseball musings uttered to date. Thus, we'll stop short in this chapter of picking only one best-ever baseball quote and declare all the entries below winners. Enjoy!

"Baseball, it is said, is only a game. True. And the Grand Canyon is only a hole in Arizona. Not all holes, or games, are created equal."

—GEORGE WILL

"Whoever wants to know the heart and mind of America had better learn baseball."

—JACQUES BARZUN

"Man may penetrate the outer reaches of the universe, he may solve the very secret of eternity itself, but for me, the ultimate human experience is to witness the flawless execution of a hit-and-run."

—BRANCH RICKEY

"Baseball is almost the only orderly thing in a very unorderly world. If you get three strikes, even the best lawyer in the world can't get you off."

—BILL VEECK

"Baseball is a harbor, a seclusion from failure that really matters, a playful utopia in which virtuosity can be savored to the third decimal place of a batting average."

—MARK KRAMER

"The one constant through all the years has been baseball. America has rolled by like an army of steamrollers. It's been erased like a blackboard, rebuilt, and erased again. But baseball has marked the time. This field, this game, is a part of our past. It reminds us of all that once was good, and what could be again."

—TERRENCE MANN, *FIELD OF DREAMS*

"Baseball is the only field of endeavor where a man can succeed three times out of ten and be considered a good performer."

—TED WILLIAMS

"I've come to the conclusion that the two most important things in life are good friends and a good bullpen."

—BOB LEMON

"There are 108 beads in a Catholic rosary. And there are 108 stitches in a baseball. When I learned that, I gave Jesus a chance."

—ANNIE SAVOY, *BULL DURHAM*

"You should enter a ballpark the way you enter a church."

—BILL LEE

"It's what you learn after you know it all that counts."

—EARL WEAVER

"Baseball is 90 percent mental. The other half is physical."

—YOGI BERRA

"Good pitching will always stop good hitting and vice versa."

—CASEY STENGEL

"Nice guys finish last."

—LEO DUROCHER

The Best Baseball Quips and Quotations

"The more self-centered and egotistical a guy is, the better ballplayer he's going to be. You take a team with twenty-five assholes and I'll show you a pennant. I'll show you the New York Yankees."

—BILL LEE

"It ain't bragging if you can do it."

—DIZZY DEAN

"Some people are born on third base and go through life thinking they hit a triple."

—BARRY SWITZER

"About the only problem with success is that it does not teach you how to deal with failure."

—TOMMY LASORDA

"This is a strange game."

—CARL YASTRZEMSKI

"It's a great day for a ball game; let's play two!"

—ERNIE BANKS

"I love doubleheaders. That way I get to keep my uniform on longer."

—TOMMY LASORDA

"A hot dog at the ball game beats roast beef at the Ritz."

—HUMPHREY BOGART

"Now, you tell me, if I have a day off during the baseball season, where do you think I'll spend it? The ballpark. I still love it. Always have, always will."

—HARRY CARAY

"When we lost I couldn't sleep at night. When we win I can't sleep at night. But when you win, you wake up feeling better."

—JOE TORRE

"You can't win 'em all."

—Connie Mack

"If a tie is like kissing your sister, losing is like kissing your grandmother with her teeth out."

—George Brett

"It's hard to win a pennant, but it's harder to lose one."

—Chuck Tanner

"A great catch is like watching girls go by; the last one you see is always the prettiest."

—Bob Gibson

"Baseball statistics are like a girl in a bikini. They show a lot, but not everything."

—Toby Harrah

"One percent of ballplayers are leaders of men. The other 99 percent are followers of women."

—John McGraw

"He doesn't drink, he doesn't smoke, he doesn't chew, he doesn't stay out late, and he still can't hit .250."

—Casey Stengel on Bobby Richardson

"Hitting is better than sex."

—Reggie Jackson

"Hitting is an art, but not an exact science."

—Rod Carew

"Keep your eye clear and hit 'em where they ain't."

—Wee Willie Keeler

"The best way to catch a knuckleball is to wait until the ball stops rolling and then pick it up."

—Bob Uecker

"Poets are like baseball pitchers. Both have their moments. The intervals are the tough things."

—Robert Frost

"Pitchers, like poets, are born not made."

—Cy Young

"It helps if the hitter thinks you're a little crazy."

—Nolan Ryan

"Show me a guy who can't pitch inside and I'll show you a loser."

—Sandy Koufax

"I hate all hitters. I start a game mad and I stay that way until it's over."

—Don Drysdale

"I remember one time going out to the mound to talk with Bob Gibson. He told me to get back behind the batter, that the only thing I knew about pitching was that it was hard to hit."

—Tim McCarver

"I ain't ever had a job, I just always played baseball."

—Satchel Paige

"My office is at Yankee Stadium. Yes, dreams do come true."

—Derek Jeter

"I have a darn good job, but please don't ask me what I do."

—Stan Musial

"It was all I lived for, to play baseball."

—Mickey Mantle

The Seventh Inning Stretch

"When I was a kid, I wanted to play baseball and join the circus. With the Yankees, I've been able to do both."

—GRAIG NETTLES

"Kids should practice autographing baseballs. This is a skill that's often overlooked in Little League."

—TUG MCGRAW

"To be good you've gotta have a lot of little boy in you. When you see Willie Mays and Ted Williams jumping and hopping around the bases after hitting a home run, and the kissing and hugging that goes on at home plate, you realize they have to be little boys."

—ROY CAMPANELLA

"There is always some kid who may be seeing me for the first or last time. I owe him my best."

—JOE DIMAGGIO

"Any ballplayer that don't sign autographs for little kids ain't an American. He's a communist."

—ROGERS HORNSBY

"Hating the New York Yankees is as American as apple pie, unwed mothers, and cheating on your income tax."

—MIKE ROYKO

"I don't put any foreign substances on the baseball. Everything I use is from the good old U.S.A."

—GEORGE FRAZIER

"I try not to break the rules, but merely to test their elasticity."

—BILL VEECK

"Why does everybody stand up and sing 'Take Me Out to the Ball Game' when they're already there?"

—LARRY ANDERSEN

"This is a game to be savored, not gulped. There's time to discuss everything between pitches or between innings."

—BILL VEECK

"You see, you spend a good piece of your life gripping a baseball, and in the end it turns out that it was the other way around all the time."

—JIM BOUTON

THE BEST BASEBALL BELLY-LAUGHERS

[41]

THE BEST BASEBALL CARD ERROR

Please Pose for the Camera . . . In an Appropriate Manner

In this chapter we turn our attention to the most quintessential of baseball hobbies, the one that still brings out the little boy or little girl in all of us, even after so many years. No, we're not talking about fantasy baseball, or about the latest oh-so-lifelike baseball video game. We're talking about baseball card collecting and more specifically about the rare breed of card known to hobby enthusiasts as an "error." As collectors know, through the decades the card companies have found a seemingly limitless range of new and unusual ways to mess up their product. And to our lasting amusement they've also made a lot of the same old mistakes, over and over again. Cards with flaws of whatever kind are referred to as errors, and they rank right up there with rookie cards as the most coveted commodities in the collectors' market.

Usually, once an error is detected the manufacturing company that produced it moves quickly to correct the goof, destroying erroneous printing plates and creating new ones. In extreme cases, the company even goes so far as to pull errant cards from previously unopened, unsold packs of cards. By doing so, they create a market scarcity. And if the number of mistakes in circulation is exceptionally low, collectors will seek out the error for its novelty.

By delineating the different types of baseball card gaffes, we may learn much about the best, or worst, depending on your point of view, errors of all time. We might begin by observing that sometimes errors are mistakes of an informational variety. Perhaps a player's name is misspelled, as on the Cal *Ripkin* Jr. 1990 Fleer Players of the Decade card, or perhaps the player's statistics are listed erroneously, as on Roger Clemens' 1989 Score, which attributes to him 778 career wins. Other times, the mistake is an error of omission, as in the case of an anonymous 1990 Topps card that should have identified "Frank Thomas" on its front.

Another common error involves the misidentification of the player featured on the card. In 2007, for example, Topps left collectors scrambling for their

Seattle Mariners media guides upon their discovery that the exact same photograph appeared on cards supposedly belonging to Jose Guillen and Yuniesky Betancourt. This is a regrettable mix-up, to be sure, but somewhat forgivable when relatively unknown players are involved. Through the decades, however, the card manufacturers have amassed a consistent track record of misidentifying some of the game's most identifiable faces. Hank Aaron's 1956 Topps clearly shows Willie Mays sliding into home plate. Tom Seaver's 1985 Donruss showcases teammate Floyd Bannister. Barry Bonds' 1987 "Opening Day" card showed a picture of Johnny Ray. And John Smoltz's 1990 Donruss stars Tom Glavine.

In other cases, errant photos aren't wholly the fault of the photographers and editing technicians, but are, rather, the consequence of player-created chicanery. Often, the card companies send their photographers to teams' training camps in Florida and Arizona for photo shoots during spring training—as the relative proximity of camps translates into less travel than if the photographers visited all of the teams at their ballparks across the country. Spring training just happens to be when players are most relaxed and convivial as well, which suits the shutterbugs' posing purposes. However, it is also when many players are most mischievous, as Topps found out in the spring of 1969. That year the California Angels' Aurelio Rodriguez convinced team batboy Leonard Garcia to pose in his place for his card at the team's Cactus League facility, and the shoot resulted in the 1969 Rodriguez error. Years later, Gary Pettis dressed his fourteen-year-old brother, Lynn, in his uniform and sent him to a photo shoot for Topps in the spring of 1985.

Another common photo irregularity involves cards displaying reverse negatives of otherwise correct pictures. On these, players who throw or bat right-handed appear to be doing so left-handed and, likewise, lefty players appear as righties, due to a lab technician's failure to reverse the negative image. Thus, Topps muffed Hank Aaron's card for a second straight year in 1957 when it depicted the Milwaukee Braves outfielder, who was by then already a two-time All-Star, batting left-handed. Similarly, Upper Deck pictured Atlanta Braves star Dale Murphy batting from the portside in 1989, and Donruss offered a backward shot of Texas Rangers rookie Juan Gonzalez in 1990.

Sometimes an error is designated as such for more than just one reason. Displaying a sense of humor in 1976, Jesus Alou stood in a left-handed batting stance for a Topps photographer. Fortunately, someone at Topps noticed the prank, and decided to intentionally reverse the negative so that Alou would appear to be on the proper side of the plate on the card. Score one for the card manufacturers.

There was only one problem: the cursive *M* on Alou's Mets cap appeared backward. This gave life to a whole new classification of error: a purposely reversed negative necessitated by a player prank.

When it comes to errors, the ones involving pranks are definitely the most fun. Such shenanigans add character to a card or, rather, reflect in some way the character of the player it depicts. Paul Gibson's 1989 Score shows the Tigers southpaw delivering a warm-up pitch from a spring training mound while shortstop Alan Trammell can be seen clearly in the background grabbing his crotch. Who knows if Trammell realized his teammate was being shot when he made the overture or if he was just adjusting himself at an inopportune time, but it is humorous to imagine that he was trying to sneak one past the censors. In any case, Score issued a correction in which Trammell's arm is airbrushed away so that he appears to be playing shortstop with no right hand. In this case, even the correction might be deemed an error.

Sometimes the card companies play jokes on the players and on collectors too. These aren't necessarily errors in the strictest sense of the term, but they're still fun to collect. Such was the case of Billy Cowan's 1972 Topps. Unbeknownst to the Angels outfielder, he was directed by a photographer to pose in his batting stance so that the halo on the Big A sign behind the leftfield fence at Anaheim Stadium would appear directly above his head. On the card, Cowan's body obscures most of the sign's frame and *A*, leaving only a perfectly proportioned halo hovering above his head. Similarly, during the 1989 season a Score photographer snapped a shot of Royals first baseman Bill Buckner—famous for the ball that rolled between his legs in the 1986 World Series—crouching in a fielding position with his legs bowed wide—while the open end of the metal cylinder used to roll up the infield tarp appears perfectly behind him. Thus, Buckner's 1990 Score shows him crouching, as if to field a ball, with a tunnel between his legs. In 2007, Topps orchestrated a silly prank as a publicity stunt. On Derek Jeter's card, deceased Yankee icon Mickey Mantle can be seen standing in the Yankees dugout, while President George W. Bush stands in the crowd waving blithely to the camera. Topps admitted to superimposing the two famous people just to create a stir.

It is certainly debatable whether these three prank cards (and others like them) should be classified as errors, since they were created intentionally and were not corrected. One card that certainly left no doubt as to whether it was a gaffe, however, was Billy Ripken's 1989 Fleer. This card began with a player prank, taught thousands of school children a new word, and incited a frenzied cover-up that resulted in no less than ten different correction cards reaching the market. The story goes something like this: Ripken was in his first full season with the Orioles in 1988 when a Fleer photographer asked him to pose at Fenway Park. The second baseman picked up a bat, set it on his right shoulder, and smiled slightly for the camera. Six months later, collectors were pulling Ripken cards from packs and noticing the words *F*** Face* written clearly in black magic marker on the knob of the bat in Ripken's hands. The words were not only clearly visible, but horizontal with the ground for easy reading. Some conspiracy theorists speculated that Fleer must have noticed the error and let it slip through in hopes of touching off a Fleer buying spree. Others suggested that the company was responsible for writing the words on the bat, conjecturing that either the photographer had handed Ripken the obscenity-inscribed piece of lumber or the production crew had added the words afterward. These were just unfounded rumors though. For his part, Ripken attributed the inscription to jokesters on his team who had set him up. This doesn't explain, of course, why he's holding the bat with the words perfectly level. Sure, it could have been a coincidence, but it would seem that Ripken and/or the photographer was in on the joke.

In any case, as the Ripken error sold for more than $100 at card shows across the nation, Fleer hastily issued several different corrections. Among these was a whitewashed version in which the knob of the bat appeared covered by a white blob of ink. Then there was a scribbled-out version, then a scribbled out as well as partially whited-out version. Then, there were several slightly different black boxes superimposed to cover up the offensive words. True collectors did their best to acquire one of each.

And that's the story of how a marginal big leaguer, who otherwise might have been remembered merely as the less talented sibling of an iconic Hall of Famer, achieved something akin to cult status among the legion of fans who collect cards. Because it defined Lil' Rip's career, and because every serious collector has a Billy Ripken story in his past, the Billy Ripken 1989 Fleer is our choice as the best baseball card error of them all. But stay tuned. You never know what collectors will pull from next year's packs!

[42]

THE BEST BASEBALL PRANK

It Put the Jock in Jocularity

Appealing to our collective sense of good humor, baseball has proven time and time again that its fans, players, and sometimes even its pundits enjoy an occasional ballpark caper to lighten the mood. In the course of a typical season, those who scrutinize the game are apt to observe a bevy of light-hearted moments that have become so familiar through the years so as to become clichés of baseball shenanigans. To begin, there's a whole catalogue of tricks that veterans play on rookies. When a prospect comes up and gets his first hit, for example, his team-mates notify the nearest umpire, who instructs the pitcher to roll the ball into the dugout so the newcomer to baseball's special fraternity may have it as a keepsake. When the youngster returns from the base paths to the dugout, however, he is presented a ball, which, invariably, has not only the date already inscribed onto its shiny leather surface with indelible marker but also his name . . . misspelled. Only later will his teammates pull out the real ball and burst out laughing. Then there's the gag where the rookie hits his first home run and returns to the dugout trium-phantly, expecting high fives and pats on the back all around. Only his teammates sit stoically on the bench, staring blankly ahead, as if they didn't notice his feat. Then suddenly, after he turns beet red and wonders if he's done something wrong, his new friends burst into wide grins and spring to their feet to mob him.

Other baseball pranks don't discriminate on the basis of big league service time. New arrivals and cagey veterans alike are apt to be victimized by a big pink bubble of Bazooka or Big League Chew affixed discreetly to their cap top, where it remains for an inning or more, while teammates and TV viewers share a laugh. Then there's the ever-popular shaving-cream pie planted suddenly in a player's face during a pre- or postgame interview. And don't forget the hotfoot, which comes courtesy of a lit match wedged between a player's shower sandal and heel. The list of smirk-inducing antics goes on and on. But this essay isn't merely dedicated to these ordinary baseball pranks. Rather, we seek to explore the more elaborate hoaxes that have taken the game's usual gags a step further, and then a step further still. Our quest is to find the most hilarious, intricately woven, well-orchestrated, baseball prank of all, the one that took on a life of its own and brought a new level of hilarity to the ballpark.

A cadre of Philadelphia Phillies players, coaches, front-office mates, and even beat reporters pulled off a good hoax in the earliest part of what turned out to be a World Championship 2008 campaign. They even got some help from the victimized player's agent to sell the ruse. The prank unfolded like this: After a workout at the team's Grapefruit League headquarters in Clearwater, Florida, gullible pitching prospect Kyle Kendrick was called into manager Charlie Manuel's office where assistant general manager Ruben Amaro Jr. told him he'd been traded to the Yomiuri Giants of the Japanese Leagues for a player named Kobayashi Iwamura. Major League teams are not, in fact, permitted to trade players to Japan without their consent, but Kendrick didn't know that. First, Amaro produced a formal-looking trade agreement printed on Phillies letterhead, then Manuel offered Kendrick some words of encouragement based on the seasons he'd spent as a player in Japan in the 1970s. Next,

Kendrick phoned his agent, Joe Urbon, and Urbon told him that indeed he'd been swapped, and that he'd better start packing and bone up on his Japanese because he was due to board a plane for the Far East the next morning. Distraught, Kendrick reported to his locker and began collecting his belongings. Continuing the gag, several reporters began asking him questions about the trade. Frazzled, he asked *them* questions about Japanese culture and food, all the while looking like he might break into tears. Finally, after an excruciating half hour, he was put out of his misery when veteran pitcher Brett Myers announced, "You've been punked!"

In 2008 Kyle Kendrick's teammates tricked him into thinking he'd been traded to Japan. COURTESY OF WIKIMEDIA COMMONS

The Best Baseball Prank

Now that's a pretty good prank, and one fans surely enjoyed reading about in the next morning's sports pages, especially during the tediously slow news days known as spring training. But if we delve back further into baseball lore, there's an even better spring training gag. The date was April 1, 1985, and as the latest issue of *Sports Illustrated* hit newsstands, readers soon came to realize that iconic journalist George Plimpton had broken an exclusive story about a pitching phenom about to turn the baseball world on its ear. The article, which would become one of the most famous in the long history of America's premier sports periodical, appeared beneath the headline THE CURIOUS CASE OF SIDD FINCH, and the subheading, "He's a pitcher, part yogi and part recluse. Impressively liberated from our opulent lifestyle, Sidd's deciding about yoga—and his future in baseball." Now, if you read only the first letters of the subheading, they spell out "Happy April Fool's Day— ah fib." Most readers didn't pick up on the cryptic acronym, however, and instead took Plimpton's lengthy and meticulously detailed article at face value. The piece told the story of Sidd Finch, an eccentric twenty-eight-year-old who was working out as a nonroster invitee for the New York Mets at their camp in St. Petersburg, Florida. According to the article, Finch was a Harvard University dropout who spoke several different languages and also happened to be an expert French horn player. He'd spent the previous several years in the Himalayan Mountains learning *siddhi*, or the Buddhist mastery of mind over matter. Then a Mets scout discovered him in Old Orchard Beach, Maine, knocking bottles off fence posts with pinpoint precision from 60 feet away. But Finch wasn't just a control specialist. He also had a fastball that had been clocked, according to Plimpton, at a barely visible 168 miles per hour. There was only one catch. Okay, there were a few. But the main one was that Finch didn't know whether he wanted to play pro ball. Among the other issues conspiring to cast doubt on his future in the game were his refusal to throw for the Mets in any environment other than an enclosed tent and his insistence that he be allowed to wear a battered work boot on his right foot and no shoe at all on his left foot whenever he took the mound. But he threw faster than any pitcher had ever thrown, so the Mets were putting up with his eccentricities for the time being.

Contributing to the article's credibility were confessions of amazement attributed to Mets manager Davey Johnson, pitching coach Mel Stottlemyre, team owner Nelson Doubleday, baseball commissioner Peter Ueberroth, and Mets players like Lenny Dykstra and John Christensen—who'd reportedly stepped into the batter's box against Finch only to be blown away. The article was accompanied by pictures of the befuddling Buddhist, including one of him wearing a work boot on a beach in the midst of a prodigious windup.

Although the article was published on April Fools' Day, and although its details painted a picture that was utterly absurd, thousands of baseball fans hung on its every word and then wrote letters to *Sports Illustrated* begging for more information. Two weeks after the article appeared, the magazine finally admitted it had been intended as a joke, but to this day the gag remains the stuff of legend in editorial boardrooms across the country. Was it the best baseball prank ever, though? Well, it's a strong contender, but ideally our winner would be a ruse that involved a real player or two, and maybe a real ball field. So we'll keep looking.

Two summers after the Finch laugher appeared in *SI*, the magazine and many other national publications covered another fantastical baseball farce that really did occur. The prank originated not in the green fields of some writer's imagination, but on a minor league diamond before 3,258 paying spectators. It was a gorgeous August night in 1987, the kind that made you wish the home team could play two—and indeed, the hometown Williamsport Bills were scheduled to play a doubleheader against the Reading Phillies. For Bills catcher Dave Bresnahan, the situation was not so rosy though. Through his first fifty-two games, the Eastern League backup had posted a paltry .149 batting average. Clearly he would be receiving his walking papers soon. But first, there was a doubleheader to be played, and as one of the team's only two catchers, that all but guaranteed he would start one of the games. Figuring that if he was going to leave the game, he should go out in style, Bresnahan made a trip to the grocery store before he was due to head to Bowman Field and did some selective produce shopping. Back home, he peeled and pared a potato into the size and shape of a baseball. By the time he headed to the park, he was well on his way to making history.

Sure enough, Bresnahan arrived in the clubhouse to discover he was penciled in as the Bills starting catcher for the first game. So he stuffed his special baseball-shaped spud into one of his practice catcher mitts, positioned the mitt in the home dugout, and then waited for the right moment. Finally, in the top of the fifth, the catcher made his move. With a runner on third base, Bresnahan told the home plate umpire that the previous pitch had ripped the webbing of his mitt. So he ambled to the dugout to retrieve his backup glove, then returned to his spot behind the plate. As the pitcher stepped onto the mound, Bresnahan called for a slider away, then discreetly slipped the potato into his throwing hand. After the batter took the pitch outside, Bresnahan whirled and fired a pick-off throw toward third base in an attempt to nab a sleeping base runner. When his throw sailed over the third-baseman's head into leftfield, the runner came trotting home. Then, just as the runner was about to score an easy run, Bresnahan tagged him out. He'd thrown the potato into leftfield, of course, not the ball, employing a decoy that the umpires quickly deemed illegal. The runner was ruled safe. The players on both benches laughed. Bresnahan's manager removed him from the game. And afterward, the Indians, who were the Bills' parent club, gave Bresnahan his outright release. But word of the prank spread quickly and before long Bresnahan was fielding calls from journalists far and wide. Marv Albert interviewed him for a spot that ran before NBC's *Game of the Week,* and the events of the bizarre swan song were chronicled in *Time,* the *Sporting News, USA Today,* and *Sports Illustrated.*

Believe it or not, we can do one better than this great baseball prank, without even leaving the produce aisle. Our choice for the best-ever baseball gag is so honored for leaving such a lasting impression on the game that fans still refer to it today, even if they're not quite aware they're doing so. The prank explains how Florida's spring training Grapefruit League got its name. It occurred back in 1915 when the Brooklyn Dodgers were working out in Daytona Beach. Toward the end of the spring, a young rightfielder named Casey Stengel got into a playful argument with his manager, Wilbert Robinson, over whether Robinson could conceivably catch a baseball dropped from an airplane. Aviation was relatively new at this time—only about a decade old—so such flights of fancy apparently still captivated people's imaginations whenever a big bird flew overhead. And so, after a double-dog dare, Stengel set off to find a pilot, while Robinson boned up on his pop-up catching skills. At the start of practice the next day, the brash player announced that he'd arranged for a plane to fly some 500 feet above the field. And Robinson hurriedly readied himself in the center of the diamond. As the drone of the propeller began to whine into earshot, though, Stengel suddenly appeared to have second thoughts. He told his manager that it wasn't too late to call the whole thing off and just let the ball fall harmlessly to the ground, explaining that a ball falling at such a great velocity was likely to rip a hole in not only Robinson's glove but his hand. "Hogwash," the feisty manager replied, but a seed of doubt had been planted in his mind. Soon enough, the plane came into view and began circling. Then, with Robinson looking skyward, the pilot ejected his small spherical payload. Robinson staggered under the falling object, waited, staggered, and then waited some more. And then . . . splat. The manager began screaming bloody hell when he realized he was covered with what could only be the bloody chunks of his own fleshy, pulpy hand. But then he realized that he was only covered with the pulp of a pink grapefruit. Fearing that he would kill his manager, Stengel had, in fact, substituted the segmented citrus sphere for the ball at the last moment. The Dodgers had a good laugh over the practical joke, except for Stengel, who was sentenced to run wind sprints in the outfield for the rest of the afternoon. As word of the gag spread throughout the game, players began referring to the Sunshine State's spring training circuit as the Grapefruit League, and the name has stuck ever since. For Robinson's sake, we're just glad his team was working out in Florida, and not in Arizona—where many snowbound teams would head in later decades. If Stengel's dare had involved his manager's ability to jump over a cactus, there's no telling what sort of medical emergency might have ensued!

As a young Brooklyn outfielder, wise-guy Casey Stengel tricked manager Wilbert Robinson into trying to catch a grapefruit dropped from an airplane. COURTESY OF THE LIBRARY OF CONGRESS

[43]

THE BEST BIG LEAGUE MASCOT

A Diamond Dunce We Can Appreciate

Although you may think the overstuffed sack of feathers clogging the aisles at your local big league park is the product of a brand new baseball craze, this is hardly the case. Yes, the mascot as veritable *Sesame Street* character is a relatively recent phenomenon, but today's family-friendly ballpark jesters are just the latest in a long line of stadium sillymen. Through the years, a wide variety of children, adults, and even animals have provided comic relief to fans and good luck to the home team. This chapter is dedicated to exploring the very best of these charismatic comedians.

To be sure, the mascot of the twenty-first century is for the kids. This is because sometime in the 1990s, big league teams realized diehards would keep turning out at their ballparks even if they began catering to families with young children by sanitizing the ballpark experience to the point of muppetry. Enter characters like Billy the Marlin, who patrols the football field that masquerades as a baseball park in South Florida. You'd think the kids in Miami would see the absurdity of a fish with arms and legs, but Billy has been walking the concourses at Land Shark Stadium—and getting laughs—since 1993. Even in provincial Boston where the Home Towne Team had previously tinkered with tradition about as often as it changed leftfielders, Wally the Green Monster emerged, as if roused from an eighty-five-year slumber, from Fenway's beloved green wall, to the delight of youngsters.

You can count Junction Jack, the rabbit who wears an Astros uniform, Fredbird the Redbird in his Cardinals gear, the Pirate Parrot, Baxter the Bobcat in Arizona, and a bevy of other cuddly characters among this new breed too. Yes, our kids love them, and as parents we appreciate the extent to which they minimize the recurrence of questions like, "How many innings until we can go home?" and, "Can I have more cotton candy?" For grown-up fans, however, these ballpark bozos don't do as much to enhance our enjoyment of an evening at the ballyard as the better mascots once did. And that's where most newcomers miss the mark.

While they would surely make great birthday party entertainers—and indeed some do on off days—they fail to engage real fans, except for the unfortunate fellow who gets struck in the side of the head with a flying hot dog launched via slingshot into the second deck between innings who, I suppose it could be said, is in a way engaged. Furthermore, these ballpark carnival acts no longer emerge organically from the anonymous ranks of fandom, as they once did, but are ushered into our green cathedrals only after their careful creation by marketing executives who no doubt wear dark suits (but perhaps brightly colored underwear) in Madison Avenue think tanks.

Fredbird the Redbird is a fixture in St. Louis.
COURTESY OF WIKIMEDIA COMMONS

As we seek to crown the best mascot of all time, let's stipulate that first and foremost our chosen ballpark goof should be a baseball fan, not just a glorified babysitter in fluorescent polyester. And let's add the stipulation that our mascot of choice should appeal to a wide range of fans, not just the ones wearing sneakers with glow lights or wheels on the bottom. And let's also say there should be a pretty good story to explain how our best mascot came to be. Sorry, but *Wally the Green Monster and his Journey Through Red Sox Nation,* the children's book penned by Red Sox broadcaster Jerry Remy, doesn't count as a good story . . . at least not until Remy wins a Pulitzer.

Let's begin our review back in the days when mascots really were considered good luck charms for their teams. In the game's early days, you see, not every team had a mascot, which was another factor that made them special. More than that, having one gave the home team the psychological edge that came from believing fate was on its side. To wit, in the 1910s the Philadelphia Athletics had a disabled batboy named Louis Van Zelst with whom Connie Mack formed a most unusual attachment. Mack believed the youngster was lucky, and Mack's players did too. Who could argue? The A's appeared in four of five World Series between 1910 and 1914 and won three times as the hunchbacked Van Zelst toted their lumber. Batters would rub the batboy's back for good luck before walking to the plate at crucial moments during key games. But then Van Zelst died in 1915, and, just like that, the A's lost their mojo. They went 36-117 in 1916 to finish 54½ games behind the first-place Red Sox. Sure, Mack had traded away most of his best players, but many fans lamented the batboy's passing as the impetus for the freefall.

Another famous mascot of the sport's early era was Charles Victor Faust. (If you find yourself wondering if all early-day mascots had three names, sort of like serial killers, you're not alone.) A mysterious friend of New York Giants manager John McGraw, Faust was in fact a player on the team's active roster. He would dress in full uniform, warm up with the Giants pitchers, and sit on the bench all game long, all season long. As a thirty-one-year-old rookie, Faust pitched in just two games, totaling two innings for the Giants of 1911, despite remaining on the roster all year.

According to baseball lore, the Giants were preparing for an exhibition game in St. Louis early in the season that year when Faust hopped out of the stands and introduced himself to McGraw. Faust told McGraw that a fortune-teller had told him that if he pitched for the Giants they would win the pennant. So McGraw put the odd fellow on a bullpen mound and quickly deduced that he couldn't pitch a lick. Yet, Mack decided to sign Faust anyway. Why? Because the goofy hick told the esteemed baseball expert that his middle name was Victory, and McGraw liked the sound of that. Sure enough, the eccentric Faust sat beside McGraw as the Giants won the pennant in 1911. He was invited back in 1912 and the team won the title again. In 1913, too, there was a spot for him beside McGraw, and the Giants won the NL for a third straight time, even if they lost the World Series yet again. Faust's behavior eventually became more and more erratic though, relegating him to a part-time bench presence in 1914, as the Giants fell to second place. Then, in 1915, after Faust was committed to an insane asylum and died of tuberculosis, the Giants finished in last place.

While these early mascots were important to their teams and earned the attention of fans and writers of the day, something seems wrong about using physically and/or psychologically disabled people as talismans. Thus, these individuals, however unique they may have been, don't seem to warrant our best mascot ever designation. We'll have to keep looking.

Next came the happy marriage of the lucky charm and the vaudevillian, as it came to pass that teams would offer between innings shows to entertain fans. During this era, Max Patkin, the third gentleman to be crowned the Clown Prince of Baseball, stood, as if on the stilts he sometimes mounted, above the rest. A minor league pitcher before World War II, Patkin never reached the Show as a player, but he made a career for himself after the war as a big league funny-man. No less a visionary than Bill Veeck discovered him goofing on Joe DiMaggio one day during a game between servicemen during the War. A short while later, Veeck hired Patkin to attract fans to Cleveland Indians games in the 1940s, and Patkin remained in the game for the next five decades, serving dozens of major and minor league teams and even appearing as himself in *Bull Durham*. His most famous routines included mimicking a first baseman tossing warm-up balls around the infield, giving fake signs to opposing players, and shadowing players around the bases after home runs. Although Patkin was on the field for the amusement of the fans, through routines like these he interacted with the players as much as was permissible. It's hard to imagine a ballpark jester mucking it up with players in this manner today in the Post-Randall-Simon-Sausage-Racer-Assault-Incident Era, but Patkin was a favorite of the players of his day, perhaps because they knew he'd once been one.

Patkin was the best at what he did for a long time, but mascots have changed a whole lot in appearance and behavior since he got goofy in the home club's garb each night. Today, mascots aren't just men in uniform, they're creatures in ornate costumes. If you can guess their species, you're usually one up on the average fan. If you can guess their gender, you should vacate your seat, quickly freshen up, and catch a flight for Vegas, where incidentally, the mascot of the local Triple-A franchise is a not-so-terrifying alien named Cosmo.

Whether the product of intelligent design or human ingenuity, the mascot's most dramatic evolutionary step forward occurred in the 1970s, when the San Diego Chicken redefined what it meant to be a stadium stooge. Bernie Brewer, it should be noted, helped pave the way, but he was more a fan-gone-wild than part of the new guard. A handlebar-mustached Brewers fan, who in 1970 famously mounted the County Stadium scoreboard, Bernie (aka Mr. Milt Mason) refused to leave until the Brewers drew a crowd of 40,000 fans. But it was the Chicken, or rather the man inside the chicken suit, who started the trend of mascots dressing like crit-ters. With his clever antics, the Chicken rose to a place of national prominence that would eventually earn him a starring role on *The Baseball Bunch,* alongside

The Phillie Phanatic is a phan phavorite in Philadelphia. COURTESY OF WIKIMEDIA COMMONS

Johnny Bench; appearances at many of the biggest rock and roll concerts of the wild 1970s; a cameo stint in the cult classic movie *Attack of the Killer Tomatoes*; and multiple appearances on baseball cards.

Along the way, he paved a path for other excellent silly-suited characters like the Phillie Phanatic and the now-extinct Expos mascot known as Youppi. Today, this concept has been distorted to the point where mascots are merely pimple-faced ballpark interns inside hot suits, but back in the dying days of disco it wasn't so much the suit as the man inside that mattered, and the creative ways he could captivate the fans' imaginations. Back in those early days when the Chicken first sizzled, the mascot was a beautiful thing.

From the very start, fans knew Ted Giannoulas had a gift. He was just a San Diego State student on spring break when he signed with KGB radio to wear the original chicken costume in 1974. The job paid $2 an hour and required simply that Giannoulas hang out at the San Diego Zoo doling out plastic Easter eggs. It didn't take long for him to take a shining to the role. The only problem was the gig ended when Easter came and went. Undeterred, Giannoulas volunteered to wear the suit to the Padres home opener to give KGB some additional publicity. And so, out of these humble beginnings, a star was born. Giannoulas went on to reinvent his field, displaying a remarkable wit and flair for the dramatic that prompted legendary *San Diego Union* sports editor Jack Murphy to write, "The Chicken has the soul of a poet. He is an embryonic Charles Chaplin in chicken feathers," and *Time* magazine to write, "[B]aseball should learn to peddle the real nostalgia—Jackie Robinson breaking the color barrier, Lou Gehrig's farewell speech, and the first appearance of the San Diego Chicken."

In his prime, the San Diego Chicken heckled the umpires, flapped his feathers in players' faces, stomped atop dugout roofs, and acted as comic relief during some lean years for the Padres. In 1976, he took his show on the road as St. Louis Cardinals players pooled their money and made arrangements for Giannoulas to fly into town for a pair of Cardinals games. In 1978, the Chicken played his first minor league game

The Famous Chicken flies into a base. PHOTO BY V.J. LOVERO; © *2008* TFC, INC.

deep in the heart of Texas when a sell-out crowd turned out to see him work his magic in El Paso.

But then, after just a few glorious seasons, corporate America struck back, threatening to take Giannoulas's lifework from him with a lawsuit filed by KGB, claiming the Chicken suit was the radio station's property. Giannoulas was forced to sit out a few seasons but eventually had his day in court and won, setting up his triumphant return to Jack Murphy Stadium in 1979. He arrived via police motorcade inside a 10-foot-high egg from which he hatched at midfield to the delight of 47,000 screaming fans.

By the early 1980s, many other teams had introduced colorful characters of their own, attempting to replicate the Padres' success with the Chicken. Some would stick, like the Phanatic, but most would fade into obscurity before being reconceptualized in the 1990s. As for the Chicken, he wasn't about to be cooped up in one city. No longer is he exclusively the Padres mascot, and he now goes by the name the Famous Chicken, as he spreads his wings and good humor at major and minor league stadiums far and wide. He plays approximately 175 dates a year. For all of the joy he has brought baseball fans, for the interesting story of how he came to be, and for the grade-A gags he played on Tommy Lasorda on *The Baseball Bunch,* the Famous Chicken is our pick for best baseball mascot ever.

[44]

THE BEST BILL VEECK STUNT

Its Orchestration Was No Small Wonder

We could begin this chapter by declaring that ever since baseball became a multibillion-dollar industry, it's forgotten how to let its hair down and enjoy a few laughs at its own expense. And we could say there surely would be no place for a loose cannon like "Barnum Bill" Veeck in the modern game, which would, of course, be true. But beginning a review of the legendary owner's most amazing publicity stunts under such a premise would seem to suggest that the antics that came to characterize Veeck's career were ever deemed acceptable by the baseball establishment. And frankly, they were not. During his four stints as the owner of three teams between 1946 and 1980, Veeck's provocative flair for the dramatic and for the absurd always positioned him as an outsider looking in at the old-boy's club of dour team owners. Veeck's peers routinely lambasted him in the press and in person. They also regularly conspired to thwart his gimmicks before they could take place. And on multiple occasions they colluded—sometimes successfully, others not—to extract him from their prim and proper fraternity. Even when Veeck had to sell his teams, however—as in 1949 when a divorce from his first wife required that he liquidate his assets and sell the Indians; in 1953 when the other owners refused to let him move the financially failing St. Louis Browns to another city, then promptly let the new owner move the club to Baltimore; and in 1961 when he sold the White Sox due to his failing health—he always seemed to wriggle his way back into baseball.

Veeck grew up knowing all along that he wanted to follow in the footsteps of his father, who was a sportswriter who eventually became team president of the Cubs. As his own career took root in the 1940s and 1950s, critics often levied accusations that the younger Veeck didn't care about winning and losing, only putting on a good show, and that he didn't adequately respect the game's history and traditions. None of this was true, of course. Veeck just didn't take the game, or himself, quite as seriously as the other owners did. And Veeck understood that making the game appealing on as many levels as possible was integral to broadening its fan base and increasing its revenues. Yes, he staged stunts that brought baseball into waters it had never tested before—and we'll get to some of those classic Veeck stunts shortly—but what his contemporaries didn't realize, and what the Hall of Fame—which posthumously inducted Veeck in 1991—did, is that Veeck truly was a visionary. His more serious proposals usually didn't create the type of buzz his carnival stunts did, but some of them were actually implemented and have stood the test of time. Others were ahead of their time. For example, while still working under the direction of his father as a young man, Veeck planted the ivy that still grows on the outfield wall at Wrigley Field. Later, he commissioned and erected the manually operated scoreboard that stands at Wrigley today. Then, before landing in Cleveland as Indians owner, Veeck tried to purchase the Phillies in the early 1940s with a plan to field an integrated team that would include Negro Leagues stars. But commissioner Kenesaw Mountain Landis thwarted the forward-looking assault on baseball's abominable gentleman's agreement. Later, as the fledgling owner of the Indians, Veeck signed the American League's first African-American player, Larry Doby, in 1947. Then he signed the oldest rookie, former Negro Leaguer Satchel Paige, who joined the Indians at the ripe old age of forty-two in 1948. Paige proved to be much more than the sideshow Veeck's fellow owners had decried him as, but a solid contributor, going 6-1 with a 2.48 ERA for pennant-winning Cleveland. Veeck was also the first owner to put his players' names on the back of their jerseys.

And it was Veeck's voice that argued most forcefully that baseball should head west and establish franchises in budding population centers in California long before his fellow owners took the idea seriously. He argued for the sharing of television revenues among owners, and for interleague play. Later, he sided with Curt Flood and accepted the onset of free agency before his peers would. He was also the person who suggested Harry Caray sing "Take Me Out to the Ball Game" during the seventh-inning stretch at Wrigley. And he was the one who first sent fireworks into the air to celebrate home runs. And the one who first brought his team to Arizona for spring training.

But there was another side of Veeck too, a downright silly side that simply delighted in making newspaper headlines. And this chapter is dedicated to Veeck's very best stunts, the ones that caused his fellow owners to grimace, and that have since elevated the memory of this quirky baseball visionary to something approaching mythic status. After reviewing Veeck's hit list, we'll pick the one stunt that best exemplified the joy, ingenuity, and devil-may-care attitude he brought to the game.

Like most players, Veeck's career took off only after a period of trial and error in the minor leagues. Veeck's path from baseball's bushes to its bigs began in Milwaukee where he kept the turnstiles clicking during his stint at the helm of the minor league Brewers in the early 1940s. Then, after taking a hiatus to serve in World War II, he returned home eager to make his mark on a grander scale. He did just that in Cleveland. His first great stunt occurred in 1948 as his Indians were closing in on their first World Series in twenty-eight years. It was then that Veeck received a letter submitted by a fan and took it very seriously. The result was "Good Old Joe Earley Night." At a time when it was common for teams to hold special nights for players returning from war or nearing retirement, Veeck held a night for the average fan. Joe Earley was a twenty-six-year-old Clevelander who had recently returned from the war. He and his wife were struggling to keep up with their bills and to raise their family. He was thoroughly enjoying the Indians' remarkable run, but beginning to grow tired of the special days the Indians had been staging for their players who, to his mind, were already famous and doing all right financially. So, on September 28, Veeck and more than 60,000 Indians rooters turned Earley into a celebrity. Before the game, the Average Joe stood on the field to be presented a new house, which turned out to be an outhouse on the back of a truck. Then he was told the team was going to give him a new car, which, in actuality, was an old clunker. Then, all kinds of aged, useless farm animals were trotted onto the field for Earley, along with plenty of other things he couldn't possibly want. Finally, once Earley was in stitches, Veeck presented him with a shiny new convertible, several new household appliances, and a lifetime pass to Municipal Stadium. Thus, the idea of Fan Appreciation Day came to be.

After Veeck's Indians won their second—and still today most recent—World Series title, they fell to third place in 1949, but not before their melodramatic owner staged a mock funeral for them late in the season. On September 23, the day after the Indians had been mathematically eliminated from the AL pennant chase, Veeck put on his most somber funeral attire. Then, he sadly lowered the 1948 Championship banner that had flown above Municipal Stadium all season, and laid it to rest in a coffin. Next, he buried it in centerfield as fans consoled one another. The tongue-in-cheek gag helped fans come to grips with their disappointment, reminded them that there were things in life more important than baseball, and allowed them to enjoy the last week of the season even if the Tribe wouldn't be repeating.

By the time the dog days of the 1951 season arrived, Veeck had already withdrawn from the game for a while, and resurfaced in St. Louis. The hapless

Browns were going nowhere, both literally and figuratively that year, and the desperate Veeck decided to try anything he could to encourage fans to turn out at the ballpark to see a bad team that was on its way to a 52-102 finish. On August 19, Veeck pulled off what would become his most widely known stunt. He signed 3-foot 7-inch Eddie Gaedel to a big league contract, submitted the appropriate paperwork to the league president, and sent Gaedel to bat in the second game of a doubleheader against the Tigers. Wearing elf shoes and the number ½ on his back, Gaedel drew a four-pitch walk to lead off the bottom of the first inning. Then he bowed and scurried to first base where he was replaced by a pinch runner. The baseball lifers cringed, cursed, and then cringed some more. Gaedel's contract was immediately voided, but there was nothing baseball could do to strike his name from the record books. He had batted in an official game, and thus had become part of the game's history. By secretly signing a little person, and sending him to bat, Veeck had given a city of depressed fans reason to take notice of the local team. The stunt told fans that the local owner recognized the team wasn't entertaining enough on its own to merit a trip to the ballpark. And it gave them reason to turn out at Sportsman's Park over the final month of the season: They might just see something they'd never seen before.

Less than a week after Gaedel's at-bat, Veeck pulled off another stunt that is still talked about today. This time he gave fans the chance to participate in the game in a whole new way. Grandstand Manager's Day outfitted a few thousand spectators behind the Browns dugout with big placards that said YES on one side, and NO on the other. At important junctures during the game between the Browns and the Philadelphia Athletics, a stadium employee held up questions related to game strategy, such as "Bunt?" or "Change pitchers?" Then, while St. Louis manager Zack Taylor sat idly smoking a pipe in a rocking chair that had been specially installed on the field, the Browns followed the voting majority's instructions. Naturally, they won, 5–3, earning one of just eight victories they'd claim in thirty September games.

During his return to Chicago as owner not of the Cubs but the White Sox, Veeck continued to make headlines by whatever means he could think of. Shortly after purchasing the White Sox in 1959, he and general manager Roland Hemond set up a desk and phone bank in the lobby of a downtown hotel and made a number of trades while operating in plain view of the public. Little did the club executives on the other end of Veeck's calls know, but their rival fans were monitoring the most intimate details of their negotiations. Here again, fans were allowed access to an interesting facet of the game that they usually didn't get to experience up close.

Later, Veeck brought fifty-year-old Minnie Minoso out of retirement in 1976, and then pulled the same stunt again in 1980, sending him to bat in official games so that he could become the only player to play in five different decades. Minoso went 1 for 8 at the plate in his first comeback, and 0 for 2 in his second. To his credit, he only struck out two times in ten post-fifty at-bats.

The most scandalous stunt of Veeck's illustrious career took place toward the end of his team-owning days in 1979. Actually, by the time Disco Demolition Night came off, Veeck was in declining health and his son Mike was essentially running the show. The event, which resulted in the White Sox forfeiture of the second game of a doubleheader against the Tigers, took place at a time in American history when a nation of music-lovers was sharply divided. Some believed disco to be the greatest invention since the advent of radio, while others considered it an abomination. On Disco Demolition Night, members of the latter group made their voices heard, loud and clear. More than 50,000 disco-hating hippies turned out at Comiskey Park for the promotion. They arrived, as instructed, bearing vinyl disco records they'd liberated from their friends' collections. After collecting the tacky tunes between games of a doubleheader, the White Sox hoped to blow them up in a big combustion chamber in centerfield. That was the plan, anyway. After the first game, several thousand records were collected and placed in the box. But because so many more fans had turned out at the ballpark than anticipated, the box was too small to accommodate all the records fans had brought. And before long, thousands of fans had taken to Frisbee-ing their extra records out of the upper deck. As the White Sox watched the airborne projectiles sail onto the field, and began wondering how they would avoid the lawsuits certain to follow, they tried to regain control by detonating the box. When they did, the explosion simultaneously made a crater in centerfield and signaled the end of any semblance of order at the ballpark. Thousands of fans jumped out of the stands and onto the field. They demolished the batting cage, pilfered the bases, ripped up clumps of sod, and set several small fires. Police in riot gear eventually arrested dozens of people and restored the rule of law, but not before the event had become a national embarrassment for Major League Baseball. The White Sox were forced to forfeit the second game for failing to provide an adequate playing environment. Bill Veeck saw his departure from the game hastened. And Mike Veeck was blacklisted from the game.

So which was the best Bill Veeck stunt of all? Our pick is Grandstand Manager's Day, because it gave Browns fans a chance to prove they did indeed know their baseball, even if their team and ballpark were second-rate. More than that, it lent credence to the lamentation of every fan who has ever muttered—after a particularly heartbreaking loss, no doubt—that he could manage the local nine better than the current skipper. For one day, at least, the hapless Browns and their fans were winners, and they had Bill Veeck to thank. But through the years Veeck put smiles on the faces of a great many other fans through his original approaches to publicity and promotion, and for his contributions to baseball lore we should all be grateful.

45

THE WORST BASEBALL UNIFORM

It Was Uniformly Awful

Like nearly every other aspect of the game—except perhaps for such time-less traditions as players spitting tobacco juice and adjusting their athletic supporters at the most conspicuous of times—baseball uniforms have steadily evolved through the generations. Along the way there have been some fashionable looks and some downright goofy ones. This query is dedicated to the latter, to those regrettable threads that teams once wore but have since buried in the furthermost reaches of their equipment closets, from which they'll surely never return. Ultimately, our goal is to single out the least fashionable, most ridiculous uniform to ever blight a big league diamond.

To start, let's review the larger trends in clothing design that have affected player wear as our American sense of taste has developed, then we'll spend the second half of the chapter discussing the worst uniforms ever. After all, a lot's changed in the world of fashion over the years, so it will be necessary for us to grant some of the bad uniforms that have appeared through the years some grace since they were, oftentimes, merely reflections of their time. Rather, our winner should have stuck out like a sore thumb, or like a plaid blazer at a black tie affair, even in its own era. For example, once upon a time it was

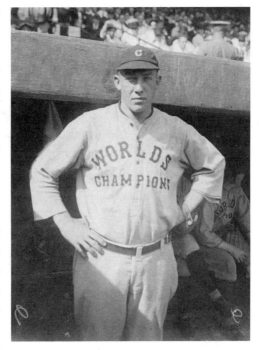

In 1921 George Uhle and his Cleveland teammates used their uniforms to brag about their success the previous year.
COURTESY OF THE LIBRARY OF CONGRESS

common for players across the league to wear jerseys clasped together just below the chin with spiffy leather laces, a reality that today makes the Chicago Cubs zippered jersey of the 1930s seem somewhat forgivable and which also exonerates a few decades worth of pre–button era teams from worst uniform ever condemnation, at least on the basis of their laces.

According to the Hall of Fame's Dressed to the Nines exhibit, Alexander Cartwright's Knickerbockers were the first team to sport uniform apparel on the field back in 1849 when their New York City team took to wearing white flannel shirts, baggy blue pantaloons, and—as if the image weren't arresting enough already—matching straw hats. Two decades later, in 1868, the Cincinnati Red Stockings took to wearing knee-highs, or knickers, a revelation that allowed them to show off their socks. And thank goodness those socks were red. Otherwise, the club might have come to be known as the Blue Stockings or Green Stockings and the Cincinnati Reds of today would be . . . well, they just might be the Greens.

In the 1880s the organized leagues experimented with a color-coded system that mandated each player on a team should wear a uniquely colored jersey in correspondence to his position in the field. The first baseman for both teams was expected to wear scarlet and white, for example, the shortstop, solid maroon, and so on. The complicated and confusing nuance made each team's uniform anything but uniform, and not surprisingly quickly faded into the early pages of the same book of ill-conceived baseball innovations that would later, no doubt, welcome into its later pages such ignominies as the orange glow ball Charlie Finley's Athletics used for two night games during the spring of 1973.

By the end of the 1880s, at least three different teams—none of which resided in New York—were wearing pinstripes. This style, of course, has remained in the game for more than a century and is now owned, so to speak, by the Yankees. In the same era, a few other teams were trying out checkered patterns, which didn't stand the test of time in quite the same way. Mind you, the flannel jerseys of these early days bore not only the aforementioned laces, but also big floppy collars. And they were made of wool, not because the material was itchier and more sweat-inducing than cotton, which it was, but because it was more expensive and those who wore it were considered to have class.

The game's first collarless jersey made its debut in 1906 when John McGraw's New York Giants not only took the field sans collars but with the words World Champions scrawled across their chests in the spot where teams normally wrote their city name or nickname. The haughty Giants failed to repeat as World Series victors, finishing twenty games behind their NL rivals from Chicago, which must have made their brash jersey jargon look pretty silly by the time September rolled around and they were already eliminated from the pennant chase. Nonetheless, other future champions followed suit, wearing boastful apparel themselves in the years to follow after championship campaigns.

In 1916 the Cleveland Indians were the first organization to place numbers on their players' jerseys. The integers were printed on the players' sleeves, which made them impossible to see from any distance. The more logical placement of numerals on players' backs finally appeared in 1929, when both the Indians and Yankees introduced the nuance and began a trend.

In the 1930s the Cubs donned the aforementioned zip-ups, which reportedly left players like Gabby Hartnett and Billy Herman fretting for their chest hair all game long. By the 1940s, the Northsiders were at it again, this time introducing a new look that had more staying power. The Cubs took to wearing sleeveless flannel vests over three-quarter-sleeve baseball shirts. Although the style only lasted a little while in Chicago, it has since undergone several revivals in other big league towns. In 1960 the crosstown White Sox became the first team to send its players onto the diamond with their names across their backs.

Then, as the 1970s blossomed, the advent of color TV catalyzed a radical rethinking of baseball-uniform design that resulted in the introduction of tele-genic, brightly colored player garb throughout the league. The eye-opening garb lasted for more than a decade until the conservative fashion sensibility of the 1980s mercifully took hold. The tide didn't turn, however, until after uniforms had well reflected the depth and scope of atrocious taste for which the 1970s are today remembered. Thus, at a time when the man-perm, thin-stache, and leather pants were all the rage, Willie Stargell sported a stiff stovepipe Pirates hat with horizontal gold striping. And George Brett went to work each night in a baby-blue Royals sleeper, which might well have come with attached footsies for those cold April nights in Kansas City. And the otherwise menacing Reggie Jackson wore a banana-yellow vest and pea-green undershirt in Oakland that caused even the taste-insane fans of the day to wonder if Old Mr. Finley had gone color-blind or simply lost his mind.

But we're getting ahead of ourselves in singling out these superstars now destined to live in baseball card and bedroom-poster infamy as representatives of their era's criminally tacky taste. Having to this point reviewed the historic trends in uniform design, let's now run down the laundry list of the worst ones ever, with an apology for the bad pun, and a nod to the Hall of Fame's team-by-team index, which readers can access via the Hall's Web site.

Although it seems unfair to come down too hard on any of the old-time uni's since America's sense of style was so different a century ago, we'd be remiss not to lambaste at least a few of the jerseys from the game's checkered—both figuratively and literally—past. Indeed, the worst representative of the checkered uniform craze was a blue pattern worn by the 1916 Brooklyn Robins. These pre-Dodgers might have filled in admirably for pieces of graph paper had the local schoolboys ever found themselves in need of stationery at the game, but they sure look ridiculous today.

Another bad one was the Philadelphia Athletics jersey of the early 1920s. It sported nothing on front but the profile of a blue elephant rearing up on its hind legs. A later model replaced the blue elephant with a white one—on a white jersey no less—which made the pachyderm practically invisible. The Washington Senators of the early 1930s, meanwhile, wore a jersey that featured no words or graphics at all, other than a blue *W* on the left sleeve. This must have given fans reason to grimace—especially ones sitting on the third-base side of the ballpark. Even those sitting along first base would see that their heroes wore an essentially plain white uniform, though. Seriously, could there possibly be a less inspired, less creative way to outfit a bunch of pro athletes? The Senators were a historically bad team for much of their life, but they were actually pretty good during the 1930s. And even if they hadn't been, they were still a big league squad and should have dressed like one.

Speaking of looking professional or, rather, falling short of the mark, let's return to the acid trip that began in the 1960s and spread across the league like a bad case of foot fungus in the 1970s. Despite churning out an occasional ugly duck, baseball fashion was progressing inoffensively enough until 1963 when Finley's Kansas City Athletics, hoping perhaps to herald a golden age of Barbecue City baseball, started wearing gold and green. Not to be outdone, the White Sox unveiled blue roadies the very next season. With only minor tweaks over the next several years, these two entries reigned as the worst uniforms of the sixties, until the expansion Seattle Pilots debuted in 1969 and made their sole season a memorable one by sporting what we'd later come to recognize as Smurf-blue road uniforms. By the end of the 1970s, the list of teams wearing blue on the road—in varying shades—would come to include the Blue Jays, Brewers, Cardinals, Cubs, Expos, Mariners, Phillies, Rangers, Royals, and Twins. The Braves had a darker blue shirt and the Indians waffled between blue and red tops. Dressing grown men, many of whom were not in the best of shape—here we're thinking of burly sluggers like Greg Luzinski and Steve Balboni—in what amounted to blue pajamas all summer long was sheer madness, especially beneath those unforgiving ballpark lights, which everyone knows add at least ten pounds. Surely, a pinstriped or a white approach would have been a more flattering approach for the ample-bodied players of the pre–weight room era.

As for the worst uniforms of this worst uniform era, the mustard yellow the Padres sported from head to toe during the early 1970s, accented by brown trim, ranks down near the very bottom. The burnt-orange worn by the Orioles was also particularly horrid, as was the maroon roads worn by the Phillies. And the brown-red Indians outfits of the mid-1970s were not only ugly but might have also been interpreted as racially insensitive. The White Sox jerseys of the seventies were the worst of all, though. In 1976 Bill Veeck brought back the long-extinct floppy collars of the game's earliest era so that on ordinary days, the club's navy-blue big-collared pullovers hung straight at the players' waists, rather than tucking into their pants. Having re-created the World Championship look of the early 1900s White Sox, Veeck still wasn't satisfied, though. So on August 8, 1976, he sent his players onto the field for the first game of a doubleheader against Kansas City wearing not only those floppy-collared tops but also thigh-high navy blue shorts instead of pants. At best, the afraid-to-slide White Sox looked like an improperly clad softball team; at worst, like a bunch of humiliated grown men forced by their eccentric owner to dress like fancy lads. After winning the first game despite their bizarre threads, the White Sox held a powwow in the clubhouse and then refused to slip back into their shorts for the second game, which they eventually lost in the relative comfort of their already awful, but more familiar, navy blue trousers. After the twin bill, Veeck blamed his wife, Mary Frances, for the shorts, and they were never seen again.

Thankfully, the 1980s saw a gradual return to sensibility, but not before popsicle-like Astros jerseys challenged, but ultimately fell short of, the White Sox's look of the 1970s for worst-ever uniform bragging rights. Now that those days are past, teams have returned to more traditional home whites and road grays. For marketing purposes, though, most teams also have a Sunday Special that they pull out of their closet for a few select home dates per year, mostly for the purpose of stocking their pro shop with yet another must-buy piece of apparel for fans who might otherwise think they have everything. The black pullovers the

Blue Jays sometimes wear at Rogers Centre, the camouflage Military Appreciation Day uni's the Padres occasionally don at Petco Park, and the St. Patrick's Day–inspired green pullovers the Red Sox have been known to sport at Fenway Park, come to mind as examples of these recent aberrations. As for the worst everyday uniform in the game today, none qualifies as an utter disaster, but for the sake of offending a couple of teams whose jerseys are, well, slightly offensive, we'll slap needs-improvement tags on the Florida Marlins' black and teal, which looks better suited for an Arena Football League team, and on the Padres' road grays, which spell out SAN DIEGO in cluttered letters and a *D* that's way too big. These aren't nearly as atrocious as those infamously flawed White Sox outfits of the 1970s, though, which are our pick for the worst uniform ever.

THE BEST BASEBALL
POP CULTURE

46

THE BEST FAN AMONG U.S. PRESIDENTS

His Love of the Game Was Unimpeachable

The link between our nation's chief pastime and chief executive is one that has been forged throughout generations of American life. This chapter tells the story of how that relationship has evolved as our nation and its game have grown up together. After reviewing the most significant interactions between our presidents and our favorite sport, we'll pick the one president whose love of the game ran the deepest.

In fact, the romance between the country's most popular sport and most important citizen dates back to before baseball as we currently know it even existed and to before there was even such an office as U.S. president. While still general of the Continental Army in 1778, George Washington—who did not become the nation's first president until 1789—reportedly participated in games of the baseball precursor "rounders" with troops as a way to maintain morale during their encampment at Valley Forge. Nearly a century later, Abraham Lincoln's renowned love of a slightly modernized game involving four bases, a bat, and a ball was portrayed in an 1860 political cartoon that depicted him and several political rivals on a field of play. Later, when the Civil War broke out, a version of the fledgling pastime was played by blue- and gray-clad troops across the country in their respective camps. Chester Arthur became the first U.S. president to host a big league team at the White House when he welcomed the National League's Cleveland Forest Cities in 1883 and told them, "Good ballplayers make good citizens." A decade later, Benjamin Harrison became the first commander in chief to attend a big league game when he visited Boundary Field in Washington in June 1892.

The tradition of a sitting president throwing out the first pitch at a game was born at American League Park in Washington on Opening Day of the 1910 season when William Howard Taft, a former semipro pitcher, tossed a ball from his seat to Senators starter Walter Johnson. The pitcher obligingly caught the horsehide and then pitched a one-hit shutout against the Philadelphia Athletics. A large man, who once famously got stuck in the White House bathtub, Taft is also often credited with inadvertently fathering baseball's seventh-inning stretch tradition. According to myth, he stood to relieve some stiffness in his back during the middle of the seventh of a game in Washington, and the crowd, thinking the president was about to depart, rose to salute him. When Taft merely rolled his shoulders a few times, flexed, and then sat back down, the embarrassed fans did the same, before settling in for the final two innings.

Woodrow Wilson, who in his youth played baseball at Davidson College, made his first public appearance with his future wife, Edith Galt, at Philadelphia's Baker Bowl in 1915 when the First Couple attended the second game of the World Series between the Phillies and the Red Sox. The next spring, Wilson and his new missus were back in Washington to celebrate Opening Day at Griffith Stadium. Later in the 1916 season, Wilson paved the way for another baseball tradition when he ordered that "The Star

President Woodrow Wilson throws out the first pitch on Opening Day of the 1916 season.
COURTESY OF THE LIBRARY OF CONGRESS

Spangled Banner" be played at military events and other civic gatherings as the United States inched closer to joining the "war to end all wars." The song was

Herbert Hoover (far left), Mrs. Harding, President Warren Harding, Mrs. Hoover, and H. M. Daugherty, stand in grandstands.
COURTESY OF THE LIBRARY OF CONGRESS

later played by a military band during a 1918 World Series game in Chicago, but would not become a staple of every baseball game until the onset of World War II more than two decades later. By then, an act of Congress had made the song the official National Anthem. Warren Harding succeeded Wilson, taking the oath of office in 1921. Before that, he had owned not only an Ohio newspaper but also a minor league baseball team in his hometown of Marion, Ohio. Harding attended five big league games during his short presidency, most notably the first-ever shutout at Yankee Stadium. After watching Sam Jones blank the Senators in the Bronx in April 1923, Harding attended just one more game home in Washington later that month, before suffering a fatal heart attack.

President Calvin Coolidge throws out the first pitch at Griffith Stadium on Opening Day of the 1925 season. COURTESY OF THE LIBRARY OF CONGRESS

In October 1924 Calvin Coolidge became the first president to throw out the first pitch of a World Series game, and attended three of the four October games played in the nation's capital that year—all Senator wins—including the clinching seventh game against the Giants. The next year, Coolidge turned out for Game Three of the October Classic, but the Senators bowed to Pittsburgh on their way to a seven-game defeat.

Franklin Delano Roosevelt threw out more ceremonial first pitches than any other president, showing off his strong right arm eleven times between 1933 and 1941. FDR is more importantly remembered, however, for famously giving baseball commissioner Kenesaw Mountain Landis the green light to keep the game up and running during World War II. In a letter to Landis dated January 15, 1942, Roosevelt wrote:

> I honestly feel that it would be best for the country to keep baseball going. There will be fewer people unemployed and everybody will work longer hours and harder than ever before. And that means that they ought to have a chance for recreation and for taking their minds off their work even more than before. Baseball provides a recreation which does not last over two hours or two hours and a half, and which can be got for very little cost. And, incidentally, I hope that night games can be extended because it gives an opportunity to the day shift to see a game occasionally.

Later in the letter, Roosevelt suggested that baseball teams fill their rosters with older players, who were less desirable for military duty, rationalizing, "[If] 300 teams [including major and minor leaguers] use 5,000 or 6,000 players, these players are a definite recreational asset to at least 20,000,000 of the fellow citizens—and that in my judgment is thoroughly worthwhile." Landis, of course, took the president's advice, and though many professional players left the game to serve in foreign theaters and—though many minor leagues shut down—the major leagues restocked and the games continued.

Harry Truman followed Roosevelt into office and, though historians have noted he wasn't much of a baseball fan, he attended a record sixteen games during his two terms. All were played in Washington, and the Senators were 9-7 when he was in the house, which is pretty good when you consider that the team was a perennial seventh- or eighth-place finisher during much of Truman's tenure. Truman was also the first left-handed president to throw out a first pitch, the first to attend a night game, the first to attend a game on the Fourth of July, and the first to throw out two first pitches at the same game—one left-handed, and one right-handed.

At the second of thirteen games he attended during his eight years in office, Dwight D. Eisenhower memorably sent a Secret Service agent to the plate to intercept Mickey Vernon on the way back to the dugout after the Senators batting champ hit a walk-off home run to beat the Yankees on Opening Day of the 1954 season. The president simply wanted to shake Vernon's hand and congratulate him on a job well done.

After John F. Kennedy attended just four games during his short term, including the 1962 All-Star Game in Washington, Lyndon Johnson attended four games between 1964 and 1967. Most notably, Johnson turned out for an exhibition game between the Astros and Yankees on April 9, 1965, that represented the first game ever played at the Astrodome. A Texan, Johnson was en route to his home in Johnson City, and he and wife, Lady Bird, stopped by the freshly minted "eighth wonder of the world" to tip their caps not only to modernity but also to Astros president Roy Hofheinz, who had been a campaign manager for Johnson in the 1940s. The president and his wife watched the game from Hofheinz's private box, while munching on chicken wings and ice cream. Because Johnson was a bit late in arriving, though, Texas governor John Connally threw out the first pitch.

In 1972, midway through Richard Nixon's term, the Senators departed the capital to become the Texas Rangers. Thus, one of the biggest baseball fans ever among our presidents was left without a home team. Nixon, who had attended eight games in Washington to that point, did get to attend a Royals-Angels game in his home state California in 1973, but surely missed those Senators. During his re-election campaign in 1972, he proved that he was a true baseball junkie, and a knowledgeable one, when a pool reporter asked him to name his favorite players at a press conference. With puffball questions like that, it's amazing Nixon thought he had to break the law to get re-elected, but nonetheless, he rattled off several of his favorite stars, then took it upon himself in the days ahead to advance his analysis several steps further. He drafted four All-Star teams in which he evaluated the players whose exploits he'd witnessed during all of his years as a fan, spanning 1925 to 1970. One list pertained to American League players between 1925 and 1945, while another ranked the best National Leaguers at each position during those years. The other two lists again separated players by league, but for the period of 1946 through 1970. These amazingly comprehensive All-Nixon rosters appeared in newspapers across the country, under the president's byline. Interestingly, Negro Leagues star Satchel Paige ranked as one of Nixon's best AL pitchers of the first era—even though Paige didn't make his major league debut until Bill Veeck gave him a contract in 1948. With such an enthusiastic foray into the type of baseball historical analysis a baseball writer or reader can certainly appreciate, Nixon would appear to be the most devout fan among the presidents we've discussed so far. But several of his successors also demonstrated an admirable love of the game.

President Richard Nixon throws out first pitch at a Washington Senators game in 1969.
COURTESY OF THE LIBRARY OF CONGRESS

Ronald Reagan began his professional career as a baseball broadcaster of sorts. Contrary to the myth that he was an actual Cubs announcer, he was in fact employed in the 1930s to produce studio re-creations of Chicago Cubs games based on telegraph reports. Later, he delighted in portraying pitcher Grover Cleveland Alexander in the 1952 movie *The Winning Team,* starring in a cast that also included Bob Lemon, Gene Mauch, and several other real players. In later years as president, Reagan made Baltimore's Memorial Stadium his home, visiting it three times, and in 1988 he visited Wrigley Field to throw out the first pitch and broadcast a couple of innings for old-time's sake.

Reagan's vice president and the nation's next president, George H. W. Bush, also possessed a unique personal connection to the game. During his days at Yale in the 1940s, he was a prominent member of the baseball team. His Bulldogs made it to the final round of the very first College World Series, in fact, before losing the first two games of a best-of-three finale against the University of California. The next year, with Bush serving as senior captain, the Bulldogs returned to the series but lost a three-game set against the University of Southern California. A left-handed-throwing, right-handed-hitting first baseman, Bush—whose teammates called him Poppy—batted .251 with 2 home runs and 23 RBIs in fifty-one games over two varsity seasons. Four decades later, as president, Bush attended ten games during his single term, visiting Baltimore, Anaheim, Toronto, Arlington, and San Diego.

In 1995, Bill Clinton and Al Gore became the first sitting president and vice president to attend the same game, visiting Oriole Park at Camden Yards to honor Cal Ripken Jr. on the date of the Iron Man's record-breaking 2,131st consecutive game. In addition to attending Camden Yards three times during his two terms, Clinton also threw out the first pitch at Cleveland's brand-new Jacobs Field in 1994, attended Shea Stadium on the date Jackie Robinson's Number 42 was retired league-wide in 1997, and attended single games at Wrigley Field and Pac Bell Park in San Francisco.

Clinton's seven ballpark appearances in eight years don't suggest he was a rabid fan, especially since most of the games he attended were of the "special occasion" variety, but no one could question the fanaticism of the next man to hold the office. Immediately prior to launching his political career with a stint as governor of Texas in 1994, George W. Bush had been the co-owner and managing general partner of the Texas Rangers for five years. Although he attended only nine games during his eight years in office, W made his ballpark appearances count. One stands out especially. The first president to have played Little League baseball as a child memorably threw out the first pitch of Game Three of the 2001 World Series between the Diamondbacks and Yankees at Yankee Stadium, just weeks after the terrorist attacks of 9/11. The symbolism of Bush, standing tall on the Yankee Stadium mound and delivering a perfect strike to Yankees catcher Todd Greene while the crowd chanted "U-S-A," was an important step in the country's psychological recovery from the blow it had been dealt. The Series had begun amid fear that Yankee Stadium might be the target of another terrorist attack, and Bush's presence reassured New Yorkers that they were indeed safe from harm and could relax, if only for a few hours, to enjoy a normal activity like a baseball game. Amazingly, that game also marked the only time a sitting president attended a World Series game at Yankee Stadium.

As for his other memorable ballpark appearances, Bush threw out the first pitches at the first game ever at Miller Park in Milwaukee in 2001, at the debut of the expansion Washington Nationals at RFK Stadium in 2005, and at the grand opening of Nationals Park in 2008. In all, Bush threw out first pitches at seven different ballparks during his presidency.

White Sox fan Barack Obama got off to a good start during his first year in office by attending the 2009 All-Star Game in St. Louis and delivering the ceremonial first pitch. Obama wore a White Sox jacket to the mound, which drew cheers from Chicago All-Star Mark Buehrle. Then, less than two weeks later, it was Obama's turn to cheer for Buehrle, as the president placed a phone call to the pitcher to congratulate him on the perfect game he tossed against the Rays on July 23.

So which president was the best fan of all? With nods to Reagan and George W. Bush, this lifelong Democrat has to cede the distinction to a third Republican candidate on our ballot: Richard Nixon, who in 1992 issued yet another set of All-Star rosters to rank the best players in the years since his time in office. To view the Nixon lists, readers are encouraged to visit the wonderful section of the *Baseball Almanac* (www.baseball-almanac.com) that takes a term-by-term approach to detailing the intersecting histories of our presidents and our game. For filling out his rosters so diligently and for possessing a fan's eye for the game's minutia and stats, "Nixon's the One."

[47]

THE BEST SUPERFAN

Drumming Up Support for the Home Team,
One Game at a Time

Baseball has always engendered a steady following of *famous* fans, including such modern-day celebrities as Kevin Costner, Garth Brooks, Eddie Vedder, Ben Affleck, Billy Crystal, Rene Russo, Jerry Seinfeld, Jack Welch, and Paul McCartney, to name just a few. But our current rumination isn't dedicated to fans like these individuals who became famous for reasons unrelated to the game and *then* made their rooting interests known, but rather to the otherwise ordinary people who through the years have become quasi celebrities thanks to their rooting acumen. Through their ingenuity, originality, and ability to inspire the masses in the grandstand seats, certain special fans just have it, whatever *it* is. And owing to this special quality they become easily identifiable among other fans, among the home and visiting players, and within their communities at large. In other words, they become famous for being fans. In the course of investigating the culture of these unique individuals, we hope to crown the one fanatic whose enthusiasm for the game has resulted in the greatest renown, earning him or her praise and admiration throughout the baseball world.

Let's begin back in the earliest days of the American League, when at the dawn of the Junior Circuit a Boston barkeep named Michael "Nuf Ced" McGreevy led the Royal Rooters, a rowdy cheering brigade that harassed visiting players at Boston's Huntington Avenue Grounds. McGreevy and his Rooters gained national fame in 1903 when they accompanied the Pilgrims (as those early Red Sox were known) to Pittsburgh for the middle games of the 1903 World Series. There, in the stands of Exposition Park, the Royal Rooters sang the hit Broadway tune "Tessie" over and over again, until Pirates star Honus Wagner was practically pulling his hair out of his head out at shortstop. Here was a group of Boston fans, hundreds of miles from home, taking over a visiting ballpark. Sound familiar? In any case, the beat writers of the day took note and sent dispatches across the land detailing

Boston's John "Honey Fitz" Fitzgerald was a member of the Royal Rooters. COURTESY OF THE LIBRARY OF CONGRESS

the raucous marauders who'd followed their team west. Before long the Royal Rooters were known throughout baseball, McGreevy most prominently among them, though Boston mayor John "Honey Fitz" Fitzgerald—the maternal grandfather of future president John F. Kennedy—also got his share of ink as one of the group's leaders.

By the 1930s several individuals had similarly vaulted into the national spotlight, owing to their unusually strong support of their home teams. Often these characters were the subjects of commentaries issued by radio broadcasters of the era who took special pride in weaving vivid tapestries of the ballpark atmosphere for their listeners. More than that, sometimes people tuning in to listen to games could even hear the catcalls and other noises made by these special ballpark luminaries through those early AM radio waves. "Howling Hilda" Chester was one such rabble-rouser at Ebbets Field in Brooklyn. She held a part-time pregame job bagging peanuts for the masses, then reported to her seat in the bleachers where she would sit, usually in a flowered dress, and bang on a frying pan with an iron ladle. She was also known to lead the bleacher bums through the Ebbets aisles in a long and winding Congo line. By the 1930s, she was so well-known that the Dodgers presented her with a special cowbell, which she used as a noisemaker instead of the frying pan until the team left town in the 1950s.

During that same era, "Screech Owl" McAllister was the resident superfan at Forbes Field, while the colorful Harry Throbe danced and cheered for the Reds at Crosley Field in a red-and-white-striped suit. At Sportsman's Park in St. Louis, "Screeching, Screaming" Mary Ott issued piercing cries that earned her comparisons to a horse whinnying. Loudmouthed Tigers partisan Patsy O'Toole, meanwhile, made such a ruckus at the ballpark that when he traveled to Washington, D.C., for a World Series game between the Yankees and Senators in 1933, Franklin Delano Roosevelt found him too obnoxious to stomach and requested that O'Toole be relocated to another part of the ballpark far from the presidential box. Pete Adelis was known as The Iron Lung of Shibe Park due to his extraordinary pipes, and his fame allowed him a platform as a guest columnist in a 1948 issue of the *Sporting News* in which he presented a list entitled "The Rules of Scientific Heckling." The unusual code of conduct made such suggestions as "Keep pouring it on," and "Don't be shouted down."

In later decades, Mets fanatic Karl Ehrhardt invented a new way of shouting at the ballpark. This diehard wasn't blessed with an iron lung, so he expressed himself instead with large, premade signs that he would schlep through the Shea Stadium turnstiles each night. The Sign Man was a regular behind the third-base dugout in Queens from 1964 through 1981. He would tote several dozen cleverly conceived signs to each game, separated by color-coded tabs, and then hold up the most apropos ones whenever the events of the game moved him to make his opinion heard. Some of his more memorable missives include gems like, Look Ma, No Hands, which he held up after an error by defensively challenged Mets short-stop Frank Taveras; Jose, Can You See, which he displayed whenever flailing Met Jose Cardenal struck out; and There Are No Words, which he triumphantly hoisted when the Mets won the 1969 World Series.

Another well-known fan of the 1970s and early 1980s was Orioles rooter "Wild Bill" Hagy, a Maryland cabbie who would hop on top of the home dugout at Memorial Stadium and treat fans to his trademark Roar from Thirty-Four, as his rally cry was called, owing to his preferred seating location in Section 34. Hagy is also said to have popularized the still familiar "O!" that Baltimore fans shout before each game when the National Anthem singer gets to "Oh, say does that Star-Spangled Banner yet wave." If this is indeed true, and we have no reason to doubt that it is, then Hagy deserves credit for inspiring a tradition that has lasted long beyond his days, a novelty that even traveled with his favorite team and its fans to a new ballpark.

Another universally recognizable fan whose era overlapped with those of the Sign Man and Wild Bill was Morganna the Kissing Bandit. Morganna was an exotic dancer whose most noticeable body measurements reputedly checked in at a mythic 60-by-23-by-39 inches. She used her considerable bust and bubbly personality to inject herself into the game's culture by repeatedly hopping out of the stands at ballparks across the country, running up to players on the field, and kissing them. In a "career" that spanned the early 1970s into the early 1990s, Morganna built an All-Star list of "victims" that included Frank Howard, Pete Rose, Johnny Bench, Nolan Ryan, Cal Ripken Jr., George Brett, Don Mattingly, and Steve Garvey, among many other blushing ballers. The buxom blond was arrested for disorderly conduct just about every time she pulled her stunt, of course, but along the way her legend only grew. She appeared on *The Tonight Show* with Johnny Carson and on the *Late Show with David Letterman*, did cameos in B-list movies, posed in *Playboy*, and always signed autographs under the trademark salutation "Breast Wishes." Morganna would never get away with her act in today's hypersensitive security environment, and rightly so, but in her day she was a pleasant ballpark diversion that even the players seemed to appreciate. Morganna was a bit discriminating, you see. She didn't waste her kisses on any old player; she pursued good ones. And in those pre–*SportsCenter* days, players knew that if Morganna planted a smooch on one of their cheeks, they'd be showing up on eleven o'clock news broadcasts across the country.

Another superfan known for unexpectedly popping up at ballparks across the country in the 1970s and 1980s was Rollen Frederick Stewart, or, as he was more commonly known, Rainbow Man. This eccentric born-again Christian sported a Jesus-like beard long before Johnny Damon did, but he also wore a massive rainbow-colored afro wig, which Damon, to our knowledge, has never done. Rainbow Man's modus operandi was to show up at nationally televised games, score a seat behind home plate, and display a sign that read JOHN 3:16. He would position himself so that the centerfield camera—the one fixed on the hitter for each pitch—would steer fans toward the verse in which the Bible says that God sent his only son to save man and give him eternal life. At first, broadcasters and network executives tried to ignore Stewart so as not to encourage him, in much the same way that TV broadcasts purposely don't beam home to viewers the images of those drunken fans who occasionally jump onto fields late in games today. But after a while, the baseball and sports establishment began treating Rainbow Man with something akin to grudging acceptance. After all, if Rainbow Man was in the house, then it had to be a big game. In time, Rainbow Man became a part of wider pop culture too, inspiring a skit starring Christopher Walken on *Saturday Night Live*, a Budweiser commercial, and even a documentary film. Despite his success at weaseling his way into mainstream culture, Rainbow Man wrote an unhappy end to his life story. He is currently serving three consecutive life sentences in a California state prison for a 1992 conviction on three counts of kidnapping.

Another superfan who has been the subject of a documentary film, but whose story fortunately hasn't taken such a dramatically dark and disturbing final turn, is current Wrigley Field fixture Ronnie Wickers, or Ronnie Woo Woo, as most fans know him. This friendly elderly gentleman has been attending Cubs games since the 1940s and is easily recognizable, thanks to the full Cubs uniform he dons as he wanders the Wrigley bleachers and to the high-pitched call of "Woo woo!" he frequently makes. Ronnie occupies a special place in the collective hearts of Cubs fans, to the point where they take pleasure in buying him ballpark treats and chatting with him about the team. In return, Ronnie is happy to treat them to a cheer whenever they'd like. It is common practice for Wrigley pilgrims to hold out their cell phones when Ronnie comes their way so that he can send a "Woo woo!" out to their friends in distant lands who can't be present at the ballpark but can pretend they are for a minute or two, thanks to the familiar sound of Ronnie's voice.

Ronnie possesses his own unique way of rooting for the home team, to be sure. And, in contrast to other modern day superfans like Heckling Harry—who sits in the leftfield stands in San Diego, haranguing visiting leftfielders—or Rob Szasz, the Happy Heckler in Tampa Bay who has even published a book about the heckling he does from behind home plate at Tropicana Field, Ronnie doesn't specialize in tearing down members of the opposing team, but rather in galvanizing the home fans behind their team.

Ronnie is a strong runner-up in our best superfan quest, eclipsed in terms of his renown and impact on the national pastime only by Indians rooter John Adams. While Mr. Adams's name is not likely recognizable to most readers who live outside Cleveland, the game-day din he makes at Progressive Field and formerly made at Municipal Stadium is a part of just about every fan's understanding of the Indians franchise. Adams is the fellow, you see, who bangs the big bass drum that booms through your car radio or television speakers whenever you tune in to a game taking place in Cleveland. He has been pounding away in support of the Tribe since midway through the 1973 season with a rabid devotion that has spanned good times and bad. Adams sits in the back row of the leftfield bleachers beneath the scoreboard and strikes the 26-inch drum that he props on the seat beside him. He starts thumping whenever the Indians put runners in scoring position, or get two strikes on an opposing hitter, or do anything else mildly exciting. Picking his spots in this way, he uses his percussion as a rallying cry to encourage other fans to make some noise in support of the home team. For years, he paid his own way into the local park, but today, after inspiring a bobblehead doll in his likeness, tossing out the ceremonial first pitch before a 2007 playoff game, and drumming his way through more than 2,500 games, he attends games for free as a guest of the Indians. For his devotion to his team, for the unique way he has of injecting energy into the home crowd, and for the steady beat he keeps, Adams is a superfan of the highest order and our choice for the best famous baseball rooter of them all.

48

THE BEST BASEBALL SONG

It Continues to Strike a Chord with Fans

As an important outlet for human emotion, music provides a medium for expression in which it's okay for even tough guys to lower their guard and communicate what they're feeling. In songs we laugh and we cry. We reflect on the childhood innocence we once took for granted. We wrestle with the larger questions in life, hoping to find some answers. We reach for our dreams. We lament our limitations. We fall in love. We fall out of love. If you think about it, it's funny, but you could say the same things about baseball and about the experience of rooting for a team, as imperfect as that team may be.

If music and baseball are both passions that simultaneously provide an escape from and a better understanding of our reality, then it makes sense that the game and its players have inspired scores of songs about them through the years. And these contributions to American pop culture have influenced practically every genre of music, from big band to jazz, folk, country, rock, and even Irish punk. As for the first baseball song, it is believed to have been "The Base Ball Polka," which was first published in sheet-music form in 1858, before the advent of audio recording, which, incidentally, Thomas Edison first introduced in 1877.

The best-known baseball song, of course, is "Take Me Out to the Ball Game." Interestingly, though, most Americans know only the chorus and none of the verses that vaudevillian Jack Norworth penned in 1908. Nonetheless, the song's familiar refrain is ingrained in our seventh-inning-stretch ritual at ballparks from coast to coast. Does that make "Take Me Out to the Ball Game" the best baseball song ever? Probably. But we thought it worthwhile to run down the playlist of other famous songs that have sprung to life at the happy intersection where baseball and pop culture collide.

To begin, let's give Norworth's classic its due. After all, "Take Me Out to the Ball Game" is one of the most widely recited songs in America. Paradoxically, most fans who sing the song are already at a ball game and therefore in no immediate need of being taken to one. Also paradoxically, Norworth had never attended a professional baseball game at the time he devised the lyrics, and he wouldn't attend one for another thirty-two years. Just the same, inspiration struck the twenty-nine-year-old entertainer as he rode in a New York City subway car one day. After observing a poster advertising a game at the Polo Grounds, he hastily scribbled some notes on a piece of paper. Later, his friend Albert Von Tilzer set the words to music and Norworth's wife, Nora Bayes, performed the vocals. Before long, the song was a smash hit, first on the vaudeville circuit, then on vinyl. But what's it really about? Well there were two versions—the original written in 1908, and a later one written in 1927. Both concern young ladies—Katie Casey in the first, Nelly Kelly in the second—who are obsessed with baseball. In the first verse the woman's gentleman caller comes for her, suggesting they go to a Broadway show (or to Coney Island in the second version). But being the fan she is, Katie/Nelly pleads instead to go to a baseball game. In the second verse, she is at the game, first heckling the umpire and then encouraging the home crowd. In the midst of a tie game, she implores her fellow fans to sing the chorus in the ballpark stands. The song's staying power is testament to its appeal. It's just a shame that big league teams don't take an extra minute or two to play a few more verses during the seventh inning so that fans could appreciate its whole story.

While "Take Me Out to the Ball Game" is commendable for its portrayal of a die-hard fan, more commonly baseball songs portray the heroics of vaunted players. One such ditty that was quite popular in its day was "Slide Kelly, Slide." Originally recorded in 1893, the song at once celebrated and criticized the playing style of Mike "King" Kelly, who was one of baseball's first great stars. The catcher/outfielder played for several teams, most notably the Chicago White Stockings and Boston Beaneaters in the pre–modern era. He eventually earned posthumous enshrinement in Cooperstown in 1945. Kelly is remembered as an

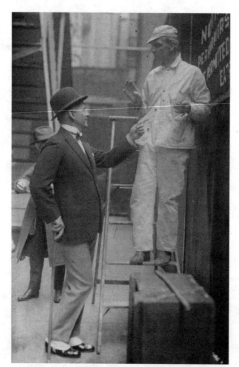

Jack Norworth (right) wrote the lyrics to "Take Me Out to the Ballgame." COURTESY OF THE LIBRARY OF CONGRESS

innovator who popularized the catcher's practices of backing up first base and of giving hand signals to the pitcher. But it was his daring on the base paths that caused fans to either love or hate him, depending upon their risk-tolerance level. Kelly was a master base stealer, owing in part to his speed and in part to his sliding ability. And also because . . . well, he is said to have cheated. Playing in a day when there was often only one umpire—positioned behind the pitcher so as to call balls and strikes and also have a clear view of first base—Kelly would allegedly run from first to third by cutting across the diamond. As the umpire looked in at the plate, Kelly would sneak behind him, bypassing second base entirely. As his legend grew, Kelly's devotees and detractors alike would chant, "Slide Kelly, Slide," whenever he reached base. Eventually George Gaskin set the mantra to music and added some sparse additional lyrics. In the early days of the recording

industry, "Slide Kelly, Slide," became America's first hit record that wasn't operatic, patriotic, or spiritual in nature, and "Slide Kelly, Slide" became a slang expression that people muttered whenever they seemed headed for a hairy situation. The lone verse goes, "Slide, Kelly, Slide!/ Your running's a disgrace!/ Slide, Kelly, Slide!/ Stay there, hold your base!"

Unlike "Slide Kelly, Slide," "Joltin' Joe DiMaggio" is in no way ambiguous about its admiration for its protagonist. The song, which became an instant classic in 1941, celebrates DiMaggio's 56-game hit streak that year. It recounts how the Yankees star tied the previous mark of forty-four games with a hit and recalls the coast-to-coast attention generated by the streak: "He tied the mark at forty-four/ July the first, you know/ Since then he's hit a good twelve mo'/ Joltin' Joe DiMaggio." The remaining verses foretell DiMaggio's eventual enshrinement in the Hall of Fame and recall the night his streak ended in Cleveland. The chorus—backed by a full orchestra and sung by Betty Bonney—is extremely catchy.

King Kelly, featured on this tobacco card from 1888, inspired a hugely popular baseball song. COURTESY OF THE LIBRARY OF CONGRESS

Jackie Robinson was another star of the 1940s and 1950s who inspired several songs. The most famous of these was the Count Basie Orchestra's "Did You See Jackie Robinson Hit That Ball?" The jazzy jingle came out in 1949—two years after Robinson broke baseball's color barrier—and rose to as high as thirteenth in the pop charts. In the song, vocalist Taps Miller applauds the talents of other African-American stars like Roy Campanella, Larry Doby, Don Newcombe, and Satchel Paige, before concluding that Jackie's the best one of all. The melodic tune concludes, "Did you see Jackie Robinson hit that ball?/ Did he hit it? Yeah, and that ain't all/ He stole home/ Yes, yes, Jackie's real gone/ Jackie's a real gone guy."

While hitting and base stealing have been popular fodder for songsmiths, pitching prowess has inspired its share of verses too. Interestingly, one of the best pitcher tributes wasn't popularized until nearly two decades after its author put words to music. Bob Dylan wrote and continues to write so many songs that "Catfish," his 1970s ode to Catfish Hunter, somehow got lost in the shuffle. Dylan junkies knew it, because they'd heard him perform it in concert or had heard a bootlegged recording of it, but it wasn't officially released until the early 1990s when Dylan produced his *Bootleg Series*. The song begins with Dylan describing a Hunter strikeout, then breaks into the chorus, "Catfish, million-dollar man/ Nobody can throw the ball like Catfish can." It recalls how Hunter used to work on "Mr. Finley's farm," as Dylan calls Charlie Finley's Oakland Athletics, and then explains that Catfish left as a free agent because Finley wouldn't pay him a fair wage. The loving tribute goes on to describe the country kid, Catfish, wearing a pinstriped suit and alligator boots while smoking a cigar. It describes him striking out Reggie Jackson, and mentions that even Athletics manager Billy Martin smiles when he looks at Catfish, who guarantees 20 wins a season and is a sure bet to make the Hall of Fame.

In 1981 songwriter and onetime minor league baseball player Terry Cashman released a song called "Willie, Mickey, and the Duke," which didn't enjoy immediate success but gained increasing airtime as the player's strike of 1981 droned on. The nostalgic song—also known as "Talkin' Baseball"—has remained popular through the years, thanks in part to its inclusion on game-day soundtracks at major and minor league parks and to its use on sports-talk radio programs, usually when the hosts and callers are talkin' baseball. Cashman's lyrics begin in the 1950s, touching upon the heroics of Bobby Thomson, the goofiness of Yogi Berra, the "Midget Gaedel," Hank Aaron, and others, before continuing through the 1960s and 1970s. Fan enjoyment of the tune led Cashman to write and record several other team-specific versions of it with lyrics to suit the storylines and memorable players of different franchises.

Another song that continues to play through ballpark speakers today is John Fogerty's 1985 hit "Centerfield." The lyrics reference Willie Mays, Ty Cobb, and Joe DiMaggio, as well as the mythic Casey and his Mudville Nine. Throughout the song, the singer implores his coach to put him into the game, in centerfield, so that he can show that he belongs. With his "beat-up glove" and "homemade bat" the singer is ready to "give this game a ride." He's "ready to play, today." Essentially, this is a song about a person who knows the time is right for him to take a chance and devote himself to something he loves. The song is inspirational in that its message could be transferred to any pursuit, not just playing professional baseball; sometimes the time just comes to take a chance and follow your dream.

Another song that is about more than "just" baseball, "The Greatest" by Kenny Rogers tells the simple but beautiful story of a young boy trying to hit a baseball out of his hand. Each time he tosses it up in the air and swings the ball eludes his bat and falls to the ground with a thud. He imagines himself in front of a big crowd, at bat with the game on the line. But he strikes out. Is the determined lad distressed? Does he realize that maybe his slow bat is a sign he's not on the fast track to big league stardom after all? Nope. Seizing opportunity from despair, he rationalizes that it must be a sign he'll make a great pitcher one day. The song ends with him proudly telling his mother, "I am the greatest, that is a fact/ But even I didn't know I could pitch like that." Because we've all stood in our backyard with a bat in our hands fantasizing about a clutch situation in which we emerge the hero, the song is easily relatable. The child's innocence and willingness to adapt his dream to fit his ability also rings true to our own lives. It is easy to see why Rogers's song became a top-twenty single in 1999.

Staying in the country genre, we come full circle with a review of a 1990s song that, like "Take Me Out to the Ball Game," portrays the magic of the fan experience. In "Cheap Seats," Alabama depicts a group of bush league bleacher creatures enraptured with their home park's flat beer and hot dogs slathered with mustard and relish. The fans heckle the umpires from afar, even if they don't know the pitcher's name. While the minor league pennant race may not be too important to them, they cherish the time they spend together above the rightfield wall doing the wave and rooting for home runs. The song captures the fun-first ethos of the minor leagues where good times with friends and family come before winning or losing, and fans—even if they don't hang on every pitch—take pride in the fact that their city has a professional team.

The most recent baseball song that makes our list comes courtesy of the Boston-based Celtic punk band known as the Dropkick Murphys, who in 2004 released a new version of the Broadway ditty Boston's famous Royal Rooters sang as early as 1903. "Tessie," in its original incarnation, was about a woman singing to her beloved parakeet. It gained popularity in 1902 as part of *The Silver Slipper*. And by the time Boston squared off against Pittsburgh in the first modern World Series, the song had been appropriated by Boston's most devout fans who, sitting in the leftfield stands of the Huntington Avenue Grounds, would sing it to their heart's content to distract opposing players (as detailed in Chapter 47). The song remained part of the Beantown baseball experience for several years, until the Rooters had a falling-out with Red Sox management after their regular seats at Fenway Park were sold to other fans for the final game of the 1918 World Series. Over the ensuing eighty-six years, Red Sox fans did not sing "Tessie" and the star-crossed team did not win another World Series. Then, early in 2004, the Dropkicks released a new version of the tune, blending parts of the original chorus with new verses that paid tribute to the Royal Rooters. The song became a hit on Boston radio, and then the Red Sox, as if on cue, won the World Series that October.

Taste in music is something that varies so greatly from person to person that fans are likely to have their own favorite baseball songs based on their own musical preferences. As the above hit list exemplifies, there are, fortunately, baseball songs aplenty for just about every type of listener. As for the best one? Well, thousands of voices rising joyously in unison, night after night, at ballpark after ballpark across the land, make a pretty strong argument. The choice has to be "Take Me Out to the Ball Game," but you already knew that.

49

THE BEST BASEBALL MOVIE

From Green Fields to Silver Screens

For serious baseball fans no leisure-time activity can compare to the exquisite pleasure of watching nine innings unfurl, but the better baseball movies come close in their ability to captivate our imaginations and hold our attention. The first-ever feature-length baseball film was released in 1909, back in the days when Ty Cobb and Honus Wagner were kings of the diamond. But it didn't focus on either of them, or on any big leaguer, but rather on an amateur. In *His Last Game*, theatergoers met a Native American named Bill Going who resisted the temptation of gamblers who wanted him to throw a game for his tribal Choctaw team. The villains then poison Going, and he winds up shooting one of them. Arrested and sentenced to death by firing squad, Going's tribal chief convinces the sheriff to allow the unfortunate protagonist to pitch one last game before his execution.

Six years later, former big leaguer and future vaudevillian "Turkey Mike" Donlin made his cinematic debut playing himself in the first baseball biopic, *Right off the Bat*. The film told the story of how Donlin made the leap from playing town ball to the professional ranks, how he caught the eye of the girl next door along the way, resisted the advances of gamblers, and fulfilled his dream of playing for the New York Giants.

In the century since the arrival of trailblazing films such

Mike Donlin—posing here with his wife, actress Mabel Hite—starred in *Right off the Bat*. COURTESY OF THE LIBRARY OF CONGRESS

as these, Hollywood has produced more than 250 feature-length baseball movies. On a rainy summer night or snowy winter afternoon, any film that includes a few cracks of the bat or thuds of the old horsehide hitting the catcher's mitt helps sate our appetite for all things hardball. But the finer cinematic efforts do more than just that. They help us put our collective finger on why we love the game so much. They remind us that baseball is the perfect metaphor for our own unpredictable, imperfect, and yet ultimately rewarding lives. And the better hardball flicks even offer levels of interpretation and understanding that enable those nonfans in our lives to appreciate the game through them in a way they might not ordinarily. In this way, baseball movies enable us to share our passion for the game with those people in our lives who usually don't quite *get* our obsession.

This chapter is dedicated to the best baseball movies, and by movies we mean feature films of the nondocumentary variety. After all, who would argue that Ken Burns' 1994 documentary *Baseball* isn't the finest hardball film ever made? Sticking to feature films then, we'll review the better ones, pick our favorite, and even tip our caps afterward to some honorable mentions that belong in any serious fan's DVD collection.

Our first nominee is *Angels in the Outfield* (1951), which tells the story of how a hapless Pittsburgh Pirates team and its rough-and-tumble manager, Guffy McGovern, are suddenly transformed into contenders with some help from on high. After a guardian angel answers a little girl's prayer, an invisible team of angels descends on Forbes Field and starts performing miracles to swing games in the Pirates' favor. The only catch is that McGovern must comport himself like a gentleman or else the angels will stop cooperating. Viewers can't see the angels—only the manager and the child can—but we do see signs of their presence as the team turns its season around. Paul Douglas, who also starred in the baseball film *It Happens Every Spring,* plays McGovern, while Joe DiMaggio and Ty Cobb make cameo appearances. This movie is a particularly enjoyable flight of fancy because bad bounces and fluke plays really do alter the outcomes of games, and *Angels in the Outfield* suggests that maybe more than just luck is the reason why.

In another movie that touches upon the game's transformational powers, Walter Matthau stars as an alcoholic former minor leaguer who agrees to coach a ragtag bunch of Little Leaguers in *The Bad News Bears* (1976). The Bears endure some early humiliations until Matthau's Morris Buttermaker recruits a couple of ringers and the Bears become a contender. As the film reaches its climax, the team squares off against the joyless Yankees and their hypercompetitive coach in the final game of the year. It is then that the Bears realize winning isn't everything, and they play for the love of the game, rather than stooping to the Yankees' level. Despite losing, the Bears are the winners in the end—kind of like Rocky Balboa in the original *Rocky* movie. While it's often remarked today that the shift in youth sports from something fun and wholesome into something perverse and virulent is a new phenomenon, *The Bad News Bears* reminds us that as long as there have been parents and children, there have been adults who miss the point of childhood.

Another film that portrays a team of misfits suddenly cast as winners, *Major League* (1989) is the most outrageously funny film on our list. Drawing from an ensemble cast that stars Corbin Bernsen, Charlie Sheen, and Wesley Snipes, it follows a fictional Cleveland Indians squad that bands together when its team owner tries to undermine the Indians' success so that she can move the club to Florida. The has-beens and never-weres hand-picked to ensure failure overcome the forces conspiring against them, though, including some squabbles in their own clubhouse, to finish the season tied with the dreaded Yankees for first place. This sets up a dramatic one-game playoff to decide the division title. One reason why the movie clicked with baseball fans was its wise choice of the Indians as the focal team. The hapless Tribe, with its frustrated but dedicated fans, translated wonderfully to the big screen. Colorful characters like Ricky "Wild Thing" Vaughn (Sheen), who has great stuff but must learn to harness it, and announcer Harry Doyle (Bob Uecker) stick in fans' minds long after the closing credits.

At the other end of the genre spectrum, *The Pride of the Yankees* (1942) may be a bit overly sentimental, but it still ranks as one of the best baseball biopics ever produced. It came out just a year after Lou Gehrig died of the mysterious illness that would come to bear his name. Actor Gary Cooper's Gehrig wrestles with a strained relationship with his immigrant mother who wants him to be an engineer, not a ballplayer. Eventually, he signs with the Yankees only so that he can come up with the money to pay for the emergency medical care she needs. Before long, Gehrig is a star and his mother forgives him. Then he woos the love of his life, promises a sick child to hit two home runs in a World Series game, and sets the record for the most consecutive games played. As illness seizes his body, he finds increasing limitations to what he can do on the field, until finally he stands behind the microphone at Yankee Stadium and delivers the immortalized line, "People all say that I've had a bad break. But today . . . today, I consider myself the luckiest man on the face of the earth." The film's heroic portrayal of a player who by all accounts really was a hero at a time when many of the game's stars didn't really embody the values and accolades often attributed to them makes *The Pride of the Yankees* an inspirational tearjerker. And as a bonus, Yankees like Babe Ruth, Bill Dickey, Mark Koenig, and Bob Meusel appear in the cast.

The Natural (1984) is perhaps the most controversial film among our nominees. Some viewers really like it, while others shake their heads and say it strays too far from the message author Bernard Malamud intended in his novel of the same name. In short, Hollywood gave Malamud's dark morality tale, which ends with a strikeout, a typically triumphant Hollywood ending. In the movie the mythic Roy Hobbs—played by Robert Redford—hits an epic light-bank-shattering home run to win the pennant for the New York Knights. And he gets the girl too. Then the movie flashes forward so that we can see Hobbs playing a contented game of catch with his future son in the happily-ever-after that awaits him. For those unfamiliar with the book, or those who are familiar with it but are willing to look past the discrepancies between it and the movie, *The Natural* succeeds in presenting the game in a sort of alternate universe where a player really can hit the cover off a ball. Part comic book, part love story, and part moral fable, it is a tense but eventually feel-good story in which the central character learns from the follies of his past and emerges not only a better man, but a winner and hero too.

Another movie that exists in a fantasy dimension at least a few degrees removed from the ordinary bounds of space, time, and, well, reality is *Field of Dreams* (1989), which was also adapted from a novel, entitled *Shoeless Joe*. If we accept the premise that there is something inherently magical about baseball, then it's not too hard to suspend our disbelief and accept that a mysterious voice is instructing Ray Kinsella to plow under his field of corn and build a baseball diamond on his struggling family farm for reasons yet unknown. Ray puts his faith in forces larger than himself, and eventually he is rewarded. Along the way to realizing that the ghost players who use his field will help save his family from financial ruin, he enlists the help of a disillusioned author, and then a long-retired player. At the same time, he struggles to convince his wife and daughter to believe in the field's magic. And he comes to appreciate that redemption, even for the dishonored Joe Jackson, is always attainable. The movie culminates with Ray having a simple game of catch on his magical field with his deceased father as the latter character appears as he did when still a young man, before the burdens of life wore him down and created the barriers that, in life, prevented him from forming a close relationship with his son.

Joe Jackson is also one of the central characters in *Eight Men Out* (1988), which, owing to its success in juxtaposing the charm and innocence of the dead-ball era with the insidious evil of organized gambling, earns inclusion here. As Arnold Rothstein's gambling syndicate entices the eight Chicago White Sox who conspire—to varying degrees—to fix the 1919 World Series, White Sox owner Charles Comiskey is portrayed as a miserly curmudgeon, Jackson as a good old Southern boy who doesn't realize the full complexity of his actions, White Sox third baseman Buck Weaver as a fairly innocent victim, and aging knuckleballer Eddie Cicotte as being driven to betrayal by Comiskey's refusal to pay him a reasonable salary. *Eight Men Out* provides a fascinating portrayal of the deal struck between the gamblers and players, of the suspicious World Series games to follow, and finally, of the court proceedings and judgments of commissioner Kenesaw Mountain Landis that sealed the eight conspirators' fate.

In *Bang the Drum Slowly* (1973), a young Robert De Niro masterfully captures the essence of simpleminded protagonist Bruce Pearson, a back-up catcher determined to play one final season before succumbing to Hodgkin's disease. The story—which is based on Mark Harris's novel—is tragic but beautiful too, as Pearson's illness eventually has the effect of pulling together a hitherto fractured group of men who haven't been functioning particularly well as a team. Ultimately, Pearson must pass away, but not before his final and best season teaches him and his fellow New York Mammoths an important lesson about overcoming differences and seeking the good in other human beings. The movie also teaches us all to appreciate just how fleeting life can be and reminds us that we should treat one another kindly.

Finally, our pick for the best baseball movie ever goes to—the envelope, please—*Bull Durham* (1988). The hilarious and poignant drama details the intersecting life paths of career minor leaguer "Crash" Davis and rising phenom "Nuke" LaLoosh. The aging catcher, Davis, played by Kevin Costner, must grapple with the realization that his career is approaching its end while he tries to mentor the reckless LaLoosh, played by Tim Robbins, who has immense talent but takes it for granted. A love triangle involving Durham Bulls resident baseball groupie, Annie Savoy, played by Susan Sarandon, further complicates the relationship between the two players. For portraying the behind-the-scenes world of bush league ball in such unapologetically crude and innocently childish fashion, for delivering poetic monologues that espouse the virtues of the "church of baseball" and of the nature of human love, for inspiring a whole new baseball-movie boom in the late 1980s and 1990s, and for even rekindling interest in the minor leagues, which in turn led to a new wave of stadium-construction projects, *Bull Durham* is our choice.

HONORABLE MENTIONS

One of the darker baseball movies, *Fear Strikes Out* (1957), is based on former big leaguer Jimmy Piersall's autobiography. The movie portrays a young Piersall, played by Anthony Perkins, who loves the game but can never play it well enough to please his domineering father. Eventually, a nervous breakdown derails his career and lands him in a mental hospital where he must rebuild his sense of self before returning to the field.

Damn Yankees (1958), the lone musical on our list, was a Broadway hit before its adaptation for film. In the play and movie alike, a Washington Senators fan named Joe Boyd makes the proverbial deal with the devil to become a big league star. The Senators start winning, but Joe's soul and the love of a good woman hang in the balance as the big game approaches and time runs out for Joe to call off the deal.

A League of Their Own (1992) introduces fans to a largely forgotten chapter in baseball history—the war-era All-American Girls Professional Baseball League, which kept fans entertained at a time when many minor leagues closed down to free players for war service. The plot, which focuses primarily on the sibling rivalry between two sisters on the Rockford Peaches, challenges gender assumptions that pervaded in the 1940s and continue even today.

Billy Crystal's made-for-HBO movie *61** (2001) provides a dramatic retelling of the 1961 season in which Yankees teammates Mickey Mantle and Roger Maris both pursued Ruth's single-season home run record. As the season progresses, we see the toll the media scrutiny being heaped on both players takes on them, and we see their personalities on and off the field come into clearer focus.

As for Ruth, we're still waiting for a top-notch movie detailing his career and larger-than-life persona. John Goodman more fairly resembled the Babe in *The Babe* (1992) than William Bendix in *The Babe Ruth Story* (1948), but neither actor came close to doing justice to the Bambino in the way Tommy Lee Jones captured *his* character in *Cobb* (1994). Jones's honest portrayal of the unlikable Georgia Peach makes *Cobb* a movie all fans should see. Roger Clemens and Hall of Fame announcer Ernie Harwell both make cameos.

50

THE BEST BASEBALL BOOKS

Their Authors Sure Knew How to Spin a Yarn

In the closing pages of our journey together, as your humble author I thought it might be helpful and appropriate to offer a reading list that might serve as a guide in your future explorations of the game. Rather than trying to whittle down the thousands of baseball titles to a short list of just the five or six most essential ones, we'll take a slightly more expansive approach than we do in other chapters. This chapter, devoted to the best baseball books, includes short summaries of some all-time favorites, followed by even shorter synopses of several honorable mentions also worthy of any serious fan's attention. Surely, avid baseball readers will be familiar with many of these titles, but I hope too, that this final chapter will introduce some hidden gems and less regaled works that may have previously gone unnoticed.

Three novels that were all later adapted for film rank among the best baseball books ever penned. Bernard Malamud's *The Natural* was published in 1952. Although Malamud and other writers soon got to work on various screenplay attempts, more than three decades would pass before Robert Redford brought Roy Hobbs to life on the big screen in 1984. Any reader who assumes it's unnecessary to read this book owing to their familiarity with the movie would be mistaken though. As is often the case with literature adapted for film, more than just a little bit of Malamud's larger meaning was lost in translation. There is a famous story in literary circles, in fact, of Malamud sitting in a movie theater and weeping upon first seeing *The Natural* and realizing how grossly distorted it had been. Throughout the book, Hobbs is a classic antihero, a not particularly likeable or redeemable character that has been dealt a bad blow by fate but is also the consistent victim of his own poor decisions and personal weakness. He chooses the wrong women, takes his immense talent for granted, and puts personal pride and greed above the good of his team. When the book ends, our sense of loss—for Hobbs the human being, as well as the player—is profound.

The second in a quartet of four baseball novels written by Mark Harris, *Bang the Drum Slowly* has remained a popular pick among literary critics ranking the best sports books since shortly after its publication in 1956. And for good reason. The narrator is a young southpaw, who despite packing on the pounds over the off-season, holding out for a larger contract in spring training, and devoting much of his time to a side job as an insurance salesman and a hobby as a card shark, is on the brink of, and then in the midst of, a career year. The story is not really about the success of Henry "Author" Wiggen though, or even of his New York Mammoths. Rather, its dominant storyline concerns Wiggen's roommate, backup catcher Bruce Pearson, who is intent on playing one final season before succumbing to Hodgkin's disease.

W. P. Kinsella's *Shoeless Joe* (1982) served as the basis for the movie *Field of Dreams*. The book requires the same suspension of disbelief as the movie, but succeeds nonetheless. This is magic realism at its finest. Those who have seen the movie may be surprised to learn that J. D. Salinger was the character upon which James Earl Jones's movie character was based, but the most essential storylines—involving the protagonist's endangered farm, his deceased father, and his faith rewarded—translate without much modification from book to film. The book takes readers on a whimsical journey through a world where dreams really do come true.

Switching gears to review the wide range of nonfiction the game has inspired, we might assert that biographies, tell-all memoirs, and season- and era-specific retrospectives outshine the more straightforward historical and statistical analyses and reference books that are useful and interesting, in their way, but stop short of delving into the lives of the game's players on a human level. Jim Bouton's *Ball Four* (1970), which opened the floodgates for the sports tell-all, is one such selection. A pitcher nearing the end of his career, Bouton secretly keeps a diary of his interactions with teammates, club officials, sportswriters, and fans during the 1969 season, which he begins with the hapless Seattle Pilots and finishes with the Astros. Bouton portrays his teammates, who never imagined their drinking, drugging, skirt-chasing exploits would become public knowledge, as glorified frat boys who somehow find time to turn up at the ballpark for a few hours a day. The book was controversial in its time, so much so that baseball commissioner Bowie Kuhn publicly demanded that Bouton renounce it, which, of course, only increased interest and sales.

An autobiography pertaining to an equally controversial figure, *Veeck—As in Wreck* (1962) offers a raucous journey through the life and times of baseball's greatest promoter, "Barnum Bill" Veeck. The master of ballpark marketing (see Chapter 44) recounts the steps involved in pulling off each of his greatest gests. Along the way, his love of the game, its players, and fans shines through.

On a more serious note, Eliot Asinof's meticulously researched *Eight Men Out* (1963) recounts one of the saddest chapters in baseball history, the Black Sox Scandal, which resulted in eight players being banned from the game for allegedly conspiring with gamblers to fix the 1919 World Series. Asinof offers a neither too sympathetic nor too judgmental appraisal of star Joe Jackson and his co-conspirators, portraying them as fallible human beings spurned to do the unthinkable by a miserly team owner and sinister figures from the gambling underworld who penetrate baseball's Garden of Eden.

Although dozens of books exist pertaining to baseball's Negro Leagues, the one credited with inventing the genre remains to this day the finest of the lot. At a time when the exploits of Satchel Paige, Josh Gibson, Cool Papa Bell, Rube Foster, Buck Leonard, Judy Johnson, and other Negro Leagues stars were beginning to fade from public consciousness, author Robert Peterson resuscitated interest in "black baseball" with *Only the Ball Was White* (1970). The book is filled with fascinating anecdotes and firsthand accounts gleaned from Peterson's interviews with many of the Negro Leagues' principal players.

In *The Glory of Their Times* (1966), Lawrence Ritter similarly shares the stories culled from his interviews with the earliest of big league stars, the ones who graced diamonds across the country at the turn of the last century. Ritter traveled thousands of miles during four years of exhaustive research so that he could preserve the memories of baseball's aging dead-ball-era heroes, goats, and role players before they passed on to the big baseball field in the sky. He sat down with Hank Greenberg, Harry Hooper, "Sad Sam" Jones, Rube Marquard, Chief Meyers, Lefty O'Doul, Fred Snodgrass, Paul Waner, Joe Wood, and many others, then got out of the way and let each of them tell their story.

Similarly, former commissioner Fay Vincent shares with readers the stories of stars from an only slightly later era in his excellent book *The Only Game in Town: Baseball Stars of the 1930s and 1940s Talk about the Game They Loved* (2006).

Another fascinating book, *The Boys of Summer* (1971) is Roger Kahn's tribute to the team he covered as a Dodgers beat writer in the 1950s. The book introduces

Pee Wee Reese, Jackie Robinson, Gil Hodges, Roy Campanella, Duke Snider, and other familiar Brooklynites in the prime of their youth, while also revisiting them nearly two decades later after they've slipped into the premature old age into which baseball forces all of its stars once their skills diminish. The result is a bittersweet ballad that explores the fragility of human hopes, dreams, and pursuits and the unyielding march of time.

So which of these best-of-the-best baseball books ranks as this author's favorite? If I had to choose just one entry to be my lone companion while stranded on the proverbial desert island, *The Glory of Their Times* would find its way into my rucksack, seeing as it's full of so many different baseball stories told from so many different perspectives. But it's hard to beat *The Natural*, *The Boys of Summer*, or *Ball Four* when settling into an easy chair beside the fireplace on a snowy day. How's that for a hedge? After picking so many winners and losers over fifty chapters, I can get away with one noncommittal chapter, can't I?

HONORABLE MENTIONS

There have been literally dozens of biographies written about Babe Ruth, and most serious Ruthians will concur that *Babe: The Legend Comes to Life* (1974), by Robert Creamer, and *The Big Bam: The Life and Times of Babe Ruth* (2007), by Leigh Montville, are the most revealing.

Montville's *Ted Williams: The Biography of an American Hero* (2005) was also regaled an instant classic upon its publication, while *The Science of Hitting*, which Williams penned with John Underwood in 1970, remains the definitive instructional book when it comes to doing the thing Williams considered the most difficult challenge in all of sports.

Baseball's Great Experiment: Jackie Robinson & His Legacy (1983), by Jules Tygiel, does well to put Robinson's groundbreaking achievement in sociopolitical perspective.

Summer of '49 (1989), by David Halberstam, is essential reading for anyone who cherishes a down-to-the-wire pennant race, and for Red Sox and Yankees fans especially.

When it comes to the book that does the best job of chronicling one game in a microcosm, *A Day of Light and Shadow* (1978), by Jonathan Schwartz, excels in its utterly mesmerizing rendering of the one-game playoff between the Red Sox and Yankees to decide the American League East title in 1978.

Two books that don't pertain to the major leagues, *The Last Best League: One Summer, One Season, One Dream* (2005), by Jim Collins, and *Slouching Toward Fargo* (2000), by Neal Karlen, chronicle summer league and independent league baseball, respectively, where the participants still take the field driven by their love of the game, but also in hopes of moving on to bigger and better pastures.

Moneyball: The Art of Winning an Unfair Game (2004), by Michael Lewis, provides as evocative a behind-the-scenes look at the business side of baseball as any book published to date.

INDEX

Italicized page references indicate photographs.

ABOUT THE AUTHOR

A Red Sox fan since birth, Josh Pahigian has done his best to put personal biases aside in this collection of essays. His previous books include *101 Baseball Places to See Before You Strike Out* (Lyons Press), selected as a finalist for the 2008 Casey Award; *The Red Sox in the Playoffs; Spring Training Handbook; The Ultimate Minor League Baseball Road Trip;* and *The Ultimate Baseball Road-Trip.* The latter title was co-written with author Kevin O'Connell.

Josh Pahigian. PHOTO BY HEATHER PAHIGIAN

In addition to writing books, Josh teaches in the English department at the University of New England in Biddeford, Maine, and contributes articles to ESPN .com and other periodicals.

He and his wife, Heather, live in Buxton, Maine.